Globalization and

Globalization and Europe
Theoretical and Empirical
Investigations

Roland Axtmann

Editor

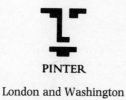

PINTER

London and Washington

PINTER

A Cassell Imprint

Wellington House, 125 Strand, London WC2R 0BB, England
PO Box 605, Herndon, Virginia 20172–0605, USA

First published 1998

British Library Cataloguing in Publication Data
A catalogue record for this book is available from the British Library.

ISBN 1-85567-436-X (Hardback)
1-85567-437-8 (Paperback)

Library of Congress Cataloging-in-Publication Data
Globalization and Europe: theoretical and empirical investigations /
Roland Axtmann, editor.
p.   cm.
Includes bibliographical references and index.
ISBN 1-85567-436-X (hardcover). – ISBN 1-85567-437-8
(paperback)
1. Europe – Foreign economic relations – History.   2. State. The
– History.   3. Competition, International – History.   I. Axtmann,
Roland.
HF1531.G58   1998
337.4–dc21   97–27667
                                                              CIP

Typeset by York House Typographic Ltd, London
Printed and bound in Great Britain by
Biddles Ltd, Guildford and King's Lynn

Contents

The Contributors

Roland Axtmann is Lecturer in political theory and political sociology in the Department of Politics and International Relations at the University of Aberdeen.

Nigel Dower is Senior Lecturer in Philosophy at the University of Aberdeen.

Paul Dukes is Professor of History at the University of Aberdeen.

Jean Houbert was Lecturer in International Relations at the University of Aberdeen until his retirement in 1997.

Douglas Kellner is Professor of Philosophy at the University of Texas at Austin.

Michael Mann is Professor of Sociology at the University of California, Los Angeles.

Zdravko Mlinar is Professor of Sociology at the University of Ljubljana.

Craig Murphy is M. Margaret Ball Professor of International Relations, Wellesley College.

Philip Resnick is Professor of Politics at the University of British Columbia.

John Rex is emeritus Professor of Sociology, University of Warwick.

George Ross is Morris Hillquit Professor in Labor and Social Thought, Brandeis University.

Franc Trček is a junior researcher in the Centre for Spatial Sociology at the Faculty of Social Sciences, University of Ljubljana.

Preface and Acknowledgements

As the new millennium approaches, we realize that we now live in a truly 'global' world of dense and ever-increasing inter- and transnational political, economic and cultural interdependence. Yet globalization is a contradictory process. Processes of global integration and interdependence are unfolding together with processes of fragmentation and regionalization. Disintegration and fragmentation of political, economic and cultural structures that spur local and regional conflicts and dislocations are counter-balanced by moves towards unification, integration and co-operation. The empirical analysis of these processes and the emergent local, regional and global structures will become the main challenge to the social sciences in the years to come.

This book offers a contribution to this task. Its main focus is the question of how the state in Europe has been implicated in, and affected by, globalization. It places the interactions between globalization and the European state in a historical perspective, going back right to the age of discovery and the formation of the modern state, yet it also addresses the complexities and uncertainties of the current age. A distinguished group of scholars from political science, international relations, sociology, philosophy and history – all of whom have been specially commissioned to write a contribution for this book – approaches the unfolding dynamics of this 'age of transition' from a multidisciplinary perspective.

It is a pleasure to express my gratitude to the authors, who all delivered their chapters within the agreed deadline. All authors responded with good grace to my editorial suggestions which, in some instances, involved substantial cuts in order to stay within the agreed-upon word limit. I take editorial responsibility for editing and cutting foot- and end notes in several contributions.

I should like to thank Fraser Lovie in the Department of Politics and International Relations at the University of Aberdeen for his technical assistance in processing the 'data' sent to me by the contributors in different shapes and formats – from Macintosh-generated disks to encoded e-mail messages: globalization most certainly does not mean standardization! While finalizing the volume, I enjoyed the hospitality of the Institut für Politische Wissenschaft at the University of Heidelberg, and I should like to thank its director, Professor Manfred Schmidt, for his support.

The book is dedicated to one of its contributors, Jean Houbert, who retired from the Department of Politics and International Relations at the University of Aberdeen in January 1997 after more than thirty years of service.

Roland Axtmann
Heidelberg, April 1997

For Jean Houbert, friend and scholar

Globalization, Europe and the State: Introductory Reflections

ROLAND AXTMANN

Towards a definition of globalization

If there were a competition for the word of the decade, *globalization* would be a strong contender. Like *civil society* in the 1980s, *globalization* is the 'in' term. Douglas Kellner in this volume reminds us that journalists, politicians, business executives, academics and others use it to signify that something profound is happening and that a new world economic, political and cultural order is emerging. There appears to be a consensus that we are living in an age of transition in which we have to bid farewell to the world we have known and boldly go where no one has gone before: globalization is seen as a process and a destination.

As Kellner shows in his comprehensive discussion of the literature, 'globalization' is a cover concept for a heterogeneity of processes that need to be spelled out and articulated. He is right to insist that there is a clear ideological aspect to this debate. 'Globalization' can be used as a replacement term for 'imperialism', displacing a focus on the domination of developing countries by the overdeveloped ones, or of national and local economies by transnational corporations. It can also replace 'modernization', robbing this previously legitimating ideology of its connotations of progress and improvement. In short, it could cover over the evaluative components of these discourses with a seemingly neutral term. By presenting globalization as an inexorable and irresistible process, the debate may serve an even more pronounced political purpose by suggesting certain policies – such as the destruction of the welfare state in the pursuit of international economic competitiveness – as the only adequate and appropriate domestic 'response' to this 'external' challenge. Yet the debate transcends these more immediate ideological and political connotations, since it is also caught up in the modernity/postmodernity debates. At stake in this debate is, on the one hand, the question of whether globalization is a continuation of the problematic of modernization and modernity, or whether it signifies a 'new age' (Albrow, 1996) for which we need new concepts and a new way in which to theorize this new 'global condition'. On the other hand, we also find in this debate a more empirically-oriented concern with the effect of a globalized media and consumer culture on individuals and collectivities. The 'buzz words' are homogeneity and heterogeneity, sameness and difference, diversity, multiplicity and hybridity. In his contribution to this volume, Kellner disentangles the different strands in these debates with great skill.

While it is thus evident that there can be no easy and uncontested definition of 'globalization', it is nevertheless possible to identify some of the major empirical processes and transformations which are seen as manifestations of this new 'age of globalization'. Arguably, a reference to 'globalization' contains the hypothesis that there has occurred an increase in the density of contacts between locations worldwide; that our life is structured in such a way that social interactions are embedded in global networks; and that 'local happenings are shaped by events occurring many miles away and vice versa' (Giddens, 1990: 64). We live in an era of ever-increasing global interconnectedness of people, places, capital, goods and services. Globalization is a multi-faceted process that manifests itself in such forms as global tourism and the global reach of nuclear, environmental and health risks. Arguably, however, it has been economic changes and technological innovations in transport and information systems and their worldwide diffusion that have conjured up visions of a 'global' world.

We may not yet have seen the emergence of a global economy which would be institutionalized through global capital markets and globally integrated financial systems as well as through global trade and global production networks, and in which the patterns of production and consumption in the world would be fully interdependent and income and employment determined at a global level (see Hirst and Thompson, 1996 for a sustained critique of the idea of a 'global' economy). Yet, as Castells (1996: 99) argues forcefully in his masterly study *The Rise of the Network Society*, the dominant trend points towards

> the increasing interpenetration of markets, particularly after the reasonably successful Uruguay Round of GATT, the birth of the World Trade Organization, the slow but steady progress in European unification, the signing of the North American Free Trade Agreement, the intensification of economic exchanges within Asia, the gradual incorporation of Eastern Europe and Russia [as well as China] into the global economy, and the growing role played by trade and foreign investment in economic growth everywhere. Furthermore, the quasi-total integration of capital markets makes all economies globally interdependent.

The globalization of the economy is driven forward by the interpenetration of the advanced capitalist countries, and, in particular, by the intensification of transfers among three economic macro-regions: North America, Europe, and the Asian Pacific. To the extent that capital is buzzing around the world, most of the time it finds a resting place in advanced capitalist countries. To the extent that international trade is increasing, it is an expression of the growing interdependencies of advanced capitalist countries. And despite processes of deindustrialization in the advanced capitalist countries, most of value-added manufacturing is still taking place there (Axtmann, 1996: 118–19).

Around each macro-region an economic hinterland has been created that is being gradually incorporated into the global economy through its links with the dominant region. North America serves this integrative function for Latin America; the European Union for Eastern Europe, much of Russia and the South Mediterranean; and Japan and the Asian Pacific for the rest of Asia, and for Australia and New Zealand too. In due course, the Russian Pacific, Eastern Siberia and Kazakhstan may also be incorporated into the global economy through their linkages with Japan and the Asian Pacific. However, much of Black Africa remains marginalized within the global economy, despite historical links to the advanced capitalist countries as their former colonies. This attests to the fact that entire regions and countries around the world are 'structurally irrelevant' in the new pattern of international division of labour, a fate shared, for example, by some rural regions of China, India and Latin America, as well as large segments of the population everywhere (Castells, 1996: 113, 133–6, 145–6). Arguably, this marginalization, or rather, the fact of an uneven economic globalization, may also have to be seen in the context of changes in the geopolitical order after the end of the Cold War and the European schisms and the diminution in the strategic significance of certain regions for the advanced capitalist countries (Holm and Sørenson, 1995; Rizvi, 1995: 80).

There is, then, a clear spatial aspect to economic globalization. This spatial dimension is reinforced by political attempts to institutionalize regional economic co-operation all around the world. Examples of such economic regionalization abound. In addition to the North American Free Trade Agreement (NAFTA) between the United States, Canada and Mexico and the European Union, one should mention, for example, the Association of Southeast Asian Nations (ASEAN) between Indonesia, Malaysia, the Phillipines, Singapore, Thailand and Brunei; and also the Asia–Pacific Economic Co-operation (APEC), founded in 1989, which brings together both the NAFTA and ASEAN states as well as China, Hong Kong, Japan, South Korea, Taiwan, Australia, New Zealand, Chile and Papua New Guinea. Among these regions and regional associations, Europe has developed a particularly high degree of regional cohesiveness – as the contributions of George Ross and Michael Mann in this volume show in some detail. Not only do we find in Europe a high density of translocal economic, political, cultural and social relations and interdependencies, but these relations and interdependencies have also been institutionalized in complex structures of organized co-operation. This institutionalization has occurred to such an extent that 'Europe' as organized in the European Community/European Union has achieved the capability of turning itself into an acting political subject (Hettne, 1993).

While these institutions and mechanisms of economic co-operation bring together states and 'national' economies, the global economy has also caused the rise of 'region states' (Ohmae, 1993) and 'megacities' (Castells, 1996: 403–10). Ohmae gives as examples of such cross-border region states Hong Kong and southern China; Singapore and its neighbouring Indonesian islands; Vancouver and Seattle (the Pacific Northwestern region state) and Toronto, Detroit and Cleveland (the 'Great Lakes' region state). These are examples of economically integrated regional entities whose primary linkages tend to be with the global economy and not with their 'host' nations. The same holds true for megacities which are 'connected externally to global networks and to segments of their own countries, while internally disconnecting local populations that are either functionally unnecessary or socially disruptive' (Castells, 1996: 404). Tokyo, São Paulo, New York, Mexico City and Shanghai, or Bombay, Los Angeles, Buenos Aires, Seoul and Beijing are relatively familiar examples of such megacities. But Castells's (1996: 407) description of a megacity in the making – the Hong Kong–Shenzen–Canton–Pearl River Delta–Macau–Zhuhai metropolitan regional system – highlights clearly what is at issue in these developments. In 1995, this spatial system extended itself over 50,000 km^2 and had a total population of between 40 and 50 million, depending on where the boundaries are defined:

> Its units, scattered in a predominantly rural landscape, were functionally connected on a daily basis, and communicated through a multimodal transportation system that included railways, freeways, country roads, hovercrafts, boats, and planes. New super-highways were under construction, and the railway was being fully electrified and double-tracked. An optic fiber telecommunications system was in process of connecting the whole area internally and with the world, mainly via earth stations and cellular telephony. Five new airports were under construction ... New container ports were also being built ... adding up to the world's largest port capacity in a given location.

What shines through in the description of this specific case of a megacity in the making holds true for the global economy more generally: The emergence of a global economic structure is premised on the development of a technological infrastructure regarding transportation and the generation and circulation of information. This infrastructure must provide for faster and more cost-effective rail, sea and air transportation and the establishment of more extensive interconnections between them; the global spread of communications networks and the systematic use of radio, television, telephone, telex, fax, computer and satellite facilities for the generation and dissemination of information. These technological innovations and their systematic applications in economic transactions have already resulted in the 'shrinking' of distances with faster and improved connections between places:

> Distances mean little and direction means even less. Relative location is more important than absolute location in a tightly connected and integrated world. Absolute location, via, where you are, has much less meaning today. What is more important as markets, societies, cultures and governments are becoming more connected is whether one is 'connected', how far one is from other places in time not in absolute distance, and how one is connected with other places. (Brunn and Leinbach, 1991: xvii)

It is not sufficient, therefore, to define globalization only in terms of an increase in the density of contacts between locations worldwide; we must also emphasize that many of those connections have become almost instantaneous. We experience a temporal immediacy to social events and cultural expressions far away (Castells, 1996: 461), since 'in the globalized world of today people can by various means relate with one another irrespective of their longitudinal and latitudinal position, as it were on a "supraterritorial" plane' (Scholte, 1996: 45). This reconfiguration of space and the 'temporal' shrinking of the world 'has made the identification of boundaries – and associated notions of "here" and "there", "far" and "near", "outside" and "inside", "home" and "away", "them" and "us" – more problematic than ever' (Scholte, 1996: 49). It is in that sense that we can accept Malcolm Waters's (1995: 3) definition of globalization as '[a] social process in which constraints of geography on social and cultural arrangements recede and in which people become increasingly aware that they are receding'.

Globalization and the modern European state

The main focus of this book is the question of how the state in Europe has been implicated in, and affected by, globalization. This book places the interactions between globalization and the state in a historical perspective, going back right to the age of discovery and the formation of the modern state, and approaches the unfolding dynamics from a multidisciplinary perspective.

The rise of the modern state involved the territorialization of politics and the territorial 'caging' of social relationships. The modern state project aimed at instituting the state as the supreme power across a territory with clearly demarcated boundaries that were sanctioned by international law. In 'pre-modern' Europe, political authority and sovereignty was shared between a wide variety of secular and religious institutions – between kings, princes and the nobility, bishops, abbots and the papacy, guilds and cities. As Anderson (1996: 141) rightly remarks, these 'multilevel medieval author-ities were collapsed to just one all-important level, that of the sovereign territorial state'. The replacement of these overlapping jurisdictions through the modern state was legitimized by a theory of state sovereignty. This theory claimed the supremacy of the government of any state over the people, resources, and, ultimately, all other authorities within the territory it con-trolled. 'State sovereignty' meant that final authority within the political community lay with the state whose will legally, and rightfully, commanded without being commanded by others and whose will was therefore *legibus solutus* because it was not accountable to any but itself (Axtmann, 1996: 10–14; Passerin d'Entrèves, 1967: 93).

A 'sovereign' right to ultimate authority and control does not imply an ability to exercise it. And the history of state-formation can be analysed as the protracted efforts of rulers and their staff to translate 'juridical' sover-eignty into 'empirical' sovereignty. 'Governing' took on the form of managing the 'networks of continuous, multiple and complex interaction between populations (their increase, longevity, health, etc.), territory (its expanse, resources, control, etc.), and wealth (its creation, productivity, distribution, etc.)' (Luke, 1996: 496). The artful combination of space, people and resources in territorialized containments and the policing, mon-itoring and disciplining of the population within these spaces became the foundation, and the manifestation, of state sovereignty (Axtmann, 1992, 1996; Luke, 1996). It was only in the nineteenth century that the state could impose authoritatively its control over society. Michael Mann (1993) has shown in great detail how, and why, state–society relation was tightened and social relations were 'caged' over the national rather than the local-regional or transnational terrain. It was only in the nineteenth century that ever more social relationships became bounded by the state's territorial reach and that the state could no longer be evaded.

The sovereignty of the state presupposed the eradication of internal con-tenders for supremacy. However, it was also predicated on the principle of non-interference in the internal affairs of the state from outside. This amoun-ted to the acceptance of the norm that the territorial integrity of every state was inviolate. Inayatullah and Blaney (1995: 12) formulate this concisely:

> Sovereignty constitutes states as existentially separate: in promoting their own sovereignty, states participate in their own constitution as discrete entities; in accepting the status of sovereign statehood, states also participate in constitut-ing others as outside, albeit as sovereign others.

State sovereignty as 'external' sovereignty is thus predicated upon the recognition by other, 'outside' political authorities: 'Other states participate in a fundamental way in the constitution of a state: their acts of recognition are part of creating the sovereign statehood of the others' (Inayatullah and Blaney, 1995: 12). When we bring these elements of statehood, territoriality, sovereignty and recognition, together, we can describe the imagery of the territorial state with Luke (1996: 495) as follows: 'The states have hardened borders, inviolate territorial spaces and defensible centers in an international order of other comparable states, all dedicated to maintaining territorial control over their borders and containing internal challenges to their political autonomy.'

In his contribution to this volume, Jean Houbert discusses how the European model and the institution of the territorial state was spread around the globe as a result of colonization and decolonization. He is right to insist that the universalization of the European state ideal was a major, and early, manifestation of globalization. The European state ideal and its key concept of sovereignty became a cornerstone of the interstate system after the Second World War when decolonization created new states that were modelled on the European ideal. We should also remember that the colonial rather than the traditional borders – be they ethnic or tribal – were retained as the basis for the creation of the new states. For the most part, therefore, decolonization did not proceed along national(ist) lines. The centrality of the European state ideal in the interstate system was further confirmed by the Charter of the United Nations and its support for the principle of state sovereignty. While affirming the maintenance of international peace and security as the prime purpose of the UN, the Charter defines this as the prevention of the violation of established state borders by the forces of other states. This adherence to the principles of the integrity of established state borders and non-interference in the domestic affairs of other states places the UN firmly within the history of European thinking about the state and the European states system.

Yet we should not forget that the norm of the self-determination of peoples is enshrined in the Charter of the UN, too; and it was this norm that contributed to delegitimizing colonial empires in the late 1940s and 1950s. This norm contains the seeds for progressively diminishing the priority of the norm of state sovereignty. Makinda (1996: 154) shows convincingly that the imperative to maintain peace and promote international peace and security could require the protection of people against authoritarian regimes and thus outside interference or intervention: 'In situations where domestic conflict or the breakdown of a state has the potential to destabilize neighboring states, the UN Security Council . . . can define the problem as constituting a threat to international peace and security within the region, as was the case in northern Iraq in 1991 and in Somalia in 1992.'

We may formulate the relevant issue more broadly. Nigel Dower's contribution to this volume shows the increasing importance that the international community attaches to human rights. The various declarations by the UN since its creation attest to it. In the human rights debate an assumption is made that the world is a moral community, that individuals have rights and duties as members of the community of humankind, and that the behaviour of states is rightfully judged by assessing their contribution to upholding the universal moral code. Related to this supposition is the idea that individuals, by the fact of being human, have a right to (at least minimal) satisfaction of basic human needs, such as subsistence, security, love and dignity of the person. Derived from this notion of (inalienable) human rights is the perception that servicing these basic human needs is the prime task of states and their legitimacy is heavily dependent upon their securing the basic 'human rights' (Brown, 1992: 101–14, 125–7). If we accept the human rights argument, then violation of human rights by a state may justify humanitarian intervention by an international organization, such as the UN, or a coalition of states. Such a violation of 'state sovereignty' could be justified by reference to the norm of the self-determination of peoples. It could be asserted that the right to self-determination presupposes free and autonomous persons empowered to participate in the decision-making process of the group and who are thus endowed with the conditions of agency (that is, human rights).

Hence, one interpretation of the notion of the self-determination of peoples is to understand it as the principle that the state should ultimately be responsible to the people as individual political beings. In that interpretation, the recognition of 'state sovereignty' would be conditional on the institutionalization of democracy, that is, 'popular sovereignty'. In the revolutionary upheavals of the French Revolution, the 'people' replaced the 'princes' as the sovereign subject of history. It was the sovereignty of the people that bestowed legitimacy upon the newly constituted political order after the demolition of the *ancien régime*. The people as a collectivity installed themselves as the bearers of the rights of political rule, couching their demands for political autonomy and self-determination in the rhetoric of the 'nation'. The new state was to be a 'nation'-state which was to derive its power, and exercise it, for (and not simply over) a nation, a people; it was 'to be a nation's state: the state "of" and "for" a particular, distinctive, bounded nation', expressing that nation's will and furthering that nation's interests (Brubaker, 1992: 28).

In the imagery of the 'nation', the plurality and antagonisms of 'society' were moulded into a political entity. The nation became the 'unitary' body in which sovereignty resided. In more general terms, cultural homogenization within the nation-state aims at the eradication of internal differences or else the denial of their existence. This creation of 'sameness' within goes hand in hand with the claim to 'uniqueness' *vis-à-vis* other states and therefore with highlighting substantial differences between states. Concerns with homogeneity and commonality within allow for the dramatization of differences without, but provide also a chance for making visible those individuals and groups within who fail to hold given features in common. The nation-state discourse is thus organized around the notion of 'national' authenticity and identity which translates into strategies of inclusion into, and exclusion from, the national community. And very easily, it also translates into political and cultural concerns with keeping the nation 'pure' or 'unpolluted' or with 'cleansing' and 'purifying' it again if it has become polluted.

It is important to understand that the notion of the nation-state incorporated from the very beginning the ideas both of constitutional government and of cultural homogeneity. And 'democracy' became entangled in this tension as well. During the political and social struggles of the nineteenth century, the notion of constitutionality became broadened into the idea of popular and democratic government, while the concern with cultural homogeneity retained its importance as a mechanism for drawing cultural boundaries between 'us' and 'them', and thereby defining membership in the democratic political community. The conceptualization of popular sovereignty may serve as the most prominent instance of the linkage between democracy and nation-state. In liberal democracies, individuals must be members of the state, must be its 'nationals', in order to possess citizenship rights. Democracy is thus linked to the nation-state through the institution of citizenship for members of the national community. Democratic rule by the sovereign people is exercised in the sovereign, territorially consolidated nation-state. In a liberal democracy, it is the people who have the 'undisputed right to determine the framework of rules, regulations and policies within a given territory and to govern accordingly' (Held, 1991: 150 and Held, 1995a for detailed discussion of these issues). Liberal democracy is premised on the acceptance of the notion of popular sovereignty and its institutionalization in citizenship rights. Sovereignty has been transferred from the (monarchical) ruler to the people, and the people have been defined as the sum of the legally equal citizens. In a bounded territory, people's sovereignty is the basis upon which democratic decision-making takes place; and 'the people' are the addressees, or the constituents, of the political decisions. The territorially consolidated democratic polity, which is clearly demarcated from other political communities, is seen as rightly governing itself and determining its own future through the interplay between forces operating within its boundaries. Only in a sovereign state can the people's will command without being commanded by others. Hence, 'popular sovereignty', too, has a spatial dimension in that it is premised on the occupation and possession of territory.

In the age of globalization, this 'nesting' of democracy within the nation-state has become problematic for a number of reasons. The success of the nation-state in the last two hundred years or so, as well as its universality and legitimacy, were premised on its claim to be able to guarantee the economic well-being, the physical security and the cultural identity of the people who constitute its citizens. But global forces such as global capitalism, global proliferation of nuclear weapons and global media and culture are now undermining this claim and challenge the effectiveness of the political organizational form of the nation-state (Beetham, 1984). They are thus weakening the links between the citizens and the nation-state. The citizens demand political representation, physical protection, economic security and cultural certainty. But in a global system that is made up of states, regions, international and supranational organizations and transnational corporations and that does not have a clear-cut power hierarchy, the nation-state finds it increasingly difficult to accommodate these interests and mediate between its citizens and the rest of the world (Horsman and Marshall, 1994).

As a result, in a world of global interconnectedness both people's sovereignty and state sovereignty have been challenged, since '[t]he very process of governance can escape the reach of the nation-state. National communities by no means exclusively make and determine decisions and policies themselves, and governments by no means determine what is right or appropriate exclusively for their own citizens' (Held, 1992: 21; Connolly, 1991: 216). For example, the formation of a global economy outreaches the control of any single state; multi- and transnational corporations, stock brokers and international money and securities dealers make production and investment decisions that affect the economic well-being of states and people without being accountable to them. Global communication and the processes of informationalization make it difficult for governments to control information and its dissemination; and with power adhering increasingly to those actors who have unconstrained access to information flows, 'the nation-state – with its more traditional geopolitical concerns for policing jurisdictively its territories, populations, and markets – often comes up short with nothing near complete closure over events within its boundaries' (Luke, 1993: 239). Global forces affect the life of citizens by imposing constraints and limits on democratically constituted political agency without allowing the citizens substantial control over them.

The 'place' of democracy has thus become problematic. The centralization and hierarchization of power within states and through states in the international system are steadily replaced by the pluralization of power among political, economic, cultural and social actors, groups, and communities within states, between states and across states. We move into a 'plurilateral' world of diffused and decentralized power, into a world characterized by a variety of different loci of power and cross-cutting power networks (Cerny, 1993). For Nederveen Pieterse (1994: 166), this 'plurilateralism' can be identified 'in the increase in the available modes of organisation: trans-national, international, macro-regional, national, micro-regional, municipal, and local'. These organizational levels are criss-crossed 'by functional networks of corporations, international organisations, non-governmental organisations [and social movements, R. A.] as well as professionals and computer users'. Those individuals, groups and commu-nities partaking in the creation of these networks and affected by them will become empowered and constrained by them in ways quite different from in the past, when it was the nation-state that determined, on the whole, their political 'liberty' and 'identity' and mediated the effects of the 'outside' world. In this plurilateral world, the idea of a *summa potestas* that resides in the state as that institutional arrangement empowered to make, and enforce, col-lectively binding decisions has lost, if not its appeal, then its justification. And so has the notion of the sovereignty of the people as a united, homogeneous body legitimating the sovereign power of 'its' state through a constitution that manifests the principle of *voluntas populi suprema lex*.

Several contributions in this volume address key issues raised by these transformations. As I have already noted above, Jean Houbert's chapter shows how a key institution of modernity, the territorial state, and its concomitant ideology of state sovereignty was spread around the globe as a consequence of colonialism and decolonization. Continuing the theme of 'colonialism', John Rex outlines a theory of colonial and post-colonial migration and discusses the political and economic conditions under which migration to Europe occurs. One of the themes in this richly argued chapter may be highlighted in the context of the issues raised in this introduction, namely the political interaction between transnational migrant commu-nities and the nation-state. Rex distinguishes between those migrant communities which embrace the goal of eventual return to their 'homeland' ('diasporas') and other globally dispersed communities which intend to remain dispersed and to draw advantage from this dispersal. The term 'transnational migrant communities' includes both types. One characteristic of these 'transnational migrant communities' is that they all maintain various types of transnational linkages. As Rex says, 'they represent cultural and social forms which cross-cut nation states and national cultures and are much more structures of a globalized world'. To sustain these transnational linkages, the migrant communities can avail themselves of the 'space adjusting' innovations in communication and transport (Brunn, 1996). Rex points out that 'ethnicity today often operates by E-mail', but we may easily add other elements of the global technological infrastructure that play an important part in community formation and network structures. Reduction in travel costs and in travel time as well as safer travel to many parts of the world; a global mail service, instant telephone contacts and fax connections as well as satellite TV – this technological infrastructure allows for the build-up and maintenance of transnational linkages of migrant communities around the world in an intensity and density that would not have been possible even a decade ago. And given the widespread accessibility of multimedia systems, the government, associations and clubs in the 'home-land' as well as the migrant communities themselves now find it easier to produce and publish newspapers, magazines, cassette tapes, videos, etc. for their dispersed members in which 'cultural belonging' may be represented and celebrated.

As it has become easier to maintain transnational bonds, the incorpora-tion and acculturation of immigrant minorities by the state in which they live have become more contested. As Robin Cohen (1996: 519) has sug-gested, 'many immigrants are no longer individualized or obedient prospective citizens. Instead, they may retain dual citizenship, agitate for special trade deals with their homelands, demand aid in exchange for electoral support, influence foreign policy and seek to protect family immi-gration quotas.' In short, they may organize themselves into powerful collective political actors. Rex's reference to the contested politics of multi-culturalism should be placed within this context. In the last few decades, ever more migrant communities have demanded recognition and support for their cultural identity. At stake is the acceptance of the demand for group-differentiated rights, powers, status or immunities that go beyond the common rights of citizenship. Considering political demands for self-government, Bhikhu Parekh has suggested that cohesive communities which have democratically accountable self-governing institutions and allow their members a right of exit

> have a vital role in giving their members a sense of rootedness, harnessing their moral energies for common purposes, and sustaining the spirit of cultural pluralism. Rather than seek to dismantle them in the name of abstractly and narrowly defined goals of social cohesion, integration and national unity, the state should acknowledge their cultural and political value and grant them such support as they need and ask for . . . Conducting the affairs of a society as complex as ours is too important a task to be left to the state alone. It requires partnership between the two [i.e. the state and society, R. A.], and encouraging cohesive communities to run their affairs themselves under the overall author-ity of the state is an important dimension of that partnership. (Parekh, 1994: 107)

Manifestly, contemplating such a 'partnership', as well as the acceptance of group-differentiated rights more generally, raises the question of the very nature, authority and permanence of the multicultural state of which these various cultural communities are part. Our prevailing assumptions of common citizenship, common identity, and social and political cohesion will be questioned. The question will also have to be addressed of how these communities can co-ordinate their actions in areas of common concern or common interest, for example with regard to the environment, the economy, or military security. The much more fragmented, decentralized institutional pattern emerging from this diversity would have to allow for: first, democratic communal self-government; second, a public debate on the matters communities have in common; third, protection of legitimate powers to uphold autonomy; and fourth, the political co-ordination of the communities that keeps them part of one larger community.

As I have argued above, liberal democracy as a specific institutional arrangement and political practice has always been grounded in the concrete temporal and spatial reality of territorially bounded political communities. To put it differently, the idea and reality of liberal democracy has always been linked to the idea and reality of the nation-state (Axtmann, 1996). Hence, multiculturalism challenges liberal democracy, not only because it puts demands for group-differentiated rights on the political agenda, but because it problematizes the notion of a popular sovereignty embodied in a 'unitary' nation and manifested in the 'unitary' nation-state. It radicalizes the discourse on difference which is always already implied in the conceptualization of the political community as a nation-state.

The notion of a 'unitary' collective (national) identity becomes thus problematized in the politics of multiculturalism. Two other contributions to this volume raise related issues. Zdravko Mlinar and Franc Trček discuss the transformation of territorial cultures through global forces in a number of European countries, and in Slovenia in particular. They argue that in the past territorial cultures and unique cultural identities were formed by reference to proximate and neighbouring societies. The importance of territorial proximity, or adjacency, for cultural formation, however, has declined in proportion to the increase and intensification in communication with the 'global core'. The authors do discern a current process of levelling territorial cultural differences as a result of what they call 'Americanization'. Yet their answer to the question of whether cultural localisms and traditions of variance will be swept away by the forces of Western cultural 'imperialism' (that is, 'Americanization') is not an unequivocal 'yes'. They foresee a situation in which social actors make creative use of the Internet and other means of communication that do not need mediation through global media corporations to combine selectively elements of their 'local' environment with 'global' inputs and thus create cultural diversity.

Paul Dukes analyses the relationship between Russia and 'Europe' as well as the effects of globalization on post-Soviet Russia. He discusses the formation of a territorial Russian culture and provides support for Mlinar's and Trček's thesis of the importance of 'proximity/adjacency' for identity formation. On the one hand, Dukes shows how the intensive interactions between Russia and 'Europe', and the Russian borrowing of elements of European culture, contributed to the formulation of a Russian cultural identity. But he also demonstrates how the Russian intelligentsia is currently endeavouring to formulate an 'idea' of Russia that, drawing on elements of traditional Russian (political) culture, opposes the notion of an 'end of ideology' after the end of the Cold War.

Dukes's chapter, as well as that by Mlinar and Trček, demonstrates that the process of (collective) identity formation in the age of globalization is embedded in a structure of interactivity. It is a key aspect of the contemporary stage of global interconnectedness that concrete societies situate themselves in the context of a world complex of societies; that they conceptualize themselves as part of a global order. As a result of this global self-reflection, the criteria for societal change and conduct tend to become 'matters of inter-societal, inter-continental, inter-civilizational, and inter-doctrinal interpretation and debate' (Robertson and Chirico, 1985: 237). Such a situating of societies may engender strains or even discontent within societies. It heightens the significance of the problem of societal order in relation to global order and is thus likely to give rise to a large number of political-ideological and religious movements with conflicting definitions of the location of their society in relationship to the rest of the world and the global circumstance as a whole. In short, it radicalizes and politicizes the search for identity. The resurgence of ethnonationalism across the world in recent years is arguably one manifestation of these processes. This identity, however, is the possible result of the confrontation of a particular locality with others in the emerging world of global capitalism, global information and communication networks, global transportation technology and global tourism. Particularistic identity in the age of globalization is thus constructed in full awareness of the rest of the world. It is an identity that does not aim at insulation from the world, but allows local units conscious, if potentially fraught, interactions with it (Mlinar, 1992: 5–12; Robertson, 1992: 69–70; Walker, 1993: 176–9).

As we find ourselves in the vortex of time-space compression, the 'globe' has potentially become the reference-point for our identity formation. We realize that we are all inhabitants of a fragile planet and members of a common species, that we share in common the 'one world'. This awareness of global interconnectedness has found one expression in the discourse on human rights. Nigel Dower presents a remarkably detailed and reflexive conspectus of key issues in this debate. He is of course aware that the idea of 'human rights' is a late expression of the idea of the European Enlightenment, 'with its confident assertion that there is universal knowledge, including universal values, discoverable by the use of universal reason'. His argumentative strategy is therefore to support the viability of global ethics, and the centrality of 'human rights' within it, without falling back on Eurocentric positions. I should like to add to Dower's discussion one point only. Human rights bestow entitlements, and impose obligations, on individuals irrespective of their nationality. Unlike civil, political and social rights, which are predicated on the distinction between national and alien, human rights override such distinctions. They challenge the particularism of citizenship which is grounded in the nation-state and thus is structurally related to the notion of state sovereignty and popular sovereignty. They imply a universalizing understanding of humanity, and by questioning the priority of citizenship they critique sovereignty as an ethically deficient way of organizing the international community (Sassen, 1996: 89–95; Walker and Mendlovitz, 1990).

Human rights potentially contest state sovereignty and popular sovereignty and devalue national citizenship. At the same time, however, human rights open up 'the one world' as the space and the arena in which individuals may engage politically as citizens of the world. In other words, the legitimacy of a democratic system 'beyond the nation-state', that is, a cosmopolitan democracy, could be derived from the human rights discourse. In recent years, David Held has been a particularly influential advocate for the creation of a 'cosmopolitan democracy'. His model provides for, *inter alia*, a reformed United Nations with a modification of the veto arrangement in the Security Council and a reconsideration of representation on it to allow for adequate regional accountability; the creation of regional parliaments (for example, in Latin America and Africa) as well as the enhancement of the role and power of such bodies where they already exist (and here Held refers to the European Parliament); and ultimately the formation of an authoritative assembly of all democratic states and agencies, a 'global parliament' (Held, 1995b: 106–9, 111). While some of these institutional innovations are defined as 'long-term' objectives, the '[c]reation of a UN second chamber (perhaps on the model of the European Parliament)' and '[e]nhanced political regionalization (EC and beyond)' are 'short-term' objectives (ibid.: 111).

Held's model does not aim for a world government or a federal world state. He accepts that democracy must be institutionalized on many levels, ranging from the local/municipal to the subnational and national levels and through the regional level to the global level. According to him, it is possible to identify clearly the levels on which respective issues and policy questions should be dealt with. For example, 'the issues which rightly belong to regional levels of governance are those which require transnational media- tion because of the interconnectedness of national decisions and outcomes, and because nations in these circumstances often find themselves unable to achieve their objectives without transborder collaboration' (Held, 1995b: 113).

In his chapter, Philip Resnick is sympathetic to the ideals behind global democracy. Yet he insists that there are a number of obstacles to the realization of global democracy. In a fascinating survey, he discusses uneven economic development, diverging political traditions, cultural or ethnic identities and, finally, solidarities that are primarily local or national in character as the major obstacles that have to be overcome before a common democratic space at the global level can be envisaged. His final judgement is measured. 'Whatever else global democracy incarnates', Resnick argues, 'it cannot be the political or cultural hegemony of any one state or grouping of states.' We must accept 'the need for minimal political governance at the global level' because 'the alternatives are simply too bleak'. According to Resnick, 'the best we can hope for is a form of cosmopolitanism that respects the plural character of the peoples of the earth'.

This conclusion is more cautious than Richard Falk's position in his report to the World Order Models Project *On Humane Governance* (1995: 16):

> For the sake of viability and legitimacy, the world must evolve structures of governance (not necessarily government) that offer improved prospects of achieving sustainability (that is, environmental balance enabling lifestyle to be continued at present or improving standards) and decency. Indeed, govern- ance structures should be as decentralized and localized as possible consistent with such goals as equity, implementation of human rights, promotion of democracy, environmental protection.

According to Richard Falk, transnational social movements are among the most important political forces for the realization of 'humane governance'. During the last two decades or so, the threats to the survival of the human race posed by nuclear, biological and chemical warfare and by dangers of an ecocatastrophe, as well as a concern with political and social injustice worldwide, be it with political prisoners or discrimination on the basis of race or gender, have led to the formation of movements that do not limit their activities to any one particular territory. For activists in the environmental and peace movements or in Amnesty International, the 'one world' has become the point of reference for their concerns (Falk, 1992: chs 4, 6). According to Falk, the participants in these movements act on the basis of a global consciousness. He defines them as 'citizen-pilgrims' whose commit- ment 'is radical and essentially religious in character, not depending on any validation by the prospect of immediate results' (Falk, 1992: 74):

[Their] ethos implies a reorientation of citizenship in order to go beyond loyalty and diligent participation in the collective life of a territorially delimited society that qualifies as a sovereign state. The citizen sensitive to the claims of this emergent ethos needs to extend his or her notions of participation in dimensions of both space (beyond the territory of any particular state) and time (beyond the present, reclaiming past wisdom and safeguarding future generations). (Falk, 1992: 153–4)

'Think globally, act locally' as much as 'Think locally, act globally' is the core of this ethos, that is 'necessarily deferential to the local and the diverse' (Falk, 1992: 153). Arguably, through their global orientation, the 'citizen-pilgrims' are participating in the creation of a global civil society. Many of these activists are members of nongovernmental organizations (NGOs). Gordenker and Weiss (1995: 357) report that there are well over 15,000 recognizable NGOs that operate in three or more countries and draw their finances from more than one country. There is also an increasingly dense network structure that connects NGOs globally:

New communication technologies are helping to foster the kinds of interaction and relationships that were once unthinkable except through expensive air travel. Scaling certain kinds of transnational efforts from neighbourhoods and regions to the global level and scaling down to involve grassroots organisations are no longer logistic possibilities, but may be treated as institutional imperatives. (Gordenker and Weiss, 1995: 365)

NGOs are undeniably one mechanism that articulates the global and the local and that will be an essential component of any type of global democracy. This topic cannot be pursued further in this introduction. We should, however, note that many analyses of NGOs see them as located between 'the state' and 'the market', and global civil society and global governance are discussed as if 'the economy' could be neglected analytically – or in the political struggle for global democracy. The contributions by Craig Murphy and George Ross query this assumption.

Well into the 1970s, postwar capitalism was stabilized through national economic management that quite frequently took the form of corporatist arrangements between capital, labour and the government. The Keynesian welfare state was the institutional expression of that policy. Cerny (1996: 633) rightly reminds us that the welfare state was not just concerned with

merely protecting the poor and the helpless from poverty and pursuing such welfare goals as full employment or public health, but also regulating business in the public interest, 'fine tuning' business cycles to promote economic growth, nurturing 'strategic industries' and 'national champions', integrating labour movements into corporatist processes to promote wage stability and labour discipline, reducing barriers to international trade, imposing controls on 'speculative' international movements of capital, and the like.

When in the 1970s the economic fallout of the Vietnam war led to the collapse of the American-administered Bretton Woods monetary system and the 1973 oil shock added to the turbulence in the financial system, the postwar boom in Europe ended, growth levels declined and unemployment began to grow. The welfare state consensus cracked. The welfare state was no longer seen as the solution to society's problems, but as their cause. It was argued that the welfare state eroded individual responsibility and initiative; created a large, inefficient bureaucratic welfare apparatus that intruded into and violated the privacy of the citizen, diminishing choice and individual preferences; and harmed economic productivity and growth by 'confiscating' private resources in the form of taxation for welfare expenditure, thus depriving the private sector of money needed for capitalization.

The 'neo-liberal' backlash against the welfare state aimed at replacing it by the 'competition state' (Philip Cerny). Whereas the welfare state had attempted to take certain economic activities out of the market by 'decommodifying' them, the competition state set out to pursue '*increased* marketization to make economic activities located within the national territory ... more competitive in international and transnational terms' (Cerny, 1996: 634; Cerny, 1990: ch. 8). A reduction in government spending and the deregulation of economic activities, especially financial markets, have become as much part of the policy objectives of the 'competition state' as the reduction in 'direct taxes, especially on capital and highly-skilled labour'. At the same time attempts are made 'to sustain tax base and income flows by introducing repressive value-added taxes, by borrowing in the financial markets, and by privatization of state assets' (Gill, 1992: 278). According to Gill (1992: 276), these changes amount to the 'internationalization of the state'; that is, 'states have become increasingly attuned to, conditioned and restructured by the pressures emanating from the global economy'.

Indeed, as Gill (1992, 1995), Cerny (1996), McMichael (1996) and Murphy and Ross in this volume suggest, globalization is not necessarily best understood as an independent variable that 'affects' the nation-state and its policy capabilities – although such an erosion of policy capacity and political autonomy can be discerned. Globalization may be better analysed as a 'project' aimed at stabilizing capitalism through global economic management. *This* global governance is carried through by a transnational class: 'In addittition to state managers (those embracing liberalization), there are the new financial and transnational corporate elites combined with the managers of newly-empowered multilateral institutions like the IMF, the World Bank and the World Trade Organization' (McMichael, 1996: 32). Thus we can detect a trend towards 'the centralization of power in multilateral institutions to set global rules and the internalization of those rules in national policy-making' (McMichael, 1996: 39).

In his chapter for this volume, Craig Murphy puts the issue of governance in the current age into a historical perspective. 'Governance', that is, the coherence and stability given to societies by conscious, goal-oriented administrative action, is, so Murphy asserts, an aggregate of strategic actions taken by a host of forces. Using the language of Antonio Gramsci, Murphy posits that effective governance involves the compatible functioning of the ensemble of institutions within a 'historical bloc'. He detects an incoherence and lack of compatibility among the current strategies of firms, states, international institutions and popular social forces. He is sceptical that the current mix of globalizing strategies will return industrialized countries to the higher growth rates of the 1950s and 1960s. As he says, 'while many firms, governments, and key international institutions all have begun to follow strategies oriented toward a larger paradigmatic scale of operation, it is doubtful whether this will trigger a new, high-growth industrial age, a "Third Industrial Revolution" or an "Information Age"'. He turns to a historical analysis of earlier transitions from one industrial era to the next with the expectation that it will tell us something about the prospects for the current age. He avers that some strategic reorientation on the part of socialist, labour and other mass-oriented movements, their 'globalization', may well be essential before the 'need' for reformed business and government strategies is recognized: 'In Europe, the development of continent-wide popular movements is probably an essential precondition for the European-wide reformist changes in government and business strategy that would make the next industrial age possible.' This thesis moves us close towards the previous argument regarding transnational movements, global civil society and global governance.

In his chapter, George Ross does not use the concept of 'governance' to discuss the connections between European integration and globalization. Yet he is adamant that the renewal of European integration in the 1980s was caused by the strategic decisions of key European actors to accelerate integration rather than continue national economic crises-management strategies. He points out that many of the decisions which have gone into the construction of the new European order were made on the outer margins of democratic legitimacy: 'European national leaders opted for new Europeanization *in camera*, through diplomacy, using the extensive executive powers reserved to them in foreign affairs to change Europe fundamentally and, in many cases, also to "exogenize" processes of change which they never could have implemented in their domestic political arenas.' Ross invites us to consider that the Single Market, European Monetary Union or Maastricht are not so much the result of 'globalization', but a contributory factor to 'globalization' itself: 'For a variety of reasons European leaders have pursued a course of action which has simulated what globalization is claimed to be doing everywhere, within the continental boundaries of the EU', that is, putting huge structural constraints on what national governments can do.

What will the future be for the 'European model of society' with its humane welfare states, civilized industrial relations procedures and negotiated settlements between groups? Ross raises this question but leaves the answer open. Michael Mann addresses yet another question: 'To what extent is Europe beginning to constitute a distinct "society" in the world?' Mann offers a fascinating analysis of the complex entwinings of ideological, economic, military and political power networks within and across the boundaries of Europe. He concludes that there is no 'Euro' society with overall internal cohesion and external closure, nor is it realistic to expect a singular 'Euro' society to emerge in the future. What we can expect at maximum will be a European network of interaction at the boundaries of which occurs a limited degree of cleavage. Linking his analysis up with the globalization debate, Mann accepts the validity of the claim that human networks of interaction have finally arrived up against the limits of the planet Earth: 'Global limits have indeed already been reached by military power (its weapons can destroy the earth), while global capitalism and the sum of its states endanger the Earth's global environmental limits.' Yet, this 'external closure' does not bring about 'internal cohesion'. Mann asserts that 'One world is emerging, but composed of multiple, overlapping, intersecting – and often conflicting – networks of interaction'. Within this complexity, 'Euro' is becoming one of the most significant macro-networks of human interaction on the globe.

The authors in this book offer a distinctive contribution towards a historical and comparative analysis of this complexity.

References

Albrow, Martin (1996) *The Global Age*. Cambridge: Polity Press.

Anderson, James (1996) The shifting stage of politics: new medieval and postmodern territorialities?, *Environment and Planning (Society & Space)*, **14**, 133–53.

Axtmann, Roland (1992) 'Police' and the formation of the modern state, *German History*, **10**, 39–61.

Axtmann, Roland (1996) *Liberal Democracy into the Twenty-First Century: Globalization, Integration and the Nation-State*. Manchester: Manchester University Press.

Beetham, David (1984) The future of the nation-state, in G. McLennan *et al.* (eds), *The Idea of the Modern State*. Milton Keynes: Open University Press, pp. 208–22.

Brown, Seyom (1992) *International Relations in a Changing Global System*. Boulder, CO: Westview Press.

Brubaker, W. Rogers (1992) *Citizenship and Nationhood in France and Germany*. Cambridge, MA: Harvard University Press.

Brunn, Stanley (1996) The internationalization of diasporas in a shrinking world, in G. Prévélakis (ed.), *The Networks of Diasporas*. Paris: Kykem, pp. 259–72.

Brunn, Stanley and Leinbach, Thomas R. (eds) (1991) *Collapsing Space and Time: Geographic Aspects of Communications and Information.* London: HarperCollins.

Castells, Manuel (1996) *The Rise of the Network Society.* Oxford: Blackwell.

Cerny, Philip (1990) *The Changing Architecture of Politics.* London: Sage.

Cerny, Philip (1993) Plurilateralism: structural differentiation and functional conflict in the post-Cold War world order, *Millennium,* **22,** 27–51.

Cerny, Philip (1996) Globalization and other stories: the search for a new paradigm for international relations, *International Journal,* **51,** 617–37.

Cohen, Robin (1996) Diasporas and the nation-state: from victims to challengers, *International Affairs,* **72,** 507–20.

Connolly, William E. (1991) *Identity/Difference.* Ithaca and London: Cornell University Press.

Falk, Richard (1992) *Explorations at the Edges of Time.* Philadelphia: Temple University Press.

Falk, Richard (1995) *On Humane Governance: Toward a New Global Politics.* Cambridge: Polity Press.

Giddens, Anthony (1990) *The Consequences of Modernity.* Cambridge: Polity Press.

Gill, Stephen (1992) Economic globalization and the internationalization of authority: limits and contradictions, *Geoforum,* **23,** 269–83.

Gill, Stephen (1995) Theorizing the interregnum: the double movement and global politics in the 1990s, in B. Hettne (ed.), *International Political Economy: Understanding Global Disorder.* London: Zed Books, pp. 65–99.

Gordenker, Leon and Weiss, Thomas G. (1995) Pluralising global governance: analytical approaches and dimensions, *Third World Quarterly,* **16,** 357–87.

Held, David (1991) Democracy, the nation-state and the global system, *Economy and Society,* **20,** 138–72.

Held, David (1992) Democracy: from city-states to cosmopolitan order?, *Political Studies,* **40** (special issue), 10–39.

Held, David (1995a) *Democracy and the Global Order: From the Modern State to Cosmopolitan Governance.* Cambridge: Polity Press.

Held, David (1995b) Democracy and the New International Order, in D. Archibugi and D. Held (eds), *Cosmopolitan Democracy.* Cambridge: Polity Press, pp. 96–120.

Hettne, Björn (1993) Neo-mercantilism: the pursuit of regionness, *Co-operation and Conflict,* **28,** 211–32.

Hirst, Paul and Thompson, Grahame (1996) *Globalization in Question: The International Economy and the Possibilities of Governance.* Cambridge: Polity Press.

Holm, Hans-Henrik and Sørensen, Georg (eds) (1995) *Whose World Order? Uneven Globalization and the End of the Cold War.* Boulder, CO: Westview Press.

Horsman, Mathew and Marshall, Andrew (1994) *After the Nation-State.* London: HarperCollins.

Inayatullah, Naeem and Blaney, David (1995) Realizing sovereignty, *Review of International Studies,* **21,** 3–20.

Luke, Tim W. (1993) Discourses of disintegration, texts of transformation: re-reading realism in the New World Order, *Alternatives,* **18,** 229–58.

Luke, Tim W. (1996) Governmentality and contra-governmentality: rethinking sovereignty and territoriality after the Cold War, *Political Geography,* **15,** 491–507.

McMichael, Philip (1996) Globalization: myths and realities, *Rural Sociology*, **61**, 25–55.

Makinda, Samuel M. (1996) Sovereignty and international security: challenges for the United Nations, *Global Governance*, **2**, 149–68.

Mann, Michael (1993) *The Sources of Social Power*, Vol. 2: *The Rise of Classes and Nation-States, 1760–1914*. Cambridge: Cambridge University Press.

Mlinar, Zdravko (1992) Introduction, in Z. Mlinar (ed.), *Globalization and Territorial Identity*. Aldershot: Avebury, pp. 1–14.

Nederveen Pieterse, Jan (1994) Globalisation as hybridisation, *International Sociology*, **9**, 161–84.

Ohmae, Kenichi (1993) The rise of the region-state, *Foreign Affairs*, **72**, 78–87.

Parekh, Bhikhu (1994) Minority rights, majority values, in D. Miliband (ed.), *Reinventing the Left*. Cambridge: Polity Press, pp. 101–9.

Passerin d'Entrèves, Alexander (1967) *The Notion of the State*. Oxford: Clarendon Press.

Rizvi, Gowher (1995) South Asia and the new world order, in Holm and Sørensen (eds), pp. 69–87.

Robertson, Roland (1992) *Globalization: Social Theory and Global Culture*. London: Sage.

Robertson, Roland and Chirico, J. (1985), Humanity, globalization and worldwide religious resurgence: a theoretical explanation, *Sociological Analysis*, **46**, 219–42.

Sassen, Saskia (1996) *Losing Control? Sovereignty in an Age of Globalization*. New York: Columbia University Press.

Scholte, Jan Aart (1996) Beyond the buzzword: towards a critical theory of globalization, in E. Kofman and G. Youngs (eds), *Globalization: Theory and Practice*. London: Pinter, pp. 43–57.

Walker, R. J. B. (1993) *Inside/Outside*. Cambridge: Cambridge University Press.

Walker, R. J. B. and Mendlovitz, Saul (1990) Interrogating state sovereignty, in Walker and Mendlovitz (eds), *Contending Sovereignties*. London: Lynne Rienner.

Waters, Malcolm (1995) *Globalization*. London: Routledge.

2

Globalization and the Postmodern Turn

DOUGLAS KELLNER

There is no doubt about it: globalization is the buzz word of the decade. Journalists, politicians, business executives, academics, and others are using the word to signify that something profound is happening, that the world is changing, that a new world economic, political and cultural order is emerging. Yet the term is used in so many different contexts, by so many different people, for so many different purposes, that it is difficult to ascertain what is at stake in the globalization problematic, what function the term serves, and what effects it has for contemporary theory and politics.

A wide and diverse range of social theorists are arguing that today's world is organized by increasing globalization, which is strengthening the dominance of a world capitalist economic system, supplanting the primacy of the nation-state by transnational corporations and organizations, and eroding local cultures and traditions through a global culture. Marxists, advocates of world-systems theory, functionalists, Weberians, and many other contemporary theorists are converging on the position that globalization is a distinguishing trend of the present moment. Moreover, advocates of a postmodern break in history argue that developments in transnational capitalism are producing a new global historical configuration of post-Fordism, or postmodernism as a new cultural logic of capitalism (Gottdiener, 1995; Harvey, 1989; Jameson, 1991; Soja, 1989). In significant modern and postmodern social theories, globalization is thus taken as a salient feature of our times.

Yet the conceptions of globalization deployed, the purposes for which the concept is used and the evaluations of the processes described by the concept vary wildly. For some, globalization entails the Westernization of the world (Latouche, 1996), while for others it involves a cover for the ascendancy of capitalism (Ferguson, 1992). Some see globalization as generating increasing homogeneity, while others see it producing diversity and heterogeneity through increased hybridization. For business, globalization is a strategy for increasing corporate profits and power, for government it is often deployed to promote an increase in state power, while non-government social organizations see globalization as a lever to produce positive social goods like environmental action, democratization, or humanization. Many theorists equate globalization and modernity (e.g. Beck, 1992; Giddens, 1990), while others claim that the 'global age' follows and is distinctly different from the 'modern age' (Albrow, 1996). Indeed, for some theorists, we live in a global age or epoch, in which globalization is *the* defining concept (Axford, 1995; Albrow, 1996), while others find claims for the novelty and centrality of globalization exaggerated (Hirst and Thompson, 1996).

Yet the ubiquity of the term 'globalization' suggests that it is part of a reconfiguring and rethinking of contemporary social theory and politics that is caught up in some of the central debates and conflicts of the present age. It is certainly arguable that during the past decades, the world has been undergoing the most significant period of technological innovation and global restructuring since the first decades of the twentieth century. Part of the 'great transformation' (Polanyi, 1957) to a new stage of techno-capitalism has involved a fundamental restructuring and reorganization of the world economy, polity and culture, for which the term globalization serves as a codeword. It is bound up with debates over post-Fordism, postmodernism, and a series of other 'posts' that themselves signify a fundamental rupture with the past. It is thus centrally involved in debates over the defining features and changes of the present era.

In this chapter, I will differentiate some of the dominant uses of the term globalization and will propose the need for a critical theory of globalization that overcomes the one-sidedness and ideological biases involved in most conceptions. My argument is that the discourse of globalization can be articulated with theories both of the modern and of the postmodern because we are currently involved in an interregnum period between an aging modern and an emerging postmodern era (Best and Kellner, 1997). In this period of transition, in a borderland between two epochs, globalization signifies both continuities with the past, with modernity and modernization, and novelties of the present and the already here future. I also want to argue that globalization must be seen as a complex and multidimensional phenom-enon that involves different levels, flows, tensions and conflicts, such that a transdisciplinary social theory is necessary to capture its contours, dynam-ics, trajectories, problems and possible futures.

Theorizing globalization

Talking cogently about globalization requires, first, that we establish the different uses and senses of the term and try to specify what processes it is used to describe. In a sense, there is no such thing as globalization *per se*. Rather the term is used as a cover concept for a heterogeneity of processes that need to be spelled out and articulated. The term is neither innocent nor neutral in many of its uses, and often serves to replace older discourses like 'imperialism', but also 'modernization'. As a replacement for imperialism, it could displace a focus on the domination of developing countries by the overdeveloped ones, or of national and local economies by transnational corporations. Moreover, it could serve as a cover to neutralize the horrors of colonialism and could be part of a discourse of neo-imperialism that serves to obscure the continuing exploitation of much of the world by a few super-powers and giant transnational corporations, thus cloaking some of the more barbaric and destructive aspects of contemporary development.

Yet as a replacement term for modernization it can also rob this previously legitimating ideology of the connotations that the processes (i.e. modernization, which has a positive ring to it) are necessarily bringing progress and improvement, are part of an inexorable trajectory of progress and modernity. Compared to the discourses of imperialism (negative, critical) and moderniza-tion (positive, legitimating), the discourse of globalization is on the surface neutral. It thus displaces discourses of modernization (good) and imperialism (bad), covering over their evaluative components with a seemingly neutral term. And yet it too is bound up with highly ideological discourses of the present age being used by some to represent an entirely positive process of economic and social progress, technological innovation, more diverse prod-ucts and services, a cornucopia of information and growing cultural freedom, and a higher standard of living. Pro-globalization boosters include champions of the market economy, which with the triumph of Thatcherism-Reaganism in the 1980s became a dominant ideology, Bill Gates (1995) and avatars of the 'information superhighway' and new technologies, and other political and economic elites, supported by their academic promoters and perhaps by sociological analysts who exaggerate the inexorable and irresistible trajectory of globalization while covering over its more troubling aspects.

For its critics, however, globalization is bringing about the devastating destruction of local traditions, the continued subordination of poorer nations and regions by richer ones, environmental destruction, and a homogeniza-tion of culture and everyday life. These critics include Marxists, liberals, and multiculturalists who stress the threat to national sovereignty, local tradi-tions, and participatory democracy through global forces, environmentalists who fear the destructive ecological effects of unchecked globalization, and conservatives who see globalization as a threat to national and local cultures and the sanctity of tradition.

The term globalization is thus a theoretical construct that is itself con-tested and open for various meanings and inflections. It can be described positively or negatively, or, as I shall suggest, multivalently, to describe highly complex and multidimensional processes in the economy, polity, culture, and everyday life. A critical theory of globalization attempts to specify the interconnections and interdependencies between different levels such as the economic, political, cultural and psychological, as well as between different flows of products, ideas and information, people, and technology. Critical theory describes the mediations between different phenomena, the systemic structure which organizes phenomena and processes into a social system, and the relative autonomy of the parts, such that there are both connections and disjunctions between, say, the economy and culture. Concerned to relate theory to practice, critical theory also attempts to delineate the positive potentials for greater freedom and democratization, as well as the dangers of greater domination, oppression, and destruction (Kellner, 1989). Grounded in historical vision, critical theory stresses the continuities and discontinuities between past, present and future, and the possibility of constructive political action and individual and group practice, grounded in positive potentials in the current constellation of forces and possibilities (Best, 1995).

The already highly complex articulations of the discourse of globalization are rendered more complicated because globalization is not only a replacement term for imperialism and modernization, but is caught up in the modernity/postmodernity debates as well. Some theorists are claiming that globalization is replacing concepts like modernity and postmodernity as the central thematic of contemporary theorizing (Featherstone, Lash and Robertson, 1995; Waters, 1995; Albrow, 1996), though others have assimilated the discourse, variously, to both the modernity and the postmodernity problematics. For some, globalization thus constitutes a continuation of the problematic of modernization and modernity, while for others, it signifies something new and different and is bound up with the postmodern turn, or an altogether novel and as yet untheorized global condition (Best and Kellner, 1991, 1997). Yet here too, totally different valorizations of the modern, postmodern and globalization process are possible. For some theorists, globalization is seen as a process of standardization in which a globalized media and consumer culture circulates the globe creating sameness and homogeneity everywhere, thus bringing to light the bland and boring universality and massification in the modern project. Postmodernists champion, by contrast, the local, diversity, difference, and heterogeneity, and sometimes claim that globalization itself produces hybridity and multiplicity, arguing that global culture makes possible unique appropriations and developments all over the world with new forms of hybrid syntheses of the global and the local, thus proliferating difference and heterogeneity (Hall, 1991). Postmodernists also argue that every local context involves its own appropriation and reworking of global products and signifiers, thus producing more variety and diversity.

In the following discussion, I want to argue against all one-sided and partial positions that see globalization either as a necessary and positive vehicle of progress and diversity, or as a force of insipid homogenization and destruction. Both of these positions are obviously one-sided, so, as in many cases where we encounter one-sided and opposed positions, we should move to a higher level to develop a critical and dialectical theory of globalization which articulates both its progressive and regressive features, as well as its fundamental ambivalence that mixes old and new, innovation and destruction, and the global and local.

Globalization: *economy/state/culture*

The term 'globalization' is thus often used as a code-word that stands for a tremendous diversity of issues and problems and that serves as a front for a variety of theoretical and political positions. While it can serve as a legitimating ideology to cover over and sanitize ugly realities, a critical globalization theory can inflect the discourse to point precisely to these phenomena and can elucidate a series of contemporary problems and conflicts. In view of the different concepts and functions of globalization discourse, it is important to note that the concept is a theoretical construct that varies according to the assumptions and commitments of the theory in question. Seeing the term globalization as a construct helps rob it of its force of nature, as a sign of an inexorable triumph of market forces and the hegemony of capital, or, as the extreme right fears, of a rapidly encroaching world government. While the term can both describe and legitimate and normalize capitalist transnationalism, and transnational government institutions, a critical theory of globalization does not buy into ideological valorizations and affirms difference, resistance, and democratic self-determination against forms of global domination and subordination.

A critical theory of globalization is necessarily transdisciplinary and describes the ways in which global economic, political and cultural forces are rapidly penetrating the earth in the creation of a new world market, new transnational political organizations, and a new global culture. The expansion of the capitalist world market into areas previously closed off to it (i.e. in the communist sphere or developing countries which attempted to pursue their own independent line of development) is accompanied by the decline of the nation-state and its power to regulate and control the flow of goods, people, information, and various cultural forms. There have, of course, been global networks of power and imperialist empires for centuries, accompanied by often fierce local resistance by the colonized entities. National liberation movements disrupted colonial empires of power and created a 'Third Way' between the capitalist and communist blocs, especially in the period after

World War Two, marked by the success of a large number of anti-imperialist revolutions. But as we approach the end of the twentieth century, it would seem that neither decolonization nor the end of the Cold War has loosened the hold of transnational systems of domination.

In addition to the development of a new global market economy and shifting system of nation-states, the rise of global culture is an especially salient feature of contemporary globalization. Accompanying the dramatic expansion of capitalism and new transnational political organizations a new global culture is emerging as a result of computer and communications technology, a consumer society with its panorama of goods and services, transnational forms of architecture and design, and a wide range of products and cultural forms that are traversing national boundaries and becoming part of a new world culture. Global culture includes the proliferation of media technologies that veritably create Marshall McLuhan's dream of a global village, in which people all over the world watch political spectacles like the Gulf War, major sports events, entertainment programmes, and advertisements that relentlessly promote capitalist modernization (Wark, 1994). At the same time, more and more people are entering into global computer networks that instantaneously circulate ideas, information and images throughout the world, overcoming boundaries of space and time (Gates, 1995).

Global culture involves promoting lifestyle, consumption, products and identities. Transnational corporations deploy advertising to penetrate local markets, to sell global products, and to overcome local resistance. Expanding private cable and satellite systems have been aggressively promoting a commercial culture throughout the world. In a sense, culture itself is being redefined, for previously local and national cultures have been forces of resistance to global forces, protecting the traditions, identities and modes of life of specific groups and peoples. Culture has been precisely the particularizing, localizing force that distinguished societies and people from each other. Culture provided forms of local identities, practices and modes of everyday life that could serve as a bulwark against the invasion of ideas, identities and forms of life extraneous to the specific local region in question. Indeed, culture is an especially complex and contested terrain today as global cultures permeate local ones and new configurations emerge that synthesize both poles, providing contradictory forces of colonization *and* resistance, global homogenization *and* new local hybrid forms and identities.

Globalization also involves the dissemination of new technologies that have tremendous impact on the economy, polity, society, culture and everyday life. Time-space compression produced by new media and communications technologies is overcoming previous boundaries of space and time, creating a global cultural village and dramatic penetration of global forces into every realm of life in every region of the world. New technologies in the labour process displace living labour, make possible more flexible production, and create new labour markets, with some areas undergoing deindustrialization (for example, the 'rust belt' of the Midwest in the United States), while production itself becomes increasingly transnational (Harvey, 1989). The new technologies also create new industries, such as the computer and information industry, and allow transnational media and information instantaneously to traverse the globe (Morley and Robbins, 1995). This process has led some to celebrate a new global information superhighway and others to attack the new wave of media and cultural imperialism.

Yet the very concept of globalization has long been a contested terrain described in conflicting positive and negative normative discourses. It is perhaps the early theorists and critics of capitalism who first engaged with the phenomenon of the globalization of the capitalist system. Not surprisingly, the defenders of capitalism, such as Adam Smith, saw the process positively, whereas Karl Marx and Friedrich Engels had more critical perceptions. Producing one of the first major discourses of globalization, Smith saw the European 'discoveries' of the Americas and the passage to the East Indies as creating a new world market with highly significant consequences. Smith wrote:

> Their consequences have already been great; but, in the short period of between two and three centuries which has elapsed since these discoveries were made, it is impossible that the whole extent of their consequences can have been seen. What benefits, or what misfortunes to mankind may hereafter result from these events, no human wisdom can foresee. By uniting, in some measure, the most distant parts of the world, by enabling them to relieve one another's wants, to increase one another's enjoyments, and to encourage one another's industry, their general tendency would seem to be beneficial. To the natives, however, both of the East and West Indies, all the commercial benefits which can have resulted from these events have been sunk and lost in the dreadful misfortunes which they have occasioned. These misfortunes, however, seem to have arisen rather from accident than from any thing in the nature of those events themselves. At the particular time when these discoveries were made, the *superiority of force* happened to be so great on the side of the Europeans, that they were enabled to commit with impunity every sort of injustice in those remote countries. Hereafter, perhaps, the natives of those countries may grow stronger, or those of Europe may grow weaker, and the inhabitants of all the different quarters of the world may arrive at that equality of courage and force which, by inspiring mutual fear, can alone overawe the injustice of independent nations into some sort of respect for the rights of one another. But nothing seems more likely to establish this equality of force than that mutual communication of knowledge and of all sorts of improvements which an extensive commerce from all countries to all countries naturally, or rather necessarily, carries along with it. (Smith, 1961: II, 141)

Smith thus envisaged the emergence of a world market system as one of the most important features of modernity that would eventually benefit the entire world. Although perceiving the injustices of unequal relations of power and force, Smith generally appraised the globalization of the world market as 'beneficial'. With characteristic honesty, he cited the 'misfortunes' of the process of colonization, but optimistically believed that the injustices of the process might be overcome. In *The Communist Manifesto*, Marx and Engels followed Smith in seeing the importance of the globalization of the capitalist market, although, of course, they differed in their evaluation of it. Closely following the optic of Smith, they claimed:

> Modern industry has established the world market, for which the discovery of America paved the way ... [the] need of a constantly expanding market for its products chases the bourgeoisie over the whole surface of the globe. It must nestle everywhere, settle everywhere, establish connections everywhere .... The bourgeoisie, by the rapid improvement of all instruments of production, by the immensely facilitated means of communication, draws all, even the most barbarian nations into civilization .... In a word, it creates a world after its own image. (Marx and Engels, 1976: 486ff.)

Both the classical liberalism of Smith and classical Marxism thus see capitalism as a global economic system characterized by a world market and the imposition of similar relations of production, commodities and culture on areas throughout the world, creating a new modern world-system as the capitalist market penetrates the four corners of the earth. For both classical liberalism and Marxism, the bourgeoisie constantly revolutionized the instruments of production and the world market generated immense forces of commerce, navigation and discovery, communications and industry, creating a new world of abundance, diversity and prosperity:

> In place of the old wants, satisfied by the production of the country, we find new wants, requiring for their satisfaction the products of distant lands and climes. In place of the old local and national seclusion and self-sufficiency, we have intercourse in every direction, universal interdependence of nations. And as in material, so also in intellectual production. The intellectual creations of individual nations become common property. National one-sidedness and narrow-mindedness become more and more impossible, and from the numerous national and local literatures there arises a world literature. (ibid.: 488)

This passage points to the resources and positive results of the world market that provide the basis for a higher stage of social organization. But in the Marxian vision, the globalization process is appraised more ambiguously. For Marx and Engels, the world market produced a new class of industrial proletariat that was reduced to abstract labour power, rendered propertyless, and had 'nothing to lose but its chains' and a world to win. Marx and Engels believed that the industrial proletariat would organize as a revolutionary class to overthrow capitalism and produce a new socialist society that would abolish poverty, inequality, exploitation and alienated labour, making possible the full development of the individual and a more equitable division of social wealth. They also envisaged the possibility of a world global crisis which would generate world revolution, enveloping the earth in a titanic struggle between capital and its opponents. Their working class revolutionaries would be resolutely internationalist and cosmopolitan in the Marxian vision, seeing themselves as citizens of the world rather than members of specific nations.

Curiously, the Marxian theory shared the illusions of many market liberals that the development of a world system of free trade would eliminate nationalism and the nation-state, with both downplaying their importance, in a new world economic system – be it capitalist or communist (Polanyi, 1957: 189). Both Smith and Marx present colonization and the globalization of the market society as inevitable and as the basis of material progress. Both recognize the injustices of the process for the victims of colonization and the use of violence and superior force to subjugate non-Western culture, but both are sanguine about the process and draw distinctions between 'barbarian nations' and civilizations that ultimately present globalization as a 'civilizing process' – this would indeed emerge as one of the dominant ideologies of imperialism (which the Marxian tradition otherwise opposes).

Indeed, globalization has also had important political implications. As Giovanni Arrighi (1994) documents, colonialization benefited successively the Italian city-states, Holland, and England, which accrued political power and, in the case of England, world empire through its role in trade, the establishment of colonies, and finance and industry. In the aftermath of World War Two, world-systems theory described 'the creation of a system of national states and the formation of a worldwide capitalist system' as 'the two interdependent master processes of the [modern] era' (Tilly, 1984: 147). Both Marxism and world-systems theory stress the importance of the rise to global dominance of a capitalist market economy that is penetrating the entire globe, while world-systems theory stresses the equal importance of a system of national states.

For several centuries, globalization proceeded on an increasingly rising curve, bringing more and more areas of the world into the world market-system. World War One and its aftermath produced a slowing down of this process, however, first enmeshing much of the Western world in a highly destructive war, followed by a period of economic boom and bust, protectionism, growing nationalism, and the failure of internationalist economic and political policy. World War Two once again engulfed much of the world in an even more destructive and global war, though already during the war itself events occurred that would shape the post-War world economic order. At the Bretton Woods conference in 1944, monetary arrangements were undertaken which would help produce a globalized world order. At the end of this meeting, the World Bank and IMF were founded, two major economic institutions that would be at the basis of later arrangements such as GATT and NAFTA. With the end of the war, world trade exploded with a vengeance. National trade barriers were systematically dismantled and eroded, global economic forces penetrated local economies, and a global consumer and media culture traversed the globe. The results have been auspicious: 'As we look back fifty years later, we can see that economic growth has expanded fivefold, international trade has expanded by roughly twelve times and foreign direct investment has been expanding at two or three times the rate of trade expansion' (Korten, 1996: 15).

Yet the results of these developments have been highly uneven. While economic elites and corporations have benefited tremendously the rewards have been unequally distributed. Gaps between rich and poor, the haves and the have nots, the overdeveloped and underdeveloped regions, have grown exponentially. The wealthier nations continue to exploit the people, resources and land of the poorer nations, often leaving environmental degradation behind. The debt crisis in which the poorer countries owe the richer ones astronomical sums has increased dramatically since the 1970s. There are more poor people in the world today than ever before; violence on the local, national and global scale has erupted throughout this century of unmitigated disaster and horror (Aronson, 1983); the planet's ecosystem is under siege and the 'fate of the earth' lies in immediate jeopardy. For much of the world, life is still 'nasty, brutish and short', and prosperity, health, education and welfare remain distant dreams for much of the overpopulation of the besieged earth.

Resisting globalization

The concept of globalization can be disempowering, leading to cynicism and hopelessness, a feeling that inexorable market forces cannot be regulated and controlled by the state, or that the economy cannot be shaped and directed by the people, thus undermining democracy and countervailing powers to the hegemony of capital (Hirst and Thompson, 1996). A critical theory of globalization, however, recognizes the reality of globalization, its power and effects, but also seeks forces of resistance and struggle that attempt to counter the most destructive aspects of global forces, or which inflect globalization for democratic and locally empowering ends. The present conjuncture, I would suggest, is marked by a conflict between growing centralization and organization of power and wealth in the hands of the few and opposing processes exhibiting a fragmentation of power that is more plural, multiple, and open to contestation than previously. As the following analysis will suggest, both tendencies are observable and it is up to individuals and groups to find openings for contestation and struggle.

With the collapse of the Soviet Union and its satellite nations – which provided the bulwark of a global alternative to a capitalist market system – market forces are now largely unopposed by any system of nation-states, including those that emerged out of opposition to colonial domination, with few corners of the world able to resist the global flow of capital and its products. Indeed, a world market economy disseminates throughout the planet fantasies of happiness through consumption and the goods and services that allow entry into the phantasmagoria of consumer capitalism. A world financial market circulates capital in international circuits that bind together the world in a global market dominated by the forces and institutions of finance capital. Capital thus circles the globe, furnishing new products and fashions while eroding tradition and national economies and identities.

Global economic change often has tremendous local impact. Whole regions are devastated with the shutting down of industrial production, moved to regions with lower wages and less government regulation. Such 'deindustrialization' has created vast 'rust belts' of previously prosperous industrial regions, as in the case of Flint, Michigan, which suffered major economic decline with the closing of General Motors automobile plants, an episode documented in Michael Moore's film *Roger and Me* (see Bluestone and Harrison, 1982; Harvey, 1989). Automation, computers and new technologies have eliminated entire categories of labour while corporate reorganization has abolished segments of management, producing vast unemployment. Corporations like Nike move from country to country in search of lower labour costs and more docile work forces. More than ever, the world economy is bound together so that hurricanes in Japan or financial irregularities in Britain influence the entire world.

Consequently, globalization involves new connections and the integration of economies and cultures into a world system, overcoming previous divisions and distances. Especially during the period of the Cold War arising after World War Two, the system of modern nation-states divided into two camps – capitalist and socialist – producing a shifting series of alliances and conflicts influencing countries from Vietnam to Nicaragua. During this period, nations either pursued the capitalist or socialist model of development – or in the case of some so-called Third World nations attempted to forge their own path of development. As the term suggests, the Third World nations created by decolonization were often considered to be less important in global affairs than the conflict between the world superpowers, and the binaristic Cold War model provided a convenient rubric for economic, political and cultural intervention into Third World affairs, dividing the world into a global field of conflict between the two superpowers with much of the planet caught in the middle.

But with the collapse of the communist system this period of history came to an end, and during the 1990s the capitalist market model of globalization has become dominant and practically uncontested. The analogue of such economic globalization is said to be the triumph of democracy throughout the world with its discourse and institutions of a pluralistic system of checks and balances, parties, elections and human rights (Fukuyama, 1992; Derrida, 1994, for a critique). For some decades, indeed, democracy has been interpreted as the necessary accompaniment and/or condition of capitalism (Rostow, Friedman, Fukuyama), while a tradition of critical theory documents the tensions and conflicts between democracy and capitalism (Bowles and Gintis, 1986; Cohen and Rogers, 1983; Kellner, 1990; Wolfe, 1972).

And yet the decline of the power of the nation-state produces a new geopolitical matrix in which transnational organizations, corporations and forces challenge national and local sites of power and influence. In the wake of political developments such as decolonization, the end of the Cold War, the formation of new trade agreements and political unions, and the rise of global transnational capitalism, national borders have shifted, resulting in the increased power of transnational institutions. Accompanying such momentous political changes are the increasing prominence of world trade, financial speculations and investment, and global cultural forces that operate outside the confines of the nation-state as a discrete entity.

And yet new conflicts also have emerged exhibiting a surge of nationalism and fundamentalism and clashes of cultures (Huntington, 1996). It is curious how classical liberalism, Marxism and modernization theory downplayed the importance of culture and local forms of social association, positing the inexorable advance of the modern economy, technology, and politics which would supposedly level out and homogenize all societies and culture, producing a world global culture. Both capitalism with its world market and communism with its international socioeconomic system and political culture were supposed to erode cultural differences, regional particularities, nationalism and traditionalism. Thus, both classical liberalism and Marxism promoted or predicted globalization as the fate of the world: for capitalist ideologues, the market was going to produce a global world culture, whereas for Marxism the proletariat was going to produce communism that would eliminate nationalism and create a communist international without exploitation or war. Both saw the significance of national borders being eliminated and both seriously underestimated the endurance of nationalism and the nation-state.

Missing from both Marxist and liberal models has been an understanding of how race, ethnicity and nationalist sentiment might intersect with class to produce local, political struggles with complex causes. Indeed, from the late 1980s to the present there has been a resurgence of nationalism, traditionalism and religious fundamentalism alongside trends towards growing globalization. The explosion of regional, cultural and religious differences in the former Soviet Union and Yugoslavia – as well as explosive tribal conflicts in Africa and elsewhere – suggests that globalization and homogenization were not as deep as proponents hoped and critics feared. Culture has thus become a new source of conflict and an important dimension of struggle between the global and the local. National cultures have produced confrontations between Serbs, Muslims and Croats, Armenians and Azerbaijanis, Mohawk First Nation peoples and Québécois, and in South Africa struggles between the Inkatha party and the African National Congress. Thus, both culture and nationalism turned out to be more enduring, deep and fundamental than expected and clashes between the global and local cultures, and of various national cultures with each other, continue in a supposedly globalized world.

It is also in the realm of culture that globalization is most visible and apparent. Global media and information systems and a world capitalist consumer culture circulate products, images and ideas throughout the world. Events such as the Gulf War, social trends and fashions, and cultural phenomena such as Madonna, rap music and popular Hollywood films are distributed through global cultural distribution networks and constitute a 'global popular' (Kellner, 1995). This global culture, however, operates precisely through the multiplication of different products, services and spectacles, targeted at specific audiences. Consumer and media industries are becoming more differentiated and are segmenting their customers and audiences into more categories. In many cases, this involves the simulation of minor differences of fashion and style as significant, but it also involves a proliferation of a more highly differentiated culture and society in terms of an ever expanding variety and diversity of cultural artefacts, products and services.

However, there has also been a significant eruption of subcultures of resistance that have attempted to preserve specific forms of culture and society against globalization and homogenization. Most dramatically, peasant movements in Mexico, guerrilla movements in Peru, labour unions in France, students in Britain and the United States, environmentalists throughout the world, and a variety of other groups and movements have resisted capitalist globalization and attacks on previous rights and benefits. Seven dozen people's organizations from around the world have protested against World Trade Organization policies and a backlash against globalization is visible everywhere. Politicians who once championed trade agreements like GATT and NAFTA are now quiet about these arrangements and at the 1996 annual Davos World Economic Forum its founder and managing director published a warning entitled 'Start taking the backlash against globalization seriously' (*New York Times*, 7 February 1996: A15).

On the terrain of everyday life, new youth subcultures of resistance are visible throughout the world, as are alternative subcultures of women, gays and lesbians, blacks and ethnic minorities, and other groups that have resisted incorporation into the hegemonic mainstream culture. British cultural studies have accordingly explored both mainstream hegemonic cultures and oppositional subcultures since the 1970s. They have focused on articulations of class, race, gender, sexual preference, ethnicity, region and nation in their explorations of concrete cultural configurations and phenomena (During, 1993; Grossberg *et al.*, 1992; Hall and Jefferson, 1976; Hebdige, 1979; Kellner, 1995). More recently, cultural studies have also taken on a global focus, analysing how transnational forces intervene in concrete situations and how cultural mediations can inflect the influence of such global configurations.

Indeed, a wide range of theorists have argued that the proliferation of difference and the shift to more local discourses and practices define the contemporary scene and that theory and politics should shift from the level of globalization and its accompanying often totalizing and macro theories in order to focus on the local, the specific, the particular, the heterogeneous, and the micro level of everyday experience. A wide range of theories associated with poststructuralism, postmodernism, feminism and multiculturalism focuses on difference, otherness, marginality, the personal, the particular, and the concrete over more general theory and politics that aim at more global or universal conditions (Best and Kellner, 1991).

It can be argued that such dichotomies as those between the global and the local express contradictions and tensions between crucial constitutive forces of the present moment and that it is therefore a mistake to reject focus on one side in favour of exclusive concern with the other (Cvetkovitch and Kellner, 1997). Our challenge is to think through the relationships between the global and the local by observing how global forces influence and even structure ever more local situations, and ever more strikingly. One should also see how local forces and situations mediate the global, inflecting global forces to diverse ends and conditions, and producing unique configurations of the local and the global as the matrix for thought and action in the contemporary world.

Indeed, in many various fields and disciplines, theorists are beginning to consider how global, systemic and macro structures interact with local, particular and micro conditions and structures. Such dialectical optics attempt to theorize the intersection of the global and the local, how they interact and mediate each other, and the new constellations being produced by current interactions between these forces. In this way, one overcomes the partiality and one-sidedness of undialectical theories that fail to perceive how the global and the local interact so as to produce new social and cultural configurations.

Analogous to the question of conceptualizing the interactions of the global and the local on the level of theory, debates have emerged over the proper locus and focus of politics today. Some theorists argue that global and national problems require macro-structural solutions, while others argue that the proper sphere of the political is the local and the personal, and not the global or national. Postmodern theories of power, for instance, have stressed how power inhabits local, specific and micro realms, ignored by modern theories that located powers in centres such as the economy, the state, or patriarchy. Postmodern politics urges local and specific actions to intervene in discursive sites of power ranging from the bedroom to the classroom, from prisons to mental institutions (Best and Kellner, forthcoming).

Here too the old modern and new postmodern politics seem one-sided. Power resides in both macro *and* micro institutions; it is more complex than ever, with new configurations of global, national, regional, and more properly local forces and relations of power, generating new conflicts and sites of struggle, ranging from debates over 'the new world order' – or disorder as it may appear to many – to struggles over local control of schools or the environment. Rethinking politics in the present conflicted and complex configurations of both novel and established relations of power and domination thus requires thinking through the complex ways in which the global and the local are interconnected. Theorizing the configurations of the global and the local also requires the development of new multidimensional strategies ranging from the macro to the micro, the national to the local, in order to intervene in a wide range of contemporary and emerging problems and struggles. As Roland Axtmann suggests (1997), globalization yields the possibility of new concepts of global citizenship that will make us responsible and participatory in the problems and challenges of the coming global village. To the slogan 'Think globally, act locally', we may thus add the slogan 'Think locally, act globally'. From this perspective, problems concerning global environmental problems, the development of a global information superhighway, and the need for new global forums for discussing and resolving the seemingly intransigent problems of war and peace, poverty and inequality, and overcoming divisions between the haves and the have nots, may produce new conceptions of global citizenship and new challenges for global intellectuals and activists.

Axtmann also suggests that global citizenship, and thus the effects of globalization *per se*, could promote a greater acceptance of diversity, heterogeneity and otherness rather than globalization just promoting homogeneity and sameness (1997). Yet globalization could produce as well new forms of imperialist domination under the guises of universality and globality. Indeed, there remains the danger that globalization functions as a cloak disguising a relentless Westernization, or even Americanization, of the world, much as did the old modernization theory which globalization theory to some extent inherits and continues. But the resurrection of tradition, ethno-nationalism, religious fundamentalisms, and other forms of resistance to globalization are motivated at least to some extent by a rejection of the homogenization and perhaps Westernization associated with some forms of globalization.

Globalization is thus necessarily complex and challenging to both our theories and politics. But most people nowadays, including theorists who should know better, operate with binary concepts of the global and the local, the modern or the postmodern, and promote one or the other side of the equation as the solution to the world's problems. For globalists, globalization is the solution and underdevelopment, backwardness and provincialism are the problem. For localists, globalization is the problem and localization is the solution. But, less simplistically, it is the mix that matters and whether global or local solutions are most appropriate depends on the conditions in the specific context that one is addressing. In a complex, globalized world, there is no easy formula to solve the intransigent problems of the present era, yet there are so many problems on so many levels that it should not be difficult for people of imagination and good will to find opportunities for intervention in a variety of areas.

Globalization and the postmodern turn: concluding remarks

Acting in the present age involves understanding the matrix of global and local forces, of forces of domination and resistance, and of rapid change and a 'great transformation' brought about by the global restructuring of capital and multidimensional effects of new technologies. The future is up for grabs, as are characterizations of where we now are, where we are going, and what concepts and perspectives best characterize our present dilemma. I have suggested that we are living in a period between the modern and something new for which the term 'postmodern' stands as a marker. One could, of course, describe the tensions between the global and the local, the modern and the postmodern, and the old and the new, as a process of postmodernization, of increasing complexity, fragmentation, indeterminacy and uncertainty. Yet it is my position that although a postmodern turn is visible, continuities with the modern are so striking that it is a mistake to posit a postmodern rupture and exaggerate discontinuities.

This is certainly the case with globalization, for clearly the process has been going on for centuries and, as the earlier discussion of Adam Smith and Marx suggested, globalization itself is bound up with capitalist modernity and the expansion of the capitalist system and relations of production which continues to be one of the defining features of our present moment. Yet there are also striking novelties in the present age. The rapidity of globalization, with its space-time compression, its simultaneous forms of mass communication, its instantaneous financial transactions and an increasingly integrated world market, is surely a novelty. New technologies are changing the nature of work and creating new forms of leisure, including the hyperreality of cyberspace, new virtual realities, and new modes of information and entertainment. Capital is producing a new technoculture, a new form of the entertainment and information society, and everything from education to work to politics and everyday life is dramatically changing.

Yet I do not believe that these novelties are sufficiently great at present to postulate a complete postmodern rupture. Capitalist relations of production still structure most social orders and the hegemony of capital is still the structuring force of most dimensions of social life. Dramatic change and innovation have been part of modernity for centuries, as has technological development and expansion. Yet these phenomena, bound up with globalization in its current phase, have created enough novelties to require a rethinking of social theory and politics in the current situation as a response to new developments in society and culture.

In sum and to conclude: historical epochs do not rise and fall in neat patterns or at precise chronological moments. Perhaps our current situation is parallel in some ways to the Renaissance, which constituted a long period of transition between the end of pre-modern societies and the emergence of modern ones. Such periods are characterized by unevenly developing multiple levels of change, and the birth-pangs associated with the eruption of a new era. In fact, change between one era and another is always protracted and contradictory, and usually painful. But the vivid sense of 'betweenness', or transition, requires that one grasp the connections with the past as well as the novelties of the present and future. Thus it is important to capture both the continuities and the discontinuities of the postmodern with the modern, in order to make sense of our current predicament.

Living in a borderland between the modern and postmodern creates tension, insecurity, confusion, and even panic, as well as excitement and exhilaration, thus producing a cultural and social environment of shifting moods and an open but troubling future. The concept of a postmodern turn embodies awareness of the risks and dangers in the current social constellation, as well as the hope of new possibilities and excitement. The postmodern turn is thus deeply implicated in the moods and experiences of the present and is an important component of our contemporary situation (Best and

Kellner, 1997). The very ubiquity of the discourse of the 'postmodern', its constant proliferation, its refusal to fade away, and its seeming longevity – several decades is a long time for a mere 'fad' in our rapidly changing world – suggest that it is addressing current concerns in a useful way, that it illuminates salient present-day realities, that it resonates with shared experience, and that it is simply an ingrained part of the current critical lexicon that one has to come to terms with, one way or another.

Acknowledgements

I am indebted to work with Ann Cvetkovich on a book *Articulating the Global and the Local: Globalization and Cultural Studies* (1997) and to work with Steven Best on *The Postmodern Turn* (1997).

References

Albrow, Martin (1996) *The Global Age*. Cambridge: Polity Press.
Aronson, Ronald (1983) *The Dialectics of Disaster*. London: Verso.
Arrighi, Giovanni (1994) *The Long Twentieth Century*. London and New York: Verso.
Axford, Barrie (1995) *The Global System*. Cambridge: Polity Press.
Axtmann, Roland (1997) Collective identity and the democratic nation-state in the age of globalization, in Cvetkovich and Kellner, pp. 33–54.
Best, Steven (1995) *The Politics of Historical Vision*. New York: Guilford Press.
Best, Steven and Kellner, Douglas (1991) *Postmodern Theory: Critical Interrogations*. London and New York: Macmillan and Guilford.
Best, Steven and Kellner, Douglas (eds) (1997) *The Postmodern Turn*. New York: Guilford Press.
Best, Steven and Kellner, Douglas (forthcoming) *The Postmodern Adventure*. New York: Guilford Press.
Bluestone, Barry and Harrison, Bennett (1982) *The Deindustrialization of America*. New York: Basic Books.
Bowles, Samuel and Gintis, Herbert (1986) *On Democracy*. New York: Basic Books.
Cohen, Joshua and Rogers, Joel (1983) *On Democracy*. New York: Penguin.
Cvetkovich, Ann and Kellner, Douglas (1997) *Articulating the Global and the Local: Globalization and Cultural Studies*. Boulder, CO: Westview Press.
Derrida, Jacques (1994) *Specters of Marx*. London and New York: Routledge.
During, Simon (ed.) (1993) *The Cultural Studies Reader*. London and New York: Routledge.
Featherstone, Mike, Lash, Scott and Robertson, Roland (eds) (1995) *Global Modernities*. London: Sage.
Ferguson, Marjorie (1992) The mythology about globalization, *European Journal of Communication*, **7**, 69–93.

Fukuyama, Francis (1992) *The End of History and the Last Man.* New York: The Free Press.

Gates, Bill (1995) *The Road Ahead.* New York: Viking.

Giddens, Anthony (1990) *Consequences of Modernity.* Cambridge and Palo Alto: Polity and Stanford University Press.

Gottdiener, Mark (1995) *Postmodern Semiotics.* Oxford: Blackwell.

Grossberg, Lawrence, Nelson, Cary and Treichler, Paula (eds) (1992) *Cultural Studies.* London and New York: Routledge.

Hall, Stuart (1991) The local and the global: globalization and ethnicity, and Old and new identities, old and new ethnicities, in King (ed.), pp. 19–40, 41–68.

Hall, Stuart and Jefferson, Tony (eds) (1976) *Resistance Through Rituals: Youth Subcultures in Post-War Britain.* London: Unwin Hyman.

Harvey, David (1989) *The Condition of Postmodernity.* Cambridge: Blackwell.

Hebdige, Dick (1970) *Subculture: The Meaning of Style.* London and New York: Methuen.

Hirst, Paul and Thompson, Grahame (1996) *Globalization in Question.* Cambridge, UK: Polity Press.

Huntington, Samuel (1996) *The Clash of Civilizations and the Remaking of World Order.* New York: Simon & Schuster.

Jameson, Fredric (1991) *Postmodernism, or the Cultural Logic of Late Capitalism.* Durham, NC: Duke University Press.

Kellner, Douglas (1989) *Critical Theory, Marxism and Modernity.* Cambridge, UK and Baltimore, MD: Polity Press and Johns Hopkins University Press.

Kellner, Douglas (1990) *Television and the Crisis of Democracy.* Boulder, CO: Westview Press.

Kellner, Douglas (1995) *Media Culture.* London and New York: Routledge.

King, Anthony D. (ed.) (1991) *Culture, Globalization and the World-System: Contemporary Conditions for the Representation of Identity.* Binghamton, NY: SUNY Art Dept.

Korten, David C. (1996) The limits of the earth, *The Nation* (15/22 July), 14–18.

Latouche, Serge (1996) *The Westernization of the World.* Cambridge: Polity Press.

Marx, Karl and Engels, Frederick (1976) *Collected Works,* Vol. 6. New York: International Publishers.

Morley, David and Robbins, Kevin (1995) *Spaces of Identity.* London and New York: Routledge.

Polanyi, Karl (1957 [1944]) *The Great Transformation.* Boston: Beacon Press.

Smith, Adam (1961) *An Inquiry into the Nature and Causes of the Wealth of Nations,* 2 vols. London: Methuen.

Soja, Edward (1989) *Postmodern Geographies.* London: Verso.

Tilly, Charles (1984) *Big Structures, Large Processes, Huge Comparisons.* New York: Russell Sage.

Waters, Malcolm (1995) *Globalization.* London: Routledge.

Wark, McKenzie (1994) *Virtual Geography: Living with Global Media Events.* Bloomington and Indianapolis, IN: Indiana University Press.

Wolfe, Alan (1972) *The Limits of Legitimacy.* New York: Basic Books.

Further reading

Appadurai, Arjun (1990) Disjuncture and difference in the global cultural economy, in Featherstone (ed.), pp. 295–310.

Bird, Jon *et al.* (eds) (1993) *Mapping the Futures: Local Cultures, Global Change.* London and New York: Routledge.

Featherstone, Mike (ed.) (1990) *Global Culture: Nationalism, Globalization and Modernity.* London: Sage.

Gilroy, Paul (1993) *The Black Atlantic: Modernity and Double Consciousness.* Cambridge, MA: Harvard University Press.

Grewal, Inderpal and Kaplan, Caren (eds) (1994) *Scattered Hegemonies: Postmodernity and Transnational Feminist Practices.* Minneapolis, MN: University of Minnesota Press.

Held, David (1995) *Democracy and the Global Order.* Cambridge and Palo Alto: Polity Press and Stanford University Press.

Lash, Scott and Urry, John (1994) *Economies of Signs and Space.* London: Sage.

Robertson, Roland (1991) *Globalization.* London: Sage.

3

Decolonization in Globalization

JEAN HOUBERT

Globalization, whatever else it may mean, refers to the globe, to planet Earth. Globalization is used here to mean the worldwide extension of one of the outstanding institutions of modernity: the interstate system. States existed in Europe, and in other parts of the world, before modern times, but they did not form a single interstate system. The Cold War was the first time in history when the whole globe was structured by one and the same interstate system. This was preceded, however, by a European-centred interstate system which had crystallized at the Westphalia settlement, at the end of the Thirty Years' War, and lasted until its terminal breakdown in the 'New Thirty Years' War': 1914–45.

The necessary preconditions for the emergence of an interstate system covering the whole globe were the conquest of the sea, the most formidable of the natural barriers to human contacts across global distances, and the arrival of the modern state. The European-centred interstate system and the modern state were inextricably part and parcel of each other; there could have been no modern state without the interstate system. The modern state as a part of an interstate system originated at the same time as Europe embarked on its overseas colonial expansion.

Settler colonization in the genesis of the global system

America

The Europeans encompassed the world in early modernity rapidly. In 1492, when Columbus embarked on his historic voyage, Europeans had not crossed any oceans, yet only thirty years later, in 1522, part of Magellan's fleet returned to Europe, having gone right round the world, crossing all the oceans. Almost as rapidly as the Europeans discovered the sea, they imposed their hegemony over all the oceans of the planet. The gunned sailing ship of Atlantic Europe drove the ships of all other civilizations out of the seas of the world. Henceforth, all possible threats to the security of Europe from the sea

were removed. With the monopoly of sea power, Europe in effect extended its
frontiers to the coastline of all the other continents. As the sea makes up over
two-thirds of the globe, the gunned sailing ship had effectively put a
European straitjacket around the world in early modernity. The sea power
which Europe acquired in this early phase of expansion has remained to the
present day; but one of its erstwhile settler colonies, the United States, is now
playing the dominant role.

Power over the sea was translated immediately into power over the land in
the Americas. The New World was discovered accidentally by the European
sailors in their search for a new route to the fabulous riches of Asia. The pre-
Columbian Americans had no knowledge of the market and were not
producers of the luxuries the Europeans were after. There were precious
metals in the New World and these were highly coveted. Gold in particular
was regarded as the measure of the power of states as well as the purpose of
trade in the mercantilist era. The native Americans were not very numerous;
they had an immense homeland and no idea of private property; and they
had a 'stone age' technology. The few European conquistadors, with swords,
guns and horses, got the better of the two existing native empires – that of the
Aztecs and that of the Incas – helped by the antagonism of the recently
conquered subjects. The natives did not take readily to hard labour in the
mines and on the plantations. They had little resistance to the diseases
inadvertently introduced by the Europeans. The natives were largely
replaced by settlers and by African slaves. The animals and the plants of
America were also largely replaced by those of Europe. The colonization of
the Americas was thus, from very early on, thorough and irreversible.
Europe, alone among all the other civilizations, thanks to the tall ships, found
and appropriated a new hemisphere; it transplanted itself to the New World,
creating a gigantic extension of European culture across the ocean. Later,
the same process was repeated in the other relatively empty lands overseas:
in Australia and New Zealand. Overland, in Eurasia, Russia, uniquely,
paralleled this kind of European expansion through settler colonization.

Power overseas was correlated with power in Europe; but this correlation
was not as close as has been made out. The fundamental reason is that power
overseas rested on sea power while power in Europe rested on land power.
France, for instance, was a very great power on land which could make a
credible bid for hegemony in Europe but failed to defeat Britain at sea and
therefore ultimately failed overseas. Holland did succeed to some extent in
translating its considerable power overseas into power in Europe. The Dutch
played a predominant part in the establishment of the principle of the
freedom of the high seas and the freedom for all to trade overseas. The Dutch
aversion to any one European state having a monopoly overseas went hand
in hand with its opposition to hegemony in Europe and preference for an

equilibrium between the Great Powers. In this way the sea power of Holland contributed to the crystallization of the interstate system in Europe.

Britain triumphed over all its rivals for power at sea and overseas because of its insular location combined with its having no territorial interests on the continent of Europe in modern times. The island state could therefore be single-minded in the development of sea power and the pursuit of interests overseas. The condition for this policy, however, was that a balance of power prevailed on the continent of Europe and that, should a would-be hegemonic power arise in Europe, Britain would be able to find a continental ally to fight an anti-hegemonic war. Sea power, in the context of the European-centred interstate system, was essentially defensive power. With superior sea power, Britain could prevent an enemy in Europe from using the sea to mount an invasion of the island state. On the offensive, Britain could conduct raids but could not, without a major ally, mount a seaborne invasion of a powerful continental state. Blockade of the enemy's commerce by sea was not sufficient to defeat a great land power. Britain, in command of the sea, retained its links with the world overseas and could supply its allies on the continent; but the decisive wars in Europe were always fought on the land. The ability to supply and finance allies on the continent was due more to Britain's economic lead than to its command of the sea. Arguably, the insular location, sea power, colonies and trade over the seas contributed to the earlier and faster development of capitalism in Britain.

The varying fortunes of European states in colonization overseas were directly affected by power at sea, and so was the decolonization of the settler colonies in the Americas. The word 'colony', in its original sense in Ancient Greece, meant a group of settlers who emigrated from their parent city-state to settle abroad and create a new city-state. The colony kept cultural and sentimental links with the parent state but no domination was involved. This type of colony has not existed in its pure form in modern history for two reasons: first, wherever the settlers went, the land was already inhabited; and, second, the parent state kept its sovereignty over the colony. Thus, settler colonization, in modern history, involved a double domination: that of the settlers over the natives, and that of the parent state over the settlers. When the natives were few and/or weak and the settlers were numerous and powerful, the settlers displaced the natives and became themselves the new natives, so to speak. The leading settlers, and not the natives, took the initiative in pressing for decolonization.

The interests of the settlers and those of the parent states, which had coincided when the colonies were first created, began to diverge and became more conflictual. There were a number of reasons for this development. The colonies in the New World were tied to their respective parent states; when the parent state went to war the colony had to follow suit, even though this may not have always been in the interest of the settlers. Under the mercantilist system, the colonies had to do all their trading with or through their parent states and all the cargoes had to be transported in their ships. The colonies had to pay taxes to the parent states, but were not sufficiently represented in the decision-making process in Europe. In the Spanish colonies, more so than in the British ones, the top positions in colonial government were reserved for Europeans from the metropolis. However, the settlers, particularly in the British colonies, had taken with them from Europe the tradition of self-government and were fully able to run their own administrations. The ideas of the European Enlightenment, which were influential with the elites in the British as well as the Spanish colonies, enabled the settlers in the New World to 'imagine' themselves as national communities and to formulate and implement the doctrine of national self-determination – a development which by and large occurred earlier here than in Europe.

Decolonization in the New World could only mean the transfer of power to the settlers. Except in the cases of Canada and Brazil, decolonization in the New World involved large-scale force. When force was used, geography and the international circumstances favoured the settlers. They were fighting on home ground, the parent states were thousands of miles across the Atlantic, and sea power was not effective away from the coastal zones. The settlers, unlike the natives when they first came in contact with Europeans, had modern arms and knew how to use them; and they were more highly motivated than the forces of the colonial powers. It is important to reiterate here that these wars of decolonization in the New World were between the settlers and their European parent states. The original natives of America were involved in these wars only to the extent that the colonial powers used them in their forces to combat the settlers. This was one more reason for the settlers to be determined to settle the 'native question' once and for all.

The decolonized settler states of America, whose culture was European, and whose political institutions were, in some cases, more modern than those of their former parent states, became members of the European-centred interstate system. For a long time, however, these settler states of the New World decided not to get involved in the balance of power in Europe. Two factors enabled them to make that choice: their geographical location across the Atlantic and British sea power. As long as Britain itself presented no threat to the security and independence of the American states, they had no reason to get involved in Europe. Furthermore, none of the settler states, not even the United States for a long time, had the means to cross the Atlantic and land an army in Europe. For the states of the New World, membership in the European-centred interstate system, in terms of military power, was in a sense a defensive membership: they were able, with the collaboration of Britain, to prevent the states of Europe from intervening in America. By the time one of the settler states of the New World, the United States, had acquired the means and the will to intervene militarily in Europe, it was too late to 'redress the balance' of the Old World: the European-centred interstate system had already entered its terminal breakdown. Overseas expansion was not the cause of this breakdown. But colonization and decolonization in the New World did contribute to the new global interstate system, which came to replace the European-centred one, as the United States became one of the dominant states of the new order.

Russia

The only European settler colonization which took place in Asia was that by Russia. At the same time as the overseas expansion of Western Europe in the sixteenth century, the Russians started to expand in the vast, thinly populated lands of Eurasia to the north of the steppes. In expanding overland, Russia was doing, in a reverse direction, what Asiatic conquerors had done over Russian territory. Consequently, the peoples the Russians encountered were not as foreign to them as the peoples which Europeans came across when they expanded overseas. Indeed, one of these peoples, the Tatars, had ruled Russia for centuries before the tables were turned. Russia had expanded through settler colonization and integration of indigenous inhabitants in Europe before crossing the Ural. Consequently, the Russians were well used to this form of colonization by the time they crossed into Asia.

The state, and in particular the army, played a much bigger part in the overland settler colonization of Siberia than in overseas settler colonization. The settlers who followed the army into Siberia were not the carriers of the modern nation-state and the capitalist mode of production but peasants and small townsfolk. Unlike overseas settlers, the Russians in Siberia remained linked overland with Russia, as part of one and the same state. Settler nationalism did not arise in Siberia. In the Eurasian land mass, it was impossible for another European state to intervene in Siberia, short of defeating and crossing over Russia. Although China did sign the treaty of Nerchinsk with Russia in 1689, on the whole the great Asiatic civilizations did not interfere with Russia's expansion in Siberia. It was much later that Japan, modernized and expansionist, would come into conflict with Russia in the Far East. Russia thus had a free hand for a long time to entrench its position in Asia. The natives of Siberia were somewhat more advanced than those of America and they were more resistant to European diseases. The natives were not very numerous, however, and were composed of small groups, often at war with one another. Soon, the natives were outnumbered by the settlers, and Siberia, including the territories of the Far East, became an irreversible settler colony. Decolonization of this immense settler colony took the form of complete integration with the parent state and not of the transfer of sovereignty to the settlers. Siberia was made an integral part of the Russian Federation in the Soviet Union, which it remained when the USSR was dissolved.

Just as the overseas expansion of Europe had removed possible threats to its security from the sea, so did the overland expansion of Russia reduce the likelihood of threats to the security of Europe from the land. The major exception was that of the Ottoman Turks, who posed a threat to Europe long after Russia had reached the shores of the Pacific. Nonetheless, Russia became the implacable foe of the Ottoman Empire and would in all likelihood have demolished it but for France's and Britain's preference of keeping a weakened Turkey alive on the edge of Europe rather than face a powerful Russia.

Russia, by expanding all the way across Eurasia to the Pacific, not only gained access to the open sea all the year round, but, like America, also spanned the globe from ocean to ocean. With Siberia, Russia occupied the bulk of Eurasia. Because of its geographical size and location, Russia, unlike the other European states, did not have to take to the sea to be a colonial power; it was a state that simultaneously played a key role in the balance of power in Europe and was a colonial power in Asia. Britain, the dominant sea power, eventually became also a formidable land power in Asia through the large modern army it created in India. Later still, Britain developed a policy of containing Russia inside the Eurasian land mass.

Russia was an indispensable part of the European balance of power system. Unlike Britain, which could be relatively detached from the continent, when the land powers were in equilibrium, Russia was required for that equilibrium. Russia played as decisive a role as Britain in the failure of France's bid for hegemony in Europe under Napoleon and thus ensured the continuation of the interstate system. The collapse of Russia through revolution and civil war, which coincided with the entry of the United States on the European scene, was part of the terminal breakdown of the European-centred interstate system. Russia, however, unlike the other European colonial powers, had been permanently enlarged through settler colonization. Metamorphosed as the core of the Soviet Union, Russia became one of the two superpowers of the global interstate system which emerged out of the New Thirty Years' War.

Decolonization in the global system

After the Second World War, decolonization took place in an interstate system that was global, bipolar, heterogeneous, and dominated by nuclear weapons. In such a system the nation-states of Western Europe were condemned through lack of size to mediocrity in terms of power. Except for the very special case of Russia, the colonial phase had not provided long-lasting size to the states of Europe. The immensity of Russia, spanning Europe and Asia, put the Soviet Union in the category of superpower, together with an erstwhile settler colony, the United States. Two gigantic states the size of continents, one entirely created by settler colonization, the other enormously augmented by the same kind of colonization, made the interstate system of the Cold War literally global. Over the Arctic, the frontiers of the two giants were virtually in contact. In the East–West dimension, these two enormous states faced each other across the oceans and covered practically the whole of the earth. An interstate system is proportional in size to that of its main actors. Once the United States and the Soviet Union became the principal players, the interstate system covered the whole globe. Furthermore, through membership of the United Nations, and possessing the formal elements of modern statehood, all states belonged to one and the same interstate system.

The interstate system of the Cold War was bipolar in that the two main actors, the United States and the Soviet Union, outclassed all other states. Each of the two superpowers was able to mobilize armies of several millions and to project power into all parts of the planet. There could only be a balance of power in the system if these two states were on opposite sides. Thus the very geometry of forces made for the rivalry of the two superpowers. But the configuration of power was not a sufficient cause of the Cold War. The system was also heterogeneous in the sense that the internal political regimes and ideologies of the two superpowers were radically different. The Cold War therefore concerned not only interstate relations but internal politics as well. Another factor added to the heterogeneity of the interstate system. All states were members of the same interstate system. But the states of the North, in the Soviet bloc as well as in the American bloc, had all the elements of modernity, while many states of the South, and almost all Black African states, had only the formal elements of the modern state, that is, sovereignty, territoriality and recognition.

The two heterogeneities, the East–West and the North–South, were not taken to be permanent features of the global interstate system. There were two long-term projects to homogenize the system: the Cold War and 'development'. The winner of the Cold War would homogenize the planet along Soviet or American lines. 'Development' would eliminate the North–South heterogeneity. The two projects were linked in that 'development' of the South was a stake in the East–West Cold War. The Soviet Union and the West became most concerned with the alignments of the states of the South in the Cold War. This was not just an issue of interstate relations; the alignment in military terms of this or that state of the South with one or the other of the Cold War blocs did not make much difference to the global balance of force. It was the internal regimes of the states of the South, more than their external alignments, that were really at stake in the Cold War. The West and the Soviet Union projected their respective model of the modern state in the South. The adoption of the Soviet model by a state of the South, even if it was a small 'Ruritania', was regarded as a loss by the West and vice versa. The states of the South themselves would have preferred to develop into real modern states without getting too involved in the Cold War. But if non-alignment in the Cold War was possible in terms of foreign policy, there could be no non-alignment in terms of internal regimes. India, for instance, adopted non-alignment in its foreign policy, but its internal regime was Western, inherited from decolonization. If a state of the South adopted the Soviet model, as Cuba did, such a state would in effect be aligned, although it might belong to the Non-aligned Movement. The United Nations also endeavoured to reduce the North–South heterogeneity by helping its 'developing' members to acquire more of the elements of the modern state.

The model of the modern state which the new states inherited from the former colonial powers, and which was fostered by the United Nations, put the emphasis on sovereignty, on non-intervention in the internal affairs of states, and also on 'nation-building'. Yet these new states were at the same time subjected to the transnational ideologies of the Cold War: communism and liberalism. It was the choice of the political regimes based on these ideologies which was at stake in the Cold War in the South, rather than the values of the nation-state stressed by the United Nations.

Finally, the interstate system of the Cold War was characterized by what Aron called a new technology of conflict: nuclear weapons brought a qualitative change to the nature of war. The Cold War remained 'cold' at least in part because of the terror of the consequences of a 'hot' war fought with nuclear weapons. This in turn made the weapons of the kind used by guerrillas, and in small-scale hot wars, very effective in bringing about political changes – notably in the context of decolonization. Nuclear terror found a counterpart in the terror of the terrorist. Large-scale war between the Great Powers was replaced by deterrence, subversion, propaganda and wars by proxy in the Third World. In this context, the 'developing' states of the South acquired power in the global interstate system out of all proportion to their military capabilities. This was indeed a complete reversal of the situation which had made colonization possible.

A different kind of colony altogether from the kind which has been discussed so far had been created in Asia and Africa. This kind of colony can be called an 'administrative colony'. A small number of administrators, soldiers and entrepreneurs from Europe maintained colonial rule. The decolonization which took place in the Cold War was a phase in the long-term process of change in Asia and Africa brought about through contacts with Europe. Colonial rule was a revolution in Asia and Africa. The introduction of modern medicine cut down the death rate while the birth rate remained high, causing the populations to rise rapidly. This, together with the establishment of private property in land, created a vast landless peasantry and mass urbanization. The capitalist mode of production did not grow sufficiently either in the countryside or in the colonial cities to absorb the surplus labour. The implantation of elements of the modern state eroded the authority of traditional elites. 'Development', as the replacement of traditional political institutions by the elements of the modern state, went on under colonial rule and continued after decolonization.

The transfer of some elements of the modern state to Asia and Africa had been necessary in order to conquer and 'pacify' the colonies. The colonial powers had to train a number of natives in the use of modern arms and the discipline of modern armies. In the Indian subcontinent, for instance, a few thousand Britons trained an enormous army which enabled Britain to conquer yet more countries in Asia. To maintain 'law and order' in the colonies, the other coercive apparatuses of the modern state had to be established: police forces, prisons, judges. For the collection of taxes elements of the modern administrative apparatus had to be introduced. All these elements of the modern state were manned by Europeans at the top but the rank and file were natives who had been trained by the colonizers. This training in turn called for schools providing modern European-type education. This type of colonial rule necessitated the collaboration of native groups. These collaborators included, at first, the traditional elites, but, increasingly, as the elements of the modern state were implanted, it was the modern, European trained, elites which became collaborators with the colonizers.

The more successful the colonial powers were in transferring their models to their colonies the more they made the colonial empires redundant. It was not the traditional elites but fractions of modern collaborators which led the nationalist movements, using the modern European doctrine of national self-determination. The transfer of sovereignty and membership in the interstate system could be a gain for the colonial power and for the West generally in the Cold War. The colonial power had transferred its model of the modern state and had formed the elites who inherited power in decolonization. The nationalist elite in power would not need much prompting from the West to crack down on any radical groups in the territory which might be tempted to turn to communism. Decolonization thus could be a very effective way of 'containing' communism in the Cold War. Moreover, the nationalist government was likely to continue the modernization of the state and stood a better chance of success than the colonial authorities in mobilizing the population behind 'development'. In the majority of cases, decolonization was unproblematic. There were cases, however, where decolonization was very problematic and involved a great deal of violence. These cases fall into two categories: when the nationalist movement was led by communists and when a substantial settler minority was present. When one or the other of these two categories was combined with the colonial power's attempt to decolonize the colony through integration, rather than transferring sovereignty, bitter wars of decolonization ensued. When communists led the nationalist movement, decolonization became intertwined with the Cold War. In such cases, the United States, which normally used its influence on the colonial powers for an early transfer of sovereignty to the nationalists, supported repression by the colonial authorities. The support of the United States, however, went together with an insistence that the colonial power, while repressing the communists, should foster an alternative, pro-West nationalist movement in the colony. Vietnam was the paradigm case of this policy, although it ultimately failed.

Decolonization through the integration of the colony with the colonial power was not a viable policy for the overseas colonial empires of Western Europe. Integration demands a modicum of homogeneity in demographic, geographical, cultural and economic conditions which was not present between the colonial powers and their colonies. Britain did not try to integrate any of its colonies. Integration was not even tried for the settler colonies, let alone the administrative ones. France and Portugal pursued variants of decolonization through integration and, except in a few tiny colonies, the policies failed. The paradigm case is Algeria.

There were one million settlers in Algeria but over fifteen million natives, and the birth rate of the latter was much higher than that of the former. Without their own state, the settlers were at the mercy of a change of policy in the metropolis. Algeria had been transformed by colonization, but if the modern sector was like a parcel of France across the Mediterranean, this was surrounded by a large traditional Algeria which had more in common with the Arab world than with France. The settlers occupied the best land and the good positions in Algeria which the native elite wanted. The modern native elite had to compete with the settlers, who had the advantage of being born in the dominant culture. In an Algerian Algeria the native elite would occupy the top positions. One-person-one-vote in France and Algeria taken together, which was introduced late in the day, protected the settlers rather than favouring the native elite. The settlers remained part of the majority in the greater France. The native elite, leading the nationalist movement, felt that universal suffrage, within the boundaries of greater France, could be to their disadvantage if fractions of the Arab population, rather than supporting them, were to be tempted by the material benefits that Paris could offer.

The international context was also unfavourable to decolonization through integration. Arab nationalism had been revived with the creation of the state of Israel and the independence of major Arab states, in particular Egypt. Egypt's nationalization of the Suez Canal Company in 1956 provided a pretext for France to intervene to try to dislodge Colonel Nasser, allegedly responsible for the anti-French nationalism in Algeria. Suez was a turning point in decolonization: it demonstrated that Britain and France, two former Great Powers, could no longer intimidate a Third World country without the support of the United States. It was also the one occasion in the Cold War when France and Britain acted together in a quasi-colonial affair. After Suez, Britain renewed its special relationship with the United States and accelerated decolonization. For France, the débâcle of Suez intensified the war in Algeria and numbered the days of the Fourth Republic. Yet by adopting the guerrilla form of fighting, the nationalists made it difficult for the French army to win by military means. A long war increased the political costs: France wanted good relations with the Arab world and with the Maghreb in particular, but the war made this impossible.

After the army had brought General de Gaulle back to power, it was concluded that France was losing more by continuing the war than by coming to terms with the nationalists. A sovereign Algeria, with a nationalist government linked to France through aid in modernization, was better than seeing the further radicalization of the nationalists and perhaps an eventual intervention of the Soviet Union just across the Mediterranean. In abandoning integration and opting for decolonizing Algeria through the transfer of sovereignty, de Gaulle also adopted this form of decolonization for the French colonies in Africa and Madagascar. Decolonization, far from impoverishing France, removed the burden of settlers and the 'wars of liberation'.

Israel is the unique case of an irreversible settler state established in the global interstate system of the Cold War. The two superpowers recognized Israel at birth. The Cold War, however, interacting with the conflict between the Arabs and Israel, made the Soviet Union the ally of the Arabs, while the United States supported Israel. Unlike other populations which experienced massive European settler colonization, the natives of Palestine did not disappear but were displaced into neighbouring Arab states. As Arab nationalism cuts across the frontiers, Arab states could not ignore the fate of the Palestinians. Only after a series of military defeats did the Arab states accept the irreversibility of the settler state in their midst.

Yet the military victories of Israel added more Arab lands to the settler state. These territorial conquests, however, could not provide a final solution to the conflict because with the lands more Arabs came under Israeli rule. The legitimacy of the Israeli state is based on the principle that it is the state of the Jews in the land of Zion; the land which, it is claimed, was 'promised' to the Jews by no less than the Almighty – and Lord Balfour! In any case, the state of Israel cannot integrate large numbers of non-Jews as full citizens. The military conquests therefore condemned Israel to being an imperialist state ruling over unwilling Arab subjects, besides being a colonial settler state. More recently, Israel has adopted the policy of trading off the conquered lands for recognition by the Arab states in the 'peace process'. However, this still leaves large numbers of Palestinians under Israeli rule. With the end of the Cold War, the Arabs have lost their Soviet ally, and the United States has pressured Israel to make concessions. Under the terms of the settlement between Israel and the PLO, if they are implemented, the natives of Palestine will get more than a 'reservation' and less than a sovereign state. This is more than natives generally got when their lands were taken in irreversible settler colonization. It reflects the demographic vitality of the natives in this case and the global context of decolonization.

The Soviet Union followed the doctrine of Lenin, who had equated imperialism with the monopoly stage, the 'highest stage', of capitalism. The end of colonialism, therefore, was understood to accelerate the downfall of capitalism. The anti-colonial revolution in Asia and Africa was part of the same global anti-capitalist revolution spearheaded by the Soviet Union. The Soviet Union was well placed to advocate decolonization in that the colonial powers were all the allies of the United States in the Cold War. The Soviet bloc had no colonies overseas. The situation inside the Soviet Union had never been raised in the global decolonization debate. Although 'the nation' was not central in the value system of the Bolsheviks, they had advocated national self-determination for the peoples of the Tsarist empire as part of a strategy of winning the support of the national minorities in the civil war. However, national self-determination was interpreted to mean integration in the Soviet Union.

The Soviet Union was not a *Russian* empire in that the state was not organized to give the Russian nation a dominant role over the other nations. A new revolutionary state was established in which the ex-colonizers and the ex-colonized were to be integrated on the basis of equality, that is, an equality of citizenship for the individuals as well as an equality between the nations in the socialist state. A local, cultural, national identity was to be cultivated simultaneously with the overall allegiance to the Soviet Union. In some cases national groups were revived or created as a matter of policy. Russians, however, were the majority in the Soviet Union; their territory, including Siberia, was far larger than the territories of all the other nationalities put together. Furthermore, most of the material resources were in Russia. The Bolsheviks were well aware of the problem posed by the coexistence of several nations in the same state, with one nation being so much larger than all the others. If the Soviet Union was to be a model for the future of the world, Great Russian chauvinism, as Lenin called it, had to be avoided. Indeed, according to the doctrine, all forms of 'bourgeois' nationalism had to be extirpated. Cultural national identification was to be subordinated to class allegiance. The state was the state of 'the working class' and not that of the nations. Yet, in the key institutions, where power really rested in the Soviet Union, the Politburo and the Central Committee of the Communist Party, membership, although not based on nationality, tended to be overwhelmingly Russian.

In its revolutionary beginnings, it was hoped that the Soviet state would be a viable alternative to the Western model of modernity for planet Earth. In the end it was failure in the larger revolutionary project which was the essential cause of the disappearance of the USSR. Once the state started to break up, the Soviet Union fractured along the internal boundaries that it had put in place: what were called the Union Republics. This meant that Russia, the principal Republic, would have a decisive role in the process of unravelling the Soviet Union. Russia's decision not to support the dying Soviet Union spelt the end. Russia had had enough of communism and was also anxious to lay down the 'White man's burden'. When the Soviet Union disintegrated, decolonization reverted to the 'normal', Anglo-Saxon, form: the transfer of sovereignty and membership in the interstate system. In the Republics of Central Asia, in particular, this form of decolonization was a consequence, and not a cause, of the break-up of the Soviet Union.

Conclusion

The modern state developed as part of an interstate system which crystallized in Europe as the member states expanded overseas and overland. The member states coexisted in anarchy and therefore had to be constantly prepared for war. Consequently military force was the determinant criterion for full membership in the interstate system. Armed conflicts between European member states of the system had the whole world for theatre: the oceans, the colonies in the New World, the trading outposts and, later, the colonies in Asia and Africa. Despite its global reach, the interstate system remained European-centred and relatively homogeneous until the terminal New Thirty Years' War. Even after decolonization in the Americas, the crucial balance of power remained in Europe and the decisive wars were fought on land in Europe.

Decolonization of settler colonies has been a much more important factor than that of administrative colonies in the globalization of the interstate system. The settlers carried the cultures of their European parent states with them and this, in the case of the overseas colonies of Britain, greatly facilitated the implantation of the modern state. Moreover, the settlers in the New World were not constrained by the legacies of the pre-modern institutions, as was the case with the Europeans back in Europe. Modernity found a clean slate, so to speak, in the New World, and grew lustily. The New World also innovated. For instance, the nation was first 'imagined' in the New World, and the modern state based on national self-determination was pioneered there well before it was generalized in Europe.

One of the superpowers of the interstate system of the Cold War, the United States, was born out of the decolonization of settler colonies. The one and only successful decolonization through integration of an immense European settler colony, Siberia, provided the Soviet Union with the scale and resources to be the other superpower of the Cold War. The sheer size of these two gigantic states, and their presence all around the world, gave the interstate system of the Cold War its global dimension.

Decolonization through the transfer of sovereignty and membership in the interstate system – the Anglo-Saxon way – proved less problematic than attempts at integrating colonies with the metropolitan states. Although the British Empire was by far the largest of the overseas colonial empires, its decolonization caused hardly a ripple in the internal politics of Britain. In sharp contrast, France and Portugal had army coups and changed their political regimes as a result of their attempts at decolonization through integration. In the Soviet Union, decolonization was a consequence, and not a cause, of the collapse of the state.

Decolonization of the administrative colonies was written into the colonization project in which Europe aimed to create the world in its own image. The administrative colonies, however, would not have acquired sovereignty and become members of the interstate system when they did without the Cold War. The decolonization of the administrative colonies added to globalization in that it universalized membership in the interstate system. But the new states were not members of the interstate system because of the military force they could wield, but because they were a stake in the Cold War between the two superpowers. Indeed, in some cases, the new members owed their very existence as sovereign states to their membership of the interstate system; their sovereignty was not internally generated but acquired by courtesy of the interstate system.

The global interstate system of the Cold War was doubly heterogeneous. The disappearance of the Soviet Union has put an end to the East–West heterogeneity but not to the North–South heterogeneity. The failure of the Soviet model has made liberalism and the transnational capitalist economy more salient features of globalization, reducing the North–South heterogeneity. The states, however, are not going to 'wither away'. Europe, which has given capitalism to the world, also gave the world the modern state as part of an anarchic interstate system. States, rooted in territoriality, will remain vitally preoccupied with the configuration of power in the world. The states need not necessarily be linked to the nations in the form of 'one nation one state'. *Ceteris paribus*, size – that of the territory and of the population – will remain a determinant in power. The epoch when states with the territorial size of European nations dominated the planet ended in the New Thirty Years' War. Colonial expansion could not give permanent enlargement of size to the states of Europe because the colonial empires were thalassocratic and based on national states. The one major exception was Russia, and it proves the rule: the Russian empire was overland and Russia was never a national state. One of the erstwhile European settler colonies, the United States, dwarfs the nation-states of Europe. As a result of decolonization, the states of Europe are back to their original European home where they are engaged in a process whose end-purpose is to transcend the nation-states and acquire the size and resources that would allow them to be in the same league as the United States which, for the time being, is the only super-power.

References

Space is not available to list all the books and articles which have been consulted. The following have been particularly helpful:

Anderson, Benedict (1994) *Imagined Communities*. London: Verso.

Aron, Raymond (1962) *Paix et Guerre entre les nations*. Paris: Calmann-Lévy.

Aron, Raymond (1984) *Les dernières années du siècle*. Paris: Julliard.

Cipolla, Carlo M. (1965) *Guns and Sails in the Early Phase of European Expansion 1400–1700*. London: Collins.

Crosby, Alfred W. (1993) *Ecological Imperialism: The Biological Expansion of Europe 900–1900*. London: Cambridge University Press.

Deporte, A. W. (1979) *Europe Between the Super Powers*. London: Yale University Press.

Gottmann, Jean (1952) *La Politique des Etats et leur Géographie*. Paris: A. Colin.

Jackson, Robert H. (1990) *Quasi-states: Sovereignty, International Relations and the Third World*. Cambridge: Cambridge University Press.

Jones, Archey (1989) *The Art of War in the Western World*. Oxford: Oxford University Press.

Kennedy, Paul (1988) *The Rise and Fall of the Great Powers*. London: Fontana.

Lieven, Dominic (1995) The Russian empire and the Soviet Union as imperial polities. *Journal of Contemporary History*, **30**, 607–36.

Mahan, A.T (1900) *The Problems of Asia and its Effects upon International Policies*. Boston, MA: Little, Brown & Co.

Parry, J. H. (1979) *Europe and a Wider World 1415–1715*. London: Hutchinson.

Rodinson, Maxime (1973) *Israel: A Colonial Settler State?* New York: Monad.

Scammell, G. V. (1981) *The World Encompassed: The First European Maritime Empires c800–1650*. London: Methuen.

Tolz, V. and Elliot, I. (eds) (1995) *The Demise of the USSR: From Communism to Independence*. London: Macmillan.

Watson, Adam (1992) *The Evolution of International Society*. London: Routledge.

Wolf, Eric (1990) *Europe and the People Without History*. London: University of California Press.

Wood, Alan (ed.) (1991) *The History of Siberia: From Russian Conquest to Revolution*. London: Routledge.

4

Transnational Migrant Communities and the Modern Nation-State

JOHN REX

In this chapter I begin by outlining a theory of colonial and post-colonial migration which is the most important form of migration in the British, French, and Dutch cases before going on to relate such migration to other forms of international migration, and to wider international and global perspectives. The forms of migration which I shall discuss include, first, post-colonial migration; secondly, other non-colonial forms of migration; and, thirdly, political, as distinct from economic, migration. I shall also argue that while the theory of migrant settlement has been developed primarily in the context of nation-states receiving immigrants, the position of migrant communities today has to be seen as occurring in more global circumstances.

The structure of post-colonial migrant communities

The basic unit involved in economic migration from former colonial territories is the extended family, seeking to increase and improve its estate. For such families the existence of empire provides one of several opportunities. Thus, for example, during the period of the British Empire, families in the Punjab took advantage of the economic opportunities opened up for them by the British Empire in East Africa and elsewhere. Subsequently the British metropolis itself became the target of migration. If, however, separate families, rather than whole communities or ethnic groups, were the unit actors in the migration process, this did not mean that their ethnicity did not play an important part in structuring their situation. However individualistic in their orientation separate families might have been, they nonetheless relied upon the support of other families who were recognizable by their language, religion and customs. Characteristically, moreover, such families dealt with the crises of birth, marriage and death through their own churches, mosques and temples.

Migrants in their first land of settlement had three points of reference: (1) a continued connection with the homeland; (2) their relationship to the society of present settlement and their need to survive and improve their lot within it; and (3) their interest in onward migration. In order to understand the nature of migrant ethnic minority organization and culture it is necessary to say something about each of these points of reference.

So far as continued connection with the homeland is concerned, the migrants will probably own property or aspire to own it there, and will send back remittances; there will be a continuing connection with kin and the homeland will provide the migrants with a source of spouses; the migrants may return to the homeland on holidays and may seek to arrange part of their children's education there; and, finally, there may well be a continuing interest in the homeland's unresolved political problems. Political divisions originating in the homeland may also affect the political structure of communities abroad. The divisions which they engender will produce divisions in the migrant community and the migrant community may use the relative freedom of the land of settlement to pursue political causes which are repressed at home.

Migrant communities usually maintain some sort of 'myth of return' (Anwar, 1979) and this has led to a loose usage of the term 'diaspora' to describe them. In a narrow and more precise sense, however, the term 'diaspora' is misleading if it is taken to imply an eventual goal of returning to some sort of Zion. In fact many migrant communities, far from aiming at an eventual return to the homeland, actually plan to operate in a wider international world, exploiting the opportunities which migration offers. For this reason I prefer to speak of transnational migrant communities rather than diasporas, while recognizing that, *inter alia*, the nature of migrant organization and culture does have some homeland reference and some concern with homeland politics.

The difficulty here is that the term 'diaspora' has been used in both a narrow and a more loosely defined sense. Much of the discussion of diasporas simply extends the term to include all cases in which members of an originally nationally and ethnically located community migrate to various parts of the world and maintain some links with a homeland while at the same time developing various forms of cultural hybridity (Gilroy, 1993; Hall, 1992) as they settle in other lands. Because of the narrower use of the term, however, I prefer to use the term 'transnational migrant communities' as one which includes both narrowly defined diasporas and other globally dispersed communities which intend to remain dispersed and to derive advantage from this dispersal. Some of the issues involved here are well discussed in an article by Clifford (1993), although Clifford does not discuss the case of long-distance post-colonial migrants.

The second point of orientation for migrant communities is that of the political community and the economy in their land of first settlement. As migrants they wish to have an equal place in such communities and economies. Entry into them is a prime reason for migration. An important determinant of immigrant organization and of the developing ethnic minority culture will therefore be the community's struggle for social justice and equality of opportunity. It is not the case that traditional and unchanging immigrant ethnic cultures confront a modern nation-state. The immigrant ethnic cultures are to be thought of as changing and developing in response to the situational challenges which they face. They must be thought of as containing their own internal modernizing tendencies which, far from being at odds with a democratic system, actually serve to strengthen it.

On an organizational level the migrant communities will have to relate themselves to indigenous political movements struggling for their own rights, for example, trade unions and entrepreneurial associations, though while supporting these organizations they may have to fight for their own special rights within them. They will also be committed to winning equality in the land of settlement for their children, which may mean that, insofar as they are successful, they may find that these children come to identify with the indigenous culture, including peer group culture, rather than immigrant culture. This appears to be one of the costs of migration, although it is interesting to note that even children who succeed in their achievements within the host society may still maintain links with the culture of their parents. The problems here are in fact not dissimilar to those of indigenous socially mobile children of working class parents.

While it is theoretically possible that a migrant community may become completely absorbed into its host society (so that Indians settled in Britain, for example, may become, and may come to think of themselves as, simply British), usually the members of these communities may also be keeping other possibilities open. They are seeking to improve their estates, not merely in one country, but wherever the best opportunities present themselves. Thus they may explore the possibilities of onward migration. A migrant family in Britain or elsewhere in Europe may thus be planning onward migration to North America and may be connected with kin and other networks there. Far from it being the case that kin links become weakened by physical distance it may well be the case that they actually become strengthened. A family in Britain may have a lively sense of connection with kin both in their homeland and in a land of possible future migration.

Given these conflicting pulls on the life of migrant communities it should be clear that any essentialist view on immigrant ethnic cultures is unsustainable. The culture of such communities is a changing and developing thing, best thought of as a set of responses to political challenges. Moreover, on a social rather than a cultural level, the boundaries of the community will not be totally clear. On the other hand, one should not go to the other extreme and imagine that ethnic minority culture and organization will simply disappear. They represent cultural and social forms which cross-cut nation-states and national cultures and are much more structures of a globalized world. There is a struggle between the social organizations and culture of the nation-state involved here. In part it is to be expected that nation-states will succeed in incorporating and acculturating immigrant minorities but the structure of these minorities also has transnational dimensions.

The actual numbers of post-colonial migrants are difficult to estimate. For example, the British birthplace statistics show that of about 55 million residents in Great Britain, about 3.8 million were born outside the United Kingdom and that of these 592,000 were born in the Irish Republic, about 1.7 million in the New (predominantly non-White) Commonwealth and 177,000 in the Old (predominantly White) Commonwealth. So far as ethnic feelings of belonging are concerned, the basis of the classification is highly questionable and is mainly concerned with distinguishing between 'Whites' and 'Ethnic Minorities' (who are overwhelmingly non-White). Three million of the census population of about 55 million belonged to the ethnic minorities thus defined. Of these 499,000 saw themselves as Black-Caribbean, 207,000 as Black African and 178,000 as Other Black, while 840,000 saw themselves as Indian, 475,000 as Pakistani and 160,000 as Bangladeshi. 157,000 as Chinese, 196,000 as 'other' Asian and 290,000 as 'Other-Other' (Owen, 1991).

Interpreting these figures as best one can, one could say that just under three million of Britain's residents are members of post-colonial immigrant communities. The equivalent groups in France are the Maghrebians, Africans and South East Asians. With only the nationality figures to guide us we should note that about two million French residents have Maghrebian nationalities, probably about 50,000 belong to African nations and about 111,000 to Vietnam, Laos and Cambodia. This would suggest a total of about 2.16 million post-colonial immigrants in France (OECD, 1995), but we know nothing of their subjective identifications.

The Netherlands and Portugal are countries which also have numbers of post-colonial immigrants, in the Netherlands case from Indonesia, Surinam and the Dutch Antilles and in the case of Portugal from Guinea, Angola, Mozambique, Goa, East Timor and Macao. Immigrants from the French territories, particularly Morocco, are also widely dispersed in countries other than France. These are to be added to the stock of European residents who have or feel themselves to have post-colonial origins. Adding these various groups together we could say that there are approximately six or seven million members of post-colonial immigrant communities in Europe.

Non-colonial forms of migration

It would, of course, be misleading to imagine that the model of post-colonial migration suggested here covers all cases of migrant communities. It does apply to migration from the former colonies of the European empires, but does not, for instance, adequately explain Turkish migration to Germany or migration from Southern to North West Europe.

In the German case, although there is no imperial connection, a definite political relationship has been established between Turkey and Germany. Turkey becomes a chosen area of labour recruitment and, once established, develops a special political relationship with Germany akin to that which former European colonies in Asia and the Caribbean have developed with European countries. That is to say, migration to Germany is not of the random kind which one would find in an open labour market, but a specific form developed by agreement between two countries. Similar relations have also been established between Germany, on the one hand, and Italy, the former Yugoslavia and Greece, on the other.

Other types of relationship have developed where there is a situation of economic dependency rather than of empire. Thus the economically successful countries of North West Europe drew in migrants from the poorer South in Portugal, Spain, Italy, Yugoslavia and Greece through a relatively open labour market. In these cases where the sending societies are physically and culturally close to the receiving ones, the immigrant communities will have an advantage over long-distance post-colonial migrants. They will be able to sustain continuing links with their homelands even while living as migrants, and the organizations of the migrant communities themselves are likely to be sponsored by government and political and religious organizations in the homeland. Thus, for example, amongst Portuguese migrants in France organizations concerned with education and social welfare were sponsored by the Portuguese government, by the Portuguese Catholic Church and by the Portuguese Communist Party (Rex, Joly and Wilpert, 1987). For a while the existence of such links troubled the North West European nations who saw the principles of their own nationalism as being undermined by these continuing connections.

In some respects, of course, these migrants are subject to the same pulls of the homeland and possible countries of onward migration as are post-colonial immigrants and it may be the case that the model of migration which I have outlined does apply to them. Such is certainly the case if one looks at Portuguese migration, which has an 'onward' dimension in the New World, and there are certainly similar features of the situation of Turks in Germany, excluded as they are from full citizenship in Germany, and therefore forced to maintain links with the homeland at the same time as exploring opportunities for onward migration to other European countries.

Germany is the principal country with large numbers of immigrants from non-colonial situations. In 1993, according to the Opemi statistics (OECD, 1995) it had 1.9 million residents of Turkish nationality, about 1.2 million from the former Yugoslavia, 563,000 from Greece, 133,000 from Spain, and 107,000 from Portugal. Other countries, particularly in the German-speaking world, have recruited guest-workers and some German Turks have also spread to other European countries. There were about 1.2 million immigrants of Portuguese, Spanish and Italian nationality in France, and Switzerland had about 600,000 residents with Italian, Spanish and Portuguese nationality. In Sweden in 1993 there were 108,000 with Finnish nationality, 60,000 from Denmark and Norway, 26,000 Yugoslavs, and 23,000 Turks.

A distinction has been made by Tomas Hammar (1990) between citizens and denizens (who lack citizenship rights) and estimates suggest that there are about 16 million such denizens in North West Europe (ibid.). This category will, however, overlap both with that of post-colonial immigrants and with political migrants, who will be discussed in the next section.

Political migrants

Since the immigration stop in North West Europe in the 1970s, immigrant communities descended from economic migrants have been enlarged only through family completion and by births in the lands of settlement (which means, paradoxically, that these migrant communities have become more permanent). What came to be more important in the former immigrant receiving societies was therefore an influx of asylum seekers and other political migrants.

It is obvious to all those who study this influx that some will, in effect, be using asylum seeking as a cover for economic migration. This is what the receiving societies fear, and there is continuous talk of 'bogus refugees'. From a theoretical point of view it has to be recognized that this is a means for continued economic migration, and the migrants involved are subject to many of the constraints which I have already discussed. It is to be expected therefore that there will be many ethnic minority communities in West Europe from the East and the South, based upon those who have claimed to be political refugees.

It would be quite wrong, however, to suggest that all political migrants are of this kind. There are many genuine asylum seekers who have some claim to qualify as 'Convention refugees' because they are in personal danger, and, with the collapse of the Communist system and with the breakdown of government, or the existence of political disturbances in many parts of Africa and Asia, there will be many others who are simply fleeing from civil war, ecological disaster or other intolerable conditions.

There is no single model which applies to all of these migrants. There will be some who simply seek shelter and protection and, though needing temporary employment, housing and education, may well realistically envisage a return to their homelands when circumstances change. At the other extreme are those who because of their original design, or because the possibility of return becomes less attractive than that of staying in the country of refuge, are likely to stay and become immigrants. These will establish networks which will form the basis of ethnic minority communities as well as facilitating the arrival of further political immigrants.

One thing is clear. Quite apart from the pressure from poorer countries for immigrants to migrate, the political circumstances of the world since 1989 are such that the nation-states of West Europe will not be able to isolate themselves from new political circumstances to the East and to the South, however much they may talk of 'safe havens' in the politically disturbed countries or the sponsoring of development there as an alternative to migration. In fact the advocacy of these very policies demonstrates the inability of the metropolitan nation-states to isolate themselves from a larger world. It is also to be noted that, even among economic migrants, the tendency to migrate will be accelerated by political disturbances in the homelands. Thus nation-states are drawn into global concerns, not only by the economic disparities between rich and poor countries which lead to migration, but also by the political disturbances going on in large parts of the world. This has been obvious since the collapse of Communism after 1989, but political migrants also include such groups as Iranians, Kurds from Turkey and Iraq, Chileans, and Tamils from Sri Lanka.

During the Cold War there was a continual inflow of asylum seekers from the Communist countries to the West and asylum policies towards them were generous. Other inflows came from Iran, Vietnam, Sri Lanka and East Africa and they were more reluctantly accepted. In the case of refugees from Chile (then a right-wing dictatorship), they were welcomed by the European parties of the Left, who managed to provide for them. The end of the Cold War and the break-up of Yugoslavia led to new flows and a considerable fear of East–West economic migration disguised as political migration. It is by no means easy to quantify these various flows, and legal migration and asylum seeking from East to West is in any case supplemented by illegal immigration. The numbers granted asylum have been increasingly restricted and a new category of unsuccessful asylum applicants given temporary leave to remain has necessarily come into being. One can only guess that there are now probably about two or three million political migrants of one status or another and of one geographic origin or another in North West Europe. It is not possible to disentangle their numbers from those of economic migrants of post-colonial and Eastern European origin. One important point to notice is that despite the anxiety felt in Europe over the increasing flow of asylum seekers the asylum problem is a small one compared with that which exists on a world scale. The UNHCR has estimated that there are about 15 million refugees in the world but the great majority of these are fleeing from one Southern country to another (Joly, 1997). The bulk of the world's refugee problem is a South–South one rather than a South–North or East–West one.

Like post-colonial economic migrants and like recruited guest-workers and migrants from the more economically dependent European countries, the communities which emerge among political migrants may have a threefold orientation to their original homeland, to their present land of refuge, and to the possibility of onward migration. Attitudes towards them, however, will be much more ambiguous. On the one hand, after the immigration stop it will be recognized by employers that these political migrants provide an alternative source of labour. On the other hand, their peaceful settlement depends upon an acceptance by the host population of an international obligation which is not seen as being of any economic value by the majority. Given the circumstances of their arrival and their visibility and isolation they form ready scapegoats for a general unease about all immigration in times of recession. They are even more likely to play this role if they are distinguishable by their colour or culture.

Middle class, business and professional immigrants

In all that has been said above the focus has been on working class immigrants coming largely to unwanted and unfilled jobs. We should also, however, note that there is another kind of migration which is very acceptable. Inward investment into European countries from the United States, Japan and the Middle East and from one European country to another brings with it the temporary or permanent settlement of business owners and managers who are usually not thought of as immigrants at all. There are also numerous professionals whose skills are a free gift to their countries of settlement. During the Nazi period other Western European countries gained much from the arrival of German Jewish professionals and there is a similar gain to the new host nations to be made from finding and keeping new highly qualified professionals and intellectuals who have been driven out of their own countries.

The response of West European nation-states to economic and political migration

Even after the immigration stop of the 1970s Western European societies continued to need immigrants. If it had been thought that immigration would not be necessary because of the rationalization of production or because capital went abroad in search of workers, there were nonetheless structural features of these societies which still led to a need for immigrant labour in the metropolis. For one thing there was a demographic deficit. The metropolitan countries were not replacing themselves. Perhaps more importantly, however, there were still numerous jobs and other economic opportunities which were ill-rewarded or were beneath the dignity of an increasingly educated population. Even the most technically advanced economies seem to need cleaners, delivery staff, laundry staff, shopkeepers, restaurateurs and individuals to fill other economic niches. If governments make the entry of immigrants to fill such positions illegal, the fact of the matter is that they will come illegally, and there will be many employers in the public, as well as in the private, sphere who will need such immigrants. If they are illegal and lacking in rights they are also likely to be cheaper and more docile and therefore attractive as workers.

Prima facie, the trade unions in metropolitan countries have an interest in keeping immigrants out. They do not want to have competitors, which will keep wages low and working conditions poor. If, however, conditions of corporatism apply where they share in economic planning, they may recognize that continued economic growth depends upon some immigration and may be persuaded to support it, provided that it does not undermine their members' conditions, and responsible trade union leaders will try to sell this idea to their members.

Trade unions exercising a degree of corporate power, however, usually represent better-off workers. They may have less influence over non-unionized labour in the secondary sectors of divided labour markets. Those in this position may well find that the only jobs they are qualified to fill may be filled by immigrants and, even if they are unwilling to do these jobs themselves, may well treat the physically or culturally distinguished immigrants as scapegoats who can be blamed for their situation. Those in this condition are likely to look for other forms of political action than those provided by the mainstream left-wing parties, whether this takes the form of the spontaneous violence of 'skinheads' or support for radical anti-immigrant or 'racist' parties.

Given the complexity and ambiguity of this situation, European governments and political parties have produced a variety of responses to the immigrant question. The first is to demand the cessation of immigration and, at the extreme, the expulsion or repatriation of those who have already arrived. The second is to accept immigration but to deny immigrants a legal and political status. The third is to recognize the rights of immigrants but to demand their acculturation and assimilation. The fourth is to accept some degree of multiculturalism. As we shall see, none of these policies is likely to be completely successful in maintaining unchanged the political structure of metropolitan nation-states. Rather they reflect the strains on such systems of immigration.

The first alternative is advocated by populist parties of the right, such as those of Le Pen in France or Haider in Austria, and the Vlaamse Blok in Belgium. Usually such parties are demonized in respectable politics and their leaders are simply seen as wicked. From the point of view of empirical social science, however, the fact of the matter is that such parties can mobilize up to about 20 or 30 per cent of the vote in most European countries. They may also have radical right-wing or fascist programmes, and this has been a special source of concern for democrats, but it is wrong to assume that anti-immigrant populism is simply a stalking horse for neo-fascism. What may be the case is that these extreme right-wing ideas may enlarge the constituency of populist racism by appealing to other classes and groups not necessarily threatened by immigration.

Parties of this kind have an indirect as well as a direct influence. The indirect influence derives from the fact that, though the mainstream parties may organize symbolic candle-lit protests against them, drawing attention to their anti-democratic and 'fascist' aims, they may nonetheless adjust their own policies on immigration in order to win back the anti-immigrant vote.

The second response is one more likely to be supported in the mainstream. This is to argue that, while immigration is actually necessary, those who come, or are recruited to come, to unfilled jobs are to be thought of as temporary workers only, who can be rotated. Herein lies the origin of the *gastarbeiter* system pioneered in Germany but also adopted as the basis of policy in several other countries. Despite the fact that many of the *gastarbeiters* never do return, the official policy in Germany is still that it is not an immigration country.

The third policy response is that of assimilationism. The strong revolutionary and republican tradition in France leads the mainstream parties, if they accept the necessity of immigration, to insist that immigrants must become Frenchmen or -women, enjoying civil rights, on condition that they renounce their culture and external political connections. Any group which seeks to maintain its own culture is seen as anti-secular and 'fundamentalist' and as having no place in a modern secular society. The threat to the unity of the nation-state is dealt with by the attempted elimination of minority cultures and political organization.

The final alternative is the policy of multiculturalism, which is often said to be the policy of the Netherlands, the United Kingdom and Sweden. In its ideal form multiculturalism suggests that, while all residents are entitled to the same civic rights, there is a private communal sphere in which various ethnic groups follow their own leaders, and retain their own language, religion and family customs provided that these do not interfere with the civic political culture based upon equality of individuals. The ideal was formulated clearly in Britain in 1966 by the Home Secretary, Roy Jenkins, when he defined 'integration' 'not as a flattening process of uniformity but cultural diversity coupled with equal opportunity in an atmosphere of mutual tolerance' (Rex and Tomlinson, 1979).

The actual practice of multicultural societies, however, very often falls short of this ideal and a number of writers in European countries have criticized the notion in the light of their experience. Many French social scientists suggest that the British form of multiculturalism is a mere rhetoric which disguises a process of ghettoizing the immigrants, and Michel Wieviorka has argued that the very term 'ethnicity', essential to multiculturalism, is only applied to inferior peoples (Wieviorka, 1994). In Germany, Radtke has argued that in a social-democratic pluralist society in which conflicting interests have been reconciled in the institutions of the welfare state, the setting up of a separate multicultural apparatus means in fact the marginalization or exclusion of immigrants (Radtke, 1994). Similarly, Rath, dealing with the Netherlands, suggests that Dutch multicultural policy involves the 'minorization' of immigrants so that they can be treated as inferiors (Rath, 1991), while Schierup and Alund in Sweden (1990) see official policies of multiculturalism there as essentially manipulative, seeking to control ethnic minorities through co-option of, or negotiation with, traditional elders in ways which take no account of the diversity which exists within such communities, particularly in the second generation.

All of these criticisms of the practice of multiculturalism see it as threatening orthodox liberal and socialist democratic ideals. A different kind of response comes from liberal political philosophy. Since such political philosophy is based traditionally on a conception of individual human rights, some philosophers as well as social scientists have sought to find a place within their ideal society for some recognition of group rights (Baubock, 1994; Habermas, 1994; Kymlicka, 1989, 1995; Taylor, 1992; van Gunsteren, 1994; Walzer, 1980). All of these are dealing with the problem of integration along the lines suggested in the quotation from Roy Jenkins above.

There clearly is a problem here of the difference between the ideal and the actual practice of multiculturalism. While the spelling out of the ideal shows that it is compatible with a revised conception of liberal or socialist democracy, what is often called multiculturalism seems to involve inequality or manipulation of minority groups.

This is not, however, a problem to be resolved simply on an abstract level. In order to clarify it a number of social scientists have suggested that it is necessary first to look empirically at the actual institutions which have been set up in European cities to deal with minorities (Ireland, 1994; Rex, 1996a and 1996b; Soysal, 1994). What their studies seek to show is that such institutions are not necessarily based upon ideal democracy on the one hand, or upon the control and manipulation of inferior groups on the other. What is usually the case is that the institutions have conflicting goals built into them. The case of Frankfurt, discussed by Radtke, which has been mentioned above is an especially interesting one. There, an elaborate multicultural bureau was set up to deal with the problems of Turks and others. As Radtke himself sees this, such a multicultural apparatus serves only to marginalize minorities and to prevent them from solving their problems through the normal institutions of the welfare state. Those who support the system, on the other hand, argue that without special support the problems of the minorities will not be dealt with at all. My own study with Samad in Birmingham and Bradford (Rex, 1996a) shows how cities which originally reacted very negatively to the presence of immigrants found it both necessary and convenient to set up special and elaborate forms of consultation. The existence of this earnest intellectual debate and the creation of new institutions reflects the fact that traditional accounts of democracy within the nation-state cannot be sustained. Economic and political migration of the kind occurring in the modern world seems to suggest that at least they need substantial revision. Another alternative, however, is to suggest that they can only be resolved at a supranational level.

Multiculturalism at a supranational level

While the nation-state struggles to maintain its traditional structure in the face of immigration, it also finds itself increasingly involved in supranational structures. This is very evident in the case of Western Europe as it attempts to create a supranational European Union, but it is also part of a larger problem of the emergence of a world system and the globalization of basic institutions. We must now see how far these supranational institutions affect and are affected by migration.

The European Union has three constituent elements which can affect immigration and the integration of immigrants, namely the Council of Ministers, the European Parliament and the European Commission. Only the Council of Ministers has actual legislative power.

As far as immigration is concerned, the Council of Ministers has considered this question as a part of its general concern with border controls including illegal immigration, the control of terrorism, and the question of drugs. It has sought to harmonize policy on immigration at the level of the lowest common denominator, that is to say recommending to member states the adoption of the most restrictive policies. Some of its functions have, moreover, been delegated to groups of civil servants from some member countries which have produced the Schengen and Trevi agreements. These agreements sought to create open internal borders between the countries involved while at the same time maintaining severe restrictions on entry from outside Europe. This led to the Council of Ministers being accused of creating a 'fortress Europe' involving a high degree of prosperity in Europe itself protected from invasion from the poorer South and East by firm immigration barriers.

The Council of Ministers has not been directly concerned with the question of the settlement of immigrants or of the rights which they should have. This has been left to the European Parliament and the Commission. The Parliament produced a number of reports (European Parliament, 1992) leading eventually to a 'Declaration against Racism and Xenophobia'. Any such statement, however, could only be a matter of rhetoric and it was left to the Commission to develop proposals which could be ratified by the Council of Ministers to implement the Declaration. The most important of these led to the creation of a body called 'The Migrants' Forum'. This was a body which included representatives of residents who were not EU citizens together with citizens of other countries, including Britain, who were thought to be suffering from discrimination and disadvantage.

In principle the 'Migrants' Forum' provided a means whereby non-EU residents who were not able to vote for the European Parliament could be consulted, but it also seemed to suggest that the consideration of the problem of ethnic and racial disadvantage among citizens would be marginalized, thus reproducing at an international level a problem which existed where consultative mechanisms were established at national level. Some would argue that, because all full citizens were represented in Parliament anyway, the creation of the 'Migrants' Forum' actually gave them an additional voice through which their special interests could be represented to the Parliament, but the critics of the Forum suggested that all disadvantaged ethnic minority groups were actually being treated as second-class citizens akin to the non-citizen *gastarbeiters* in Germany. There may have been some gain for the *gastarbeiters* in being included in such a body, but for the minority citizens in Britain it represented a lowering of their status. The European Union, as they saw it, was coming to be based upon the 'differential incorporation' of immigrant minorities (Smith, 1965, 1974). All black and disadvantaged minorities were being treated as *gastarbeiters*.

Beyond these questions of political representation, a wider debate developed among politicians and social scientists about the possibility of a new European identity. Any such conception, however, had to deal not only with the incorporation of outsiders, but also with the task of producing a common sense of belonging to Europe among the citizens of member states who had their own national traditions. That is to say, it dealt with a concept of Europeanness which was based upon common elements of identity between, for example, the British, German and French. Thus European identity came to be thought of in terms of a shared race, ethnicity and religion, and, though this could not be a matter for legislation, much thinking was based upon the assumption that Europeans were White and Christian. This identity debate left unresolved the question of how far Blacks and Muslims were to be thought of in Europe. Generally these problems were still left to national governments. If these governments did not have a policy of democratic multiculturalism it was not to be expected that such a policy would be reflected at a European level.

As I suggested in discussing national questions the democratic ideal of multiculturalism involved the recognition of a civic culture based upon the notion of equal citizens' rights together with the acceptance of cultural diversity. It can hardly be said that this has been achieved in Europe. The civic culture which exists seems to exist for full citizens who are represented in Parliament, although it is true that the European Court could be a means of promoting individual human rights. It would seem that this supranational organization has not yet been able to proceed very fast in facing up to the notion of individual and group rights in the way in which the political philosophers of liberalism have done at a national level.

Of course, it is still possible not merely to describe European social institutions as they are but to suggest ways in which they should develop. In this context it is interesting to notice that Habermas has suggested that the European Union should develop a philosophy and an identity based not upon some form of emotional and cultural unity but upon what he calls 'constitutional patriotism' (Habermas, 1992, 1994; Delanty, 1996). That may be an ideal worth fighting for. It would be the equivalent at an international level of what I have called, in discussing Roy Jenkins's definition of integration, the shared political culture of the public domain, which I have suggested should be based upon the ideal of equality. Constitutional patriotism at the level of supranational government could also be combined with the recognition of cultural diversity at a national and subnational level.

At a wider international level the United Nations reproduces many of the problems of the European Union in an exaggerated form. It has little in the way of legislative powers except through the Resolutions of the Security Council which are often ignored by member states. It tends, however, to be even stronger on rhetoric than the Council of Europe. It may declare a particular year to be a Year Against All Forms of Racial Discrimination and through agencies like UNESCO might produce statements and declarations on such topics as racism and race prejudice (Montagu, 1981), but these declarations are rarely specific and in any case depend for their implementation upon the member states.

It would seem, then, that such attempts as there have been to create regional and international *political* bodies have actually done little to regulate the relations between nation-states and transnational migrant communities. We should now note finally, however, that it could be argued that in a global world effective decision making does not rest with political bodies at all. National governments make their economic decisions within constraints set by multinational corporations. The international information system is no longer under the control of these governments; and the media of mass communication speak to, and reflect, the shared interests of members of an international community. It is very hard in these circumstances to say who the effective decision-makers are in the new global world. Probably they serve the interests of a small number of super-entrepreneurs, though their power will be limited by those who control the information system and the means of communication (Sklair, 1991).

The new global order will not, however, reflect the interests of nation-states, and this may be of considerable importance for transnational migrant communities. It is true that members of these communities may simply be called in to take the most unwanted and undesirable jobs. But neither the pursuit of profit nor the control of the information system and the media can be based simply upon ethnic and racial distinctions and members of transnational migrant communities may find that the new globally organized world presents them with new opportunities. If the information system comes to be crucial and some migrant groups have the skills necessary for its effective working, they may find themselves having access to the more powerful and well rewarded positions. On an international level places like Baroda in India have become very important in the development of computer software. It is equally true that within any one society some ethnic groups with the appropriate skills may be able to advance themselves. They have the power of collective action to defend and advance their interests in new ways. Ethnicity today often operates by e-mail and the members of ethnic groups may be able to gain entry into the decision-making classes, unless these classes become closed on an ethnic basis, which seems unlikely. It seems possible that the new globalized world economy will not necessarily condemn ethnic minority groups only to underclass positions. It may provide them with opportunities which they do not have in the nation-state and in regional groupings of nation-states.

Finally, however, one should note that in a world of concentrated international power there will still be those who are powerless and who will seek through their local identifications, and the forms of collective organization to which they give rise, to protect themselves. This is why it is sometimes suggested that whereas the modern condition and the modern nation-state rested upon the struggle of occupationally based classes, in the postmodern condition, social movements, including ethnic movements, are often more concerned with the assertion and defence of collective identities within a globalized world (Melucci, 1990; Touraine, 1971, 1977).

References

Anwar, M. (1979) *The Myth of Return: Pakistanis in Britain*. London: Heinemann Educational Books.

Baubock, R. (1994) *Transnational Citizenship*. Aldershot: Edward Elgar.

Clifford, J. (1993) Diasporas, *Cultural Anthropology*, **9**, 302–37.

Delanty, G. (1996) Beyond the nation-state: national citizenship and identity in a multicultural society, in *Sociological Research Online*. Guildford.

European Parliament (1992) *The Evrigenis and Ford Reports*. Strasbourg.

Gilroy, P. (1993) *The Black Atlantic*. London: Verso.

Habermas, J. (1992) Citizenship and national identity: reflections on the future of Europe, *Praxis International*, **12**, 1–19.

Habermas, J. (1994) Citizenship and national identity, in van Steenbergen (ed.).

Hall, S. (1992) The new ethnicities, in J. Donald and A. Rattansi (eds) *Race, Culture and Difference*. London: Sage.

Hammar, T. (1990) *Democracy and the Nation-state*. Aldershot: Gower.

Ireland, P. (1994) *The Policy Challenge of Ethnic Diversity: Immigrant Policies in France and Switzerland*. Cambridge, MA: Harvard University Press.

Joly, D. (1997), with Kelly, Lynette and Nettleton, Clive, *Refugees in Europe: The Hostile New Agenda*. London: Minority Rights Group.

Kymlicka, W. (1989) *Liberalism, Community and Culture*. Oxford: Oxford University Press.

Kymlicka, W. (1995) *Multicultural Citizenship*. Oxford: Oxford University Press.

Melucci, A. (1990) *Nomads of the Present: Social Movements and Individual Needs in Contemporary Society*. London: Hutchinson.

Montagu, A. (1981) *Statements on Race: An Annotated Elaboration and Exposition of the Four Statements on Race Issued by UNESCO*. London: Greenwood Press.

OECD (1995) *Annual Report of Sopemi 1994 – Trends in International Migration*. Paris: OECD.

Radtke, F.-O. (1994) The formation of ethnic minorities: the transformation of social into ethnic conflicts in a so-called multi-cultural society, the German case, in Rex and Drury (eds).

Rath, J. (1991) Minorisering – De Social Constructe van Ethnische Minderheden. PhD thesis, University of Utrecht.

Rex, J. (ed.) (1996a) Multiculturalism and political integration in European cities, *Innovation in Social Science*, **9** (1).

Rex, J. (1996b) *Ethnic Minorities in the Modern Nation-State*. Basingstoke: Macmillan.

Rex, J., and Drury, B. (eds) (1994) *Ethnic Mobilisation in a Multi-Cultural Europe*. Aldershot: Avebury.

Rex, J., Joly, D. and Wilpert, C. (eds) (1987) *Immigrant Associations in Europe*. Aldershot: Gower.

Rex, J. and Tomlinson, S. (1979) *Colonial Immigrants in a British City – A Class Analysis*. London: Routledge and Kegan Paul.

Schierup, C.-U. and Alund, A. (1990) *Paradoxes of Multiculturalism*. Aldershot: Gower.

Sklair, L. (1991) *Sociology of the Global System*. Hemel Hempstead: Harvester Wheatsheaf.

Smith, M. G. (1965) *The Plural Society in the British West Indies*. Berkeley, CA: University of California Press.

Smith, M. G. (1974) *Corporations and Society*. London: Duckworth.

Soysal, Y. (1994) *Limits of Citizenship: Migrants and Post-National Membership in Europe*. Chicago: Chicago University Press.

Taylor, C. (1992) *Multiculturalism and the Politics of Recognition*. Princeton, NJ: Princeton University Press.

Touraine, A. (1971) *The Post-Industrial Society: Tomorrow's Social History: Classes, Conflicts and Culture in the Post-Modern Society*. New York: Random House.

Touraine, A. (1977) *The Self-Production of Society*. Chicago: Chicago University Press.

van Gunsteren, H. (1994) Four conceptions of citizenship, in van Steenbergen (ed.).

van Steenbergen, B. (ed.) (1994) *The Condition of Citizenship*. London: Sage.

Walzer, M. (1980) Pluralism: a political perspective, in *Harvard Encyclopaedia of American Ethnic Groups*. Cambridge, MA: Harvard University Press.

Wieviorka, M. (1994) Ethnicity as action, in Rex and Drury (eds).

Further reading

Guibernau, M. and Rex, J. (eds) (1997) *The Ethnicity Reader*. Cambridge: Polity Press.

Marshall, T. (1950) *Citizenship and Social Class*. Cambridge: Cambridge University Press.

Massey, D., Arango, J., Hugo, G., Kourouci, A., Pellegrino, A. and Taylor, E. J. (1993) Theories of international migration: a review and appraisal, *Population and Development Review*, **19**, 431–65.

Owen, D. (1991) *Ethnic Minorities in Britain: Settlement Patterns*. Census Statistical Paper no. 1, Centre for Research in Ethnic Relations, University of Warwick, Coventry.

Rex, J. (1981) A working paradigm for race relations research, *Ethnic and Racial Studies* (London), **4**, 1–25.

Rex, J. (1991) *Ethnic Identity and Ethnic Mobilisation in Britain*. Research Monograph no. 5, Centre for Research in Ethnic Relations, University of Warwick, Coventry.

Rex, J. (1992) Ethnic mobilisation in Britain, *Revue Européenne des Migrations Internationales*, **10**, 15–31.

Rex, J. (1997) The problematic of multinational and multi-cultural societies. The Ethnic and Racial Studies Lecture, October 1996, to be published in *Ethnic and Racial Studies* (1997).

Wallerstein, I. (1974) *The Modern World System: Capitalist Agriculture and the Origins of the European World Economy in the Sixteenth Century*. New York: Academic Press.

5

Territorial Cultures and Global Impacts

ZDRAVKO MLINAR AND FRANC TRČEK

General points of departure

There are certain assumptions that underlie the current debate about the spread of trans-border connections between peoples and their cultures which do not fit the actual state of affairs. Empirical evidence shows that we *cannot accept* the following:

1. *The assumption that, as national states become more exposed to cultural influences, this exposure (or the outward projection of domestic cultural influences) increases proportionately in all directions.* On the contrary, a clear bias towards particular geographical orientations and directions of connections (to 'core' countries or 'core' centres), to the almost complete neglect of other directions or areas, can be detected.
2. *The assumption that there is a necessary and gradual decline in the intensity of cultural influences as distance increases.* As a matter of fact, cultural impacts of neighbouring countries on each other may become relatively, or even absolutely, weaker than those exerted by the distant global or world 'core'. There are even instances of a 'local–global inversion' which allows people to be better informed about world events than about those events in their geographical proximity.
3. *The assumption that greater openness of national societies and cultures signifies* eo ipso *an enrichment in the sense of greater cultural diversity.* Rather, it can also entail greater uniformity, as is shown in particular in trends towards 'Americanization' – which is an indicator of globalization, although it is nevertheless distinct from it.
4. *The assumption that the whole population of a nation-state (or any territorial community) comes into contact with other cultures and adopts them.* Rather, there are in fact characteristic, inter-generational differences and, for example, the older the generation, the greater its cultural – language – 'exclusiveness' and the narrower the territorial boundaries of its specific 'cultural profile'.
5. *The assumption that all national or territorial cultures experience the global-*

ization process in the same or a similar manner, regardless of size. Actually, smaller nations are generally more receptive to cultural influences from the global core than larger nations which tend to be more competitive.

6. *The assumption that exposure and susceptibility to global impacts are the same regardless of past experience and the history of relations with other nations and cultures.* Yet as can be seen in the case of East European nations, since the collapse of the communist system and its exclusiveness, they are now more receptive to world core impacts than Western European nations which had never been subjected to similar restrictions in trans-border contacts.

7. *The assumption that the current increase, and importance, of the cultural influence of the global 'core' will continue indefinitely.* On the contrary, in the long run globalization is likely to proceed without centralization and entail dehierarchization with a shift away from the centre–periphery paradigm – even though current empirical evidence suggests a different picture, at least in some respects. Yet the familiar entrenched territorial hierarchies are respected less and less strictly by the once-subordinate territorial and non-territorial actors as they become empowered technologically (through the new information and communication technologies), economically (through the disposal of greater financial resources) and politically (through the exercise of individual or ethnic rights). Accessibility thus increases not only horizontally, or geographically, but also vertically through the hierarchical levels of territorial organization. This brings the prospect of multilevel power sharing as national societies become more open and interactive (Mlinar, 1995b).

A detailed analysis of these assumptions is beyond the scope of this analysis. In this chapter we have set ourselves a more modest task. The territorial provenance of foreign cultural impacts is established from empirical data on selected cultural activities (that is, film, music, television programmes) in some European countries, and in Slovenia in particular. The primary purpose of this exercise is to establish the geographical origins of the main cultural influences and changes in their relative significance over time. Attention is focused in particular on shifts in the relative importance of the influence or impacts of neighbouring cultures, as compared with that of the global core. The global core is identified as the most influential source of popular culture on a world scale which today is taken to be above all the USA, together with Great Britain in some respects. Information and communication technologies are lowering the 'friction of space', that is, the time and costs involved in transferring information. Thus the time-space distance between peoples as well as between their cultures is diminishing, and the one- or two-way accessibility of territorial cultures is increasing, leading to what has been termed 'time-space compression'.

Territorial cultures, adjacency and globality

In the course of centuries territorial cultures have formed unique identities on the basis of restricted access and the 'friction of space' in general. Where communications dried up or even ceased completely, lines of demarcation appeared between territorial cultural systems. Earlier, the most typical examples of this were the physical, geographical dividing lines between languages or dialects, that is, for example, inaccessibility owing to rivers, mountains, forests, marsh areas, etc. (Ramovš, 1935). But the development of transportation and communication technologies which has occurred more or less in concert with the growth of disposable income and the dismantling of political barriers has allowed a growing number of actors to interact across, and move beyond, the borders of historically fortified territorial units. This has led to a transition from a 'space of places' to a 'space of flows'. This is similar to the better-defined transition from the 'old' to the 'new localism'. According to Strassoldo (1992), the old localism tended to minimize contacts with the outer world and maintain a firm, closed boundary, whereas the new localism is grounded in an awareness of the rest of the world and is open to contact with it. The old localism rests on a principle of insulation, whereas the new promotes association over a broader space. The former was exclusive, the latter is selectively associative, establishing supra-local linkages.

The transition to a 'space of flows' may be either uni-directional through the influx and domination of stronger cultures, or bi-directional as a result of interaction and interpenetration. Historically, in both cases influence has been exerted first through the adjacency or proximity principle. In recent years, however, political changes in Europe have encouraged national societies and cultures – which had previously been locked within the boundaries of their individual countries – to open up to the wider world. Particularly in border regions, very diverse forms of cross-border cultural co-operation have sprouted (von Malchus, 1994; Mlinar, 1996b). It may be noted that this kind of cross-border co-operation is a sort of corrective to poorly fitting and imposed dividing-lines, at least as far as state borders are concerned. But in the long run its dynamics and the interaction of adjacent regions will lose their present significance – either relatively or even absolutely. With the technological, economic and political means available for overcoming distance, the spatial dispersion of connections is increasing, and the earlier dependence on, and vulnerability to, the surroundings is declining.

To avoid making unfounded generalizations and simplifications regarding globalization, the wide differences between the flows of people, goods, information and ideas have to be taken into account. Thus, even in West Europe, flows of people are still predominantly restricted to areas within state borders (Noin and Woods, 1993) and the mobility of most people in European countries is actually limited to a local-national scale with only a small segment entering transnational streams. Trans-border flows of goods, on the other hand, are increasingly determined by supranational regional integration and the triadization of the world economy (Park, 1994), represented by Europe, East Asia and the North American Free Trade Area.

Globalization is strongest in world information flows, although here, too, there are major deviations. In several fields deterritorialized global networks and global flows dominated by the 'world core' have evolved. This suggests that the importance of the adjacency principle is receding and gives way to the principle of global organization of a 'decontextualized culture'. Thus, there is a decline in the intensity of cultural connections based on geographical and ethnical proximity as the impacts grow of the world core – which may somewhat simplistically be equated with the USA, or, in some fields like music, the USA and UK together.

The diminishing significance of connections between neighbouring cultures in Europe is a manifestation of the general trend and long-term process of autonomization or dehierarchization as presented above, which is concurrent with the process of globalization (Mlinar, 1992). The autonomization process is particularly important for small nations which were subordinated to big neighbours for centuries. Anthony Giddens (1990) calls this 'disembedding' because it involves a distancing from the immediate environment and the simultaneous intensification of connections over a wider, global expanse. The growing role of English may serve as an example of these processes. As it gains sway, the use of Swedish is declining in Finland, for example, a situation replicated with Danish in Sweden and German in Belgium (Findahl, 1989). Furthermore, major languages like French, German and Russian are not only confronted with the influx of English into almost all spheres of public life on their 'home' territory, but they are losing their former language-users abroad. These two developments have provoked the strongest reactions in France where a *mélange*, the so-called 'Franglais', had begun to emerge (Etiemble, 1973; Flaitz, 1988), along with the reorientation abroad away from French to 'global' English. The status of French culture in general seemed to be weakening and there has been a growing feeling that the language is in danger of disappearing as an international language (Domenak, 1991: 48). While small nations cannot realistically aspire to cultural self-sufficiency – although they do try to reduce foreign influences (Mlinar, 1994) – big nations have greater scope and their responses have been stronger. The French, for example, have endeavoured to distance themselves from the English language and culture at the risk of a kind of self-isolation. French government representatives from time to time assert the 'right to be different' from English and American (popular) culture, yet the same right is not granted to ethnic groups within France.

General information flows in Europe also reveal poor interconnections between the political and cultural centres of geographically and ethnically proximate nations. As the Czech political scientist Bohumil Doležal (1995: 34) points out with regard to the political sphere, links between the governments of the neighbouring East Central European countries have remained weak even after the political reforms. This may partly be attributed to pretensions to superiority by some states or cultures in relation to their neighbours. Withdrawal and non-cooperation is a typical response to such feelings of superiority. The mass media, for example, tend not to draw on local, original sources and information networks. It is still true that

> the overwhelming majority of world news flows from the developed to the developing countries, and is generated by four large transnational news agencies: AP, UPI, AFP and Reuters. Moreover, the West dominates the use of satellites, the electromagnetic spectrum, controlling the use of airwaves, telecommunications, micro-electronics, remote-sensing capabilities, direct satellite broadcasting and computer-related transmission. (Wete, 1988: 139)

In a more detailed analysis of the collection and flow of world news, Hester (1991: 45) finds that, due to historical developments and power relations, agencies that control the flow and contents of world news are centralized in three western metropoles – New York, London and Paris – and also in Moscow, while Japan's economic growth increases the importance of Tokyo as a centre of communication power (Hester, 1991: 45). As a result, in many fields of cultural activity we are often better informed about what is happening in the world centres than we are about happenings in the cities of neighbouring countries.

Reinforcement of the world core: 'Americanization'

Data on the territorial origin of the most popular music, films and television programmes, and the main sources of information and their dissemination in the world context, show a strong tendency towards the 'Americanization' of European cultures, although there are certain exceptions. Explanations of the changes that have been offered to date do not, however, suffice for a sociological interpretation of them.

Thus we cannot be satisfied with earlier explanations such as media imperialism (Schiller, 1969, 1981) or 'cultural imperialism', which contain an implicit 'conspiracy theory', namely, that the American military-industrial complex is seeking to subordinate the rest of the world. Although the USA does actively advocate the 'doctrine of the free flow of information', the trends can only be explained sociologically in the context of long-term developmental processes. The early stage of globalization, when only very few actors are capable of acting on a world scale, is characterized by centralization and hierarchization. It is only when globalization advances further that it begins to take the form of dehierarchized interconnections in a world context and thereby approaches a 'global civil society' (Mlinar, 1995a: 156).

The global dominance of American popular culture is usually explained with reference to the distinctive features of the American market. Thus Hoskins and Mirus (1990: 85) stress the fact that 'the United States constitutes a very large market in terms of *number of viewers*, as well as in terms of *income per viewer*, a mass audience with high commercial value results. Such a market can support high production quality programming at comparatively lower risk of failure than anywhere else.' The extent and financial strength of the American market thus make possible the lower prices of American programmes on the international market, assuming that a product of the same quality costs the same regardless of the size of the market (Hoskins and Mirus, 1988: 551).

Beside this typical 'economy of scale' explanation, there is a sociologically equally relevant explanation in terms of the cultural heterogeneity of the American audience (with its considerable numbers of Cubans, Mexicans, Puerto Ricans, African Americans, Native Americans and recent immigrants). Given this heterogeneity, American popular culture is built around values which are generally adopted by the majority of the diverse American population (Crane, 1992: 165). Hence the programming of popular culture is directed towards the lowest common denominator of this heterogeneous audience. Thus the ethnic and cultural diversity of American society fails to be reflected in its media programmes.

Another point that must be taken into consideration in connection with American cultural dominance is the fact that the international public is already well acclimatized to American culture (Schou, 1992). Not only is it perceived as the bearer of progress, but it is also seen as a global culture. As global media corporations prevail and launch their products on numerous markets almost simultaneously, these products – the majority of which originate in the USA – are also globally consumed at the same time. These products are designed as global cultural products based on the most general, essentially Eurocentric, cultural values.

Just as the expansiveness of American popular culture rests on English as the *lingua franca* of today, the European national cultures are bounded precisely because of the language barrier. For example, 80 per cent of

Europe's television and film production stays within national borders (Burgelman and Pauwels, 1992: 176–7). As Schlesinger (1993: 12) points out, '[i]t could fairly be said that the real common currency of the European audiovisual space is actually American television's output for the US. It is producing the moving images that most easily traverse any European national barriers.'

Proportion of American TV programmes screened on national television

In most European countries, television first developed under the aegis of the national TV monopoly, whose primary role was to provide the public with educational and informational programmes, rather than entertainment. In the former socialist countries, before the inception of satellite television, national TV was also the only form generally available, except in border regions where foreign programmes could be received. When the European tradition of national television stations as co-creators/disseminators of the national cultural identity is compared to the USA's consumerist, entertainment-oriented television (Brown, 1991), it becomes much easier to understand all the heated debate over the Americanization and consequent 'vulgarization' of European television programmes, which is seen as threatening the national identity of the European nations.

The empirical data from our study, presented in Figure 5.1, show the share of American programmes in the total number of programmes transmitted. Until the very end of the 1980s, the share was considerably lower on Slovene and Croatian television than on Austrian television. The difference stems from the high share of domestically produced programmes which reached more than 80 per cent in Slovenia and Croatia until 1986. Following the break-up of Yugoslavia and the political reforms, the proportion of American programmes on Slovene and Croatian TV showed a marked increase.

However, when individual categories of programmes are analysed the highest share of American programmes is found in fiction, which is financially and technically the most demanding part of production. In all three national networks there was a significant decline in domestic production of feature films. In the past twenty years all three stations have doubled their programme time and increased the number of feature films shown by as many as five times. The next most frequently shown foreign programmes on all three stations came from Germany, France and Italy. However, their shares were declining, as were those of programmes from other West European countries. Programmes from other geographical areas were rarely screened by any of the three national stations. Nevertheless, when the programmes are taken *as a whole*, the national television stations cannot be said to have become Americanized.

Zdravko Mlinar and Franc Trček

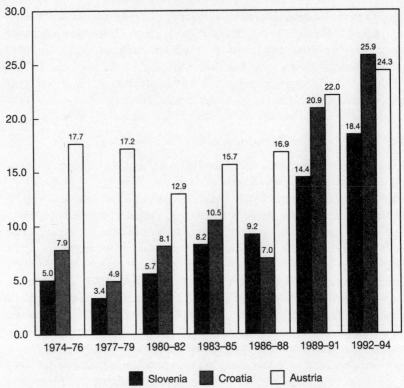

Figure 5.1 Share of American TV programmes screened on national television in Slovenia, Croatia and Austria, 1974–1994

Proportion of films of American origin

Film is another area of cultural activity that reveals the changing roles of territorial proximity and the world core. Domenak has already reported (1990: 118–23) that data on films show alienation between cultural neighbours or geographically proximate nations in Europe. Thus, for example, the French public is generally not interested in films from other European countries. Domenak also reports data showing a decline in cinema attendance at screenings of films from neighbouring and other European countries. He claims that, while cinema-goers tend to be familiar with the names of Hollywood stars, they know nothing about leading actors and directors from neighbouring countries.

Despite the fact that the growth of video-recorders and satellite and cable-TV networks is reducing the number of cinema-goers – particularly in countries where this audio-visual technology is well entrenched – there has not been any exceptionally marked decrease in feature-film production.

Output is rising in non-European countries with a high rate of film production such as India, Thailand, China and Hong Kong. Recent figures indicate that in most West European countries the decline in film production has also been halted (*Panorama of EU Industry* 94: 27–5).

However, high output of feature films does not guarantee a variety of choice of cinema programmes. For example, although it is the biggest producer, Asia has not managed to penetrate beyond the Asian market and certain African countries. The European film industry is in a similar situation to some extent, for out of every ten European films only one makes a profit, two cover production costs, while the remaining seven incur a loss (Burgelman and Pauwels, 1992: 176–7).

The French film industry was the only one to respond proactively to Americanization trends. But the endeavour was not a success from the financial point of view as government subsidies led to soaring production costs. The industry gained the benefits of new state financing, but in the process lost its competitiveness in relation to the USA. Moreover, notwithstanding the national strategy, its share of the domestic market also fell as the share of American films rose (Hayward, 1993: 386). Still, France is the only country to have maintained its volume of output and to have reached the global market with some of its films by following American global prescriptions. Yet it should be emphasized that the Hollywood film industry is the only one that manages to distribute its films worldwide. Its films dominate in the cinemas of numerous countries. Its market share is slightly lower only in certain African, Arabic and Asian countries (*Statistical Yearbook*, 1995: 8.7–8.11).

Fears that the influx of non-American capital into Hollywood would affect the production style of its films have not been borne out (McAnany and Wilkinson, 1992). There is even an evident trend towards adopting American production techniques in numerous national film industries. A good example of this is the new wave of high-budget French films (Crane, 1992: 165), which are again attracting relatively good attendance by international standards.

The Slovene cinema repertoire is dominated by American films (Figure 5.2). Over the past eighteen years their proportion has doubled and since 1990 it has levelled out at over 80 per cent. During the same period, with the exception of 1983, American films' share of attendance was constantly higher than their share of the total number of films shown and reached a peak of 90 per cent of total attendance. A surprisingly similar trend, with a time-lag, is shown by data on the rising share of American films in all films screened in Moscow.

Attendance figures for films in Slovenia according to their geographical origin show that, until the mid-1980s, West European and Hong Kong films

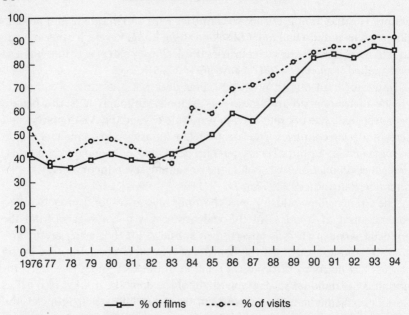

—□— % of films   --○-- % of visits

Figure 5.2 Americanization of Slovenian cinema programmes, 1976–1994

(popularly called 'karate' films) typically attracted relatively high attendance. But subsequently it dropped drastically. From 1990 onwards, the non-American films shown included only an occasional European high-budget 'Americanized' film (mainly French and Spanish) and, quite exceptionally, Asian, East European and Australian films which had won awards at prestigious film festivals. Other films simply do not appear in Slovenian cinemas. During the period 1976–94, for example, only one African film appeared in the cinema repertoire.

Although certain West European films (e.g. those of the Spanish director Almodóvar) and Australian films did attract fairly high attendance, in the past three years they have never reached ranking among the top fifteen films in terms of attendance figures. Consequently, in Slovenia the cinema repertoire rates as the most Americanized part of mass culture.

The territorial origin of popular music

Unlike film and TV production, the creation of new popular music does not necessarily involve high production costs and expensive, ultra-modern technology. At least theoretically, then, musicians recording with small independent companies can compete with the leading record labels in the world music market (Crane, 1992: 169). Nevertheless, their competitiveness is generally restricted to the national level, or the level of broad transnational ethno-linguistic regions (e.g. Latin America, countries with a German-speaking population, the newly-emerged states on the territory of the former Yugoslavia, etc.).

The global music market is effectively dominated by an oligopoly of six transnational companies (Sony-CBS, Time Warner, PolyGram, Thorn EMI, Bertelsmann Music Group, and Matsushita MCA). According to the figures for 1991, the share of the big six in the overall profits on the world music market amounted to 91.1 per cent. Following them in seventh place, with 3.4 per cent, was the English company Virgin Music, which in the meantime has already been taken over as a subsidiary of one of the six mega-corporations (it was bought up by Thorn EMI), while a trifling 5.5 per cent of profits remained for all the other music companies together. In such an oligopolistic situation, as Burnett notes: 'It is now almost impossible for a small company to establish itself and compete in the marketplace' (Burnett, 1992: 750).

In Slovenia before the Second World War, musical influences from neighbouring countries predominated – although to a small extent only – because the media were undeveloped. However, in the 1950s and 1960s, musical innovations began to percolate through on the air-waves from foreign radio stations (e.g. the then highly popular Radio Luxembourg). Out of a total of 210 big hits in the past two decades, 90 (43 per cent) were British and 83 (40 per cent) American songs. Consequently only 37, or 17 per cent of, hits came from elsewhere. Since that means that all other hits were sung in English, except for some German and Italian songs, it may be concluded that the English language has been absolutely dominant among the most popular foreign songs (198 hits, or 94 per cent). Except for some personal appearances at foreign ethnic music concerts, which attract only small audiences, there are no musical influences/incursions by Asian, African or South American popular music in Central Europe. Anglo-American popular music alone is globally dominant.

Foreign music influences and listening rates show considerable inter-generational and educational variation. Thus, for example, the SJM 92 Media research study clearly shows that rock and pop music is listened to exclusively by the younger generation, while the audience for domestic folk and popular light music expands with rising age. A similar trend is also noted with regard to education. The audience for opera, classical music and jazz is made up of more educated listeners who also attend rock and pop concerts more frequently than the less educated. Popular folk and light music is listened to considerably more by the less educated (for example, the folk/light programmes are listened to by 78.5 per cent of those who have completed primary school, by 72.9 per cent of those with vocational training at a college for further education, and by 45.4 per cent of secondary school leavers, but only by 35.3 per cent of those with higher or tertiary education). Hence, age-groups and educational levels are relevant to music appreciation patterns, in both narrow and broad territorial frameworks. The music preferences of the younger and more educated indicate the path of the future.

Adjacency, global core and transnational cultures

The findings of our research substantiate, at least broadly, the general premises that have been presented in our introduction as a critique of popular assumptions. Whereas territorial (national) cultures are becoming relatively, or even absolutely, less susceptible to the influence of neighbouring or proximate cultures there is a rising trend of receptivity to the influence and presence of the global core. The trend designated as 'Americanization' is evident in all three fields of cultural activity (TV, film, music). Nevertheless, it should be noted that the significance and content of this process are gradually changing. Earlier Americanization stood for a manifest form of 'cultural imperialism' and specifically a form of American national domination. Today, the USA is continuing to export its popular culture, of course. Indeed, as Schiller has noted, 'American cultural imperialism, dominated by the big US companies, has simply given way to a form of *transnational* corporate *cultural domination* under the sway of the big "stateless" transnationals ... . Cultural conglomerates now are not exclusively American owned. US *cultural styles and techniques* ... have ... become *transnationalized*' (Schiller, 1992: 12–13, emphases added). In this way, the particularism of American cultural domination is being erased and there is growing scope for mutual penetration of the world core and national cultures. This, however has a dual effect: a trend towards national–global convergence, as well as a concomitant trend towards increased sensitivity to preservation of a distinctive territorial cultural heritage. Rapprochement is taking place, for example, through 'joint venturing' in the aforementioned transnationalization of American cultural production. In the broader context it is also coming about through the rapid expansion of new means of computer-mediated and other communication, such as the Internet.

Endeavours to preserve national particularities take different forms such as import quotas (typical of France, Canada and India, and since 1996 the European Union as well) which are a reaction to the US 'free flow' doctrine. Restrictive measures like this, however, can only be of short duration. More promising are affirmative programmes aimed at mitigating the uneven territorial distribution of cultural production. This can involve the build-up of new cores (polycentrism) or a rapprochement and co-participation at the world core as a way of overcoming past domination and subordination.

From Americanization to global diversification

This essay dealt with the cultural changes that take place in the context of time-space compression. Intrusions and direct impacts by the global core on territorial cultures of national societies are intensifying just as there is a relative and even absolute decline in the impacts of proximate and neighbouring societies. An analysis of cultural changes affecting television, film and popular music in the case of some Central European countries indicates marked one-way American impacts. The opening-up of national societies, then, does not of itself guarantee a greater wealth of diversity of cultural influences, or at least not a linear process of globalization.

This opening-up does not proceed equally in all geographical directions; rather, it is directed primarily towards the world core. Initially, then, one particularity predominates but as its inclusiveness with respect to world heterogeneity grows its particularity diminishes and it becomes internally differentiated and gradually more representative of the world as a whole. Thus as the process of Americanization proceeds it changes such that in time it assumes the features of globalization.

In earlier times national cultures took shape through regional particularities that distinguished them from other cultural identities on the same or lower territorial levels. This particularity then spread on a 'one to many' communication pattern from the centre to the whole territory of the country. Local and regional cultures and the cultures of neighbouring nations arose as disruptions or even threats to standarized national cultures.

The process of Americanization also follows a 'one to many' logic, travelling from America to the whole world. Today neighbouring territorial cultures are drawing closer through their intensified communications with the world core rather than direct interaction with each other. Although this trend is currently predominant, there are signs of deviation from the pattern. There is a diversification, demassification and an individualization which are evident for example in CNN's system of gathering information by engaging local reporters from around the world; in the trend to 'world music' with global distribution of previously unknown ethno-music; in the diversification of television programmes; and in the introduction of interactive television and so forth.

We are facing an emerging, radically different pattern of networked global communications with a high degree of individualization of cultural production, that is, a 'many to many' pattern. This pattern is based on computer-mediated communications like the Internet in the context of a decentralized society and unmediated global communications between actors in contrast to the presently predominant corporate media structure.

In times past, differences arose between territorial cultures according to time and place and insofar as communications were weak or broken. The intensification of communication is eroding the foundations of these cultural differences. But instead of universal territorial uniformity this is leading towards growth of diversity through the creativity of actors who selectively combine elements of their local environment with global inputs. It is to be expected that the tendencies towards homogenization from the standpoint of both traditional territorial and imported American mass culture will be undermined at some point in the future.

Acknowledgements

We wish to extend our thanks for their assistance in collecting materials for this analysis to our students of spatial sociology, and in particular Bojan Korenini, Boštjan Kovačič, Boštjan Novak, and Katarina Zajc.

References

Brown, Duncan H. (1991) Citizens or consumers: US reactions to the European Community's Directive on television, *Critical Studies in Mass Communication*, **8**, 1–12.

Burgelman, Jean-Claude and Caroline Pauwels (1992) Audiovisual policy and cultural identity in small European states: the challenge of a unified market, *Media, Culture and Society*, **14**, 169–83.

Burnett, Robert (1992) The implications of ownership changes on concentration and diversity in the phonogram industry, *Communication Research*, **19**, 749–69.

Crane, Diana (1992) *The Production of Culture: Media and the Urban Arts*. Newbury Park, CA: Sage.

Doležal, Bohumil (1995) Zdravo bi bilo, navaditi se na razlike [We have to get used to the differences], *Delo – Sobotna priloga*, Ljubljana, 1 July, 34.

Domenak, Žan-Mari (Domenach, Jean-Marie) (1991) *Evropa: Kulturni izazov (Europe: le défi culturel)*. Beograd: Prosveta.

Etiemble, René (1973) *Parlez-vous franglais?* Paris: Gallimard.

Findahl, Olle (1989) Language in the age of satellite television, *European Journal of Communication*, **4** (2).

Flaitz, Jeffra (1988) *The Ideology of English*. Amsterdam: Mouton de Gruyter.

Giddens, Anthony (1990) *The Consequences of Modernity*. Oxford: Polity Press.

Hayward, Susan (1993) State, culture and the cinema: Jack Lang's strategies for the French film industry 1981–93, *Screen*, **34**, no. 4, Winter.

Hester, Al (1991) The collection and flow of world news, in John C. Merrill (ed.), *Global Journalism*. New York: Longman, pp. 29–50 (2nd edn).

Hoskins, Colin and Mirus, Rolf (1988) Reasons for the US dominance of the international trade in television programmes, *Media, Culture and Society*, **10**, 499–515.

Hoskins, Colin and Mirus, Rolf (1990) Television fiction made in USA, in Larsen (ed.), pp. 83–90.

Larsen, Peter (ed.) (1990) *Import/Export: International Flow of Television Fiction.* Paris: UNESCO.

McAnany, Emile G. and Wilkinson, Kenton T. (1992) From cultural imperialists to takeover victims? Questièns on Hollywood's buyouts from the critical tradition, *Communication Research,* **19,** 724–48.

Mlinar, Zdravko (ed.) (1992) *Globalization and Territorial Identities.* Aldershot: Avebury.

Mlinar, Zdravko (1994) Deterritorialization and reterritorialization of cultural identities, *Small Societies in Transition,* special issue of *Druboslovne razprave* (Ljubljana: Slovene Sociological Society), **15–16,** 141–53.

Mlinar, Zdravko (1995a) Local responses to global change, *Annals of the American Academy of Political and Social Science,* **540,** 145–56.

Mlinar, Zdravko (1995b) Territorial dehierarchization in the emerging new Europe, in Josef Langer and Wolfgang Pollauer (eds), *Small States in the Emerging New Europe.* Eisenstadt: Verlag für Soziologie und Humanethologie.

Mlinar, Zdravko (1996a) Transnational flows and language identity of a small nation: the case of Slovenia, *International Journal of Sociology of Language,* **119,** 141–53.

Mlinar, Zdravko (1996b) Managing the openness of border regions in the context of European integration. Paper presented to the European Regional Science Association 36th European Congress, ETH Zurich, Switzerland, 26–30 August 1996.

Noin, Daniel and Woods, Robert (eds) (1993) *The Changing Population of Europe.* Oxford: Blackwell.

Panorama of EU Industry 94, Luxemburg: EU, 1994.

Park, Jong H. (1994) Trading blocks and US–Japan relations in Pacific trade and cooperation, in M. Landeck (ed.), *International Trade, Regional and Global Issues.* Basingstoke: Macmillan.

Ramovš, Fran (1935) *Historièna gramatika slovenskega jezika [Historical Grammar of the Slovene language].* VII – Dialekti, Ljubljana.

Schiller, Herbert I. (1969) *Mass Communications and American Empire.* New York: Beacon Press.

Schiller, Herbert I. (1981) *Who Knows: Information in the Age of Fortune 500.* Norwood, NJ: Ablex Publishing Corporation.

Schiller, Herbert (1992) *Mass Communications and American Empire,* 2nd edn, update. Boulder, CO: Westview Press.

Schlesinger, Philip (1993) Wishful thinking: cultural politics, media, and collective identities in Europe, *Journal of Communication,* **43,** 6–17.

Schou, Soren (1992) Postwar Americanisation and the revitalisation of European culture, in M. Skovmand and Kim C. Schroder (eds), *Media Cultures: Reappraising Transnational Media.* London: Routledge, pp. 142–58.

Statistical Yearbook (1995). Paris: UNESCO.

Strassoldo, Raimondo (1992) Globalism and localism: theoretical reflection and some evidence, in Z. Mlinar (ed.) (1992).

von Malchus, Viktor (1994) Towards sustainable economic and social development of border regions. Paper presented at the 6th European Conference of Frontier Regions, Ljubljana (Slovenia), 13–15 October 1994.

Wete, F (1988) The new world information order, in C. Schneider and B. Wallis (eds), *Global Television*. New York: Wedge Press.

Further reading

Lopes, Paul D. (1992) Innovation and diversity in the popular music industry, 1969 to 1990, *American Sociological Review*, **57**, 56–71.

Lull, James (1995) *Media, Communication, Culture: A Global Approach*. Cambridge: Polity Press.

6

Globalization and Europe: The Russian Question

PAUL DUKES

There are two problems here: one very new, one very old. Globalization is a
new phenomenon; the relationship of Russia to Europe goes back beyond the
dawn of historical time, to the aeons of geology. Of course, as always, lateral
(or is it vertical?) thought could lead to arguments in the opposite direction.
Obviously, there was a closer connection between the continents before they
began to drift apart (Crosby, 1994: ch. 1). Moreover, if the word 'globalization' and much that is associated with it is of recent provenance (a 1990s
computer spellcheck is unaware of its existence), the process itself is of older,
even ancient, lineage. As far as the relationship of Russia to Europe is
concerned, events since 1989 have posed the question with a new intensity.
To look at the two problems in yet another way, one of them makes the other
redundant, or at least of minor significance, since the process of globalization
has reduced the importance of intracontinental relationships. On the other
hand, if Russia extends Europe to the Far East, as at least some members of
the Vladivostok intelligentsia would argue, we are dealing here with a
sizeable chunk of planet Earth. And, in any case, the historical approach
must be more conventional, not forgetting its stock in trade, the passage of
time through centuries, nor the adjurations of Lucien Febvre concerning its
intimate link with the geographical approach and *its* basic dimension of
space (Febvre, 1925: 364).

This contribution, then, will proceed as follows. The first section will be
concerned with the evolution of the relationship of Russia to Europe, the
second with the onset of globalization, including the degree of its responsibility for the collapse of Soviet control over Eastern Europe, then for the
dissolution of the Soviet Union itself and subsequent events. A third section
will consider Russia's post-Soviet position in a Europe itself increasingly
affected by the process of globalization, mainly from the point of view of its
impact on historical analysis.

However, before we proceed, a further preliminary observation is necessary, about the peculiar character of Russia. Not only is it very big, it is also
constantly changing. To put the point in another way, the frontier adjust-

ments accompanying the change from Russia to Soviet Union and back again might seem to make the twentieth century exceptional: the loss of a large swathe of Europe after 1917, the reincorporation of most of this in 1940/1945 and its renewed loss in 1991 were all of huge significance. But so was the acquisition of most of the Central Asian and Far Eastern parts of the empire in the nineteenth century, of the Baltics and slices of Poland in the eighteenth century, and so on back through the period centred on Moscow to that centred on Kiev. To be sure, the twentieth century *is* exceptional in its political revolutions from tsarist autocracy to Soviet Union to democratic republic. But as far as involvement in the process of globalization is concerned, especially when considered literally, the varying dimensions of Russia have been of key significance, even more so from the point of view of the relationship to Europe.

The relationship of Russia to Europe

The alphabet is just one of the indicators of the necessity of beginning in classical times. For while the 'alpha-beta' and so on of most of the continent is written after the Roman manner, Russia and just a few others have always followed the original Greek forms. But that is not the whole beginning of the story, since before Russia received its alphabet and much else from Byzantium, the Eastern Slavs had developed a distinctive culture in their boundless forests and steppe. 'Primitive animism' it may have been, but its influence pervaded all aspects of life, and did not disappear when the Grand Prince Vladimir of Kiev adopted Christianity in or around the year 988 (Franklin and Shepard, 1996: 162–3).

If social scientists might be wondering what is this all about, they might be reassured by turning to the outcome of US Department of State Contract no. 1722–420119 published in revised form by Harvard Professor Edward Keenan in 1986 (Keenan, 1986). Keenan was asked to tell the US government what constituted 'Russian political culture'. His essential response was that Christianity and other imports from Byzantium made no more than a superficial impact on a culture centred on the peasant commune. Mutual responsibilities made necessary by a harsh environment reduced the significance of the individual, and produced a collective outlook which adapted rather than changed right up to the end of the nineteenth century. There ensued an anomalous period including the last years of tsarism and the first Soviet years before a reversion to the main trajectory of development in the 1930s. Stalinism was the expression of a force much deeper than 'the cult of personality'.

Dmitry Obolensky (1971: 35) is among those who would not agree, arguing that far from constituting a kind of 'mark of the beast', Byzantine influence had a profound internal effect and also brought Russia into Europe. Even if this were so, however, this does not bring the story to a successful conclusion, for Orthodox and Roman Catholic Europe lived far from happily ever after: in spite of several attempts to maintain or restore the unity of Christendom, the schism appeared irreparable even before the arrival of the Reformation in the early sixteenth century. Coincidentally (or more than coincidentally), just as Luther and Calvin were rejecting Rome soon after the 'discovery' of the 'New World' beyond Europe by Columbus and others, a Russian monk, Filofei, looked landwards to the eternal city as a source of inspiration. With the capture of Byzantium by the Ottoman Turks in 1453 still fresh in his mind, no doubt, he declared that two Romes had fallen, but that Muscovite Russia had become the Third Rome and would never fall (Crummey, 1987: 135–8).

There were evident echoes of this concept when a new capital city was built at the beginning of the eighteenth century. For the choice of the name reflected more than the egocentricity of the founder, St Petersburg recalling the rock on which the Christian church had first been founded (a necessary reassurance, perhaps, as wooden piles were driven into the marshy banks of the river Neva) as well as a new European spirit in the adoption of a Western suffix (the Germanic -*burg* rather than the Slavonic -*gorod* or -*grad*) (Hughes, 1997). More than coincidentally (and this time we can be more certain), Peter the Great opened his 'window on the West' at the very time that 'Europe' was becoming widely adopted as a secular concept, as opposed to a synonym for Christendom (Dukes, 1990: 211).

The Enlightenment of the eighteenth century fell short of the ecumenical communication of medieval academia, but was nevertheless a cosmopolitan movement serving to consolidate the continent in a modern manner as questions about the whole world were posed against a background of further circumnavigation by Captain James Cook (Scott, 1996) and others, including Russians across Siberia and beyond. Towards the end of the eighteenth century, Catherine the Great, like Peter the Great at the century's beginning, looked mostly to the West for ideological inspiration, and encouraged Russian artists and scientists to do likewise. But the American and French Revolutions, from 1776 and 1789 respectively, brought about a profound reappraisal leading to a series of great debates in Russia, especially after the epic victory over Napoleon in 1812 (Dukes, 1990: 201, 217).

There were two broad tendencies in the debates. On the one hand, there were those who drew their inspiration from the USA, France and elsewhere in the West. On the other hand, there were those who looked inwards for their ideology, to the Orthodox Church, the commune and further indigenous sources. Towards the end of the nineteenth century, as Russia became increasingly involved in the global struggle for empire, the heirs to the

Westerners and Slavophiles updated old arguments while adding new dimensions to them (Venturi, 1952). At the neo-Westerner extreme, socialism was confronted by the Marxist challenge, although Karl Marx himself spent much of his later energy on coming to terms with an institution which had also attracted the Slavophiles – the commune (White, 1996: ch. 5). Could Russia proceed from feudalism to socialism without fully undergoing the experience of capitalism?

Various answers were given to this question after tsarist Russia collapsed in the *dénouement* of imperialism constituted by the First World War. In the difficult days of the Civil War and Intervention following the October Revolution of 1917, a confident positive (if short-lived) response was given in the policy of War Communism. This was followed by the New Economic Policy from 1921, marking a compromise between proletarian aspirations and peasant realities. Meanwhile, opponents of the new Soviet regime searched for explanations of and alternatives to the overwhelming deluge, most of them adapting world views already in existence. But there was one significant fresh departure – the Eurasian, or Europasian, which found a key to Russia's past, present and (to a lesser extent) future in its unique position straddling two continents (Burbank, 1986: 215–22). Soon, in the 1930s, there would be interpretations of Stalinism as the attempt to catch up and overtake the West using Eastern methods. While Stalin himself could be considered the living embodiment of such a view, for his own part the Leader looked mostly in the opposite direction for inspiration, citing American efficiency along with Russian revolutionary drive as the necessary 'Leninist' components for the successful completion of Soviet aims (Stalin, 1970: 120).

The Great Patriotic War, as Russians to this day conventionally call their leading part in the Second World War, brought about a degree of devastation still beyond the appreciation of most of the former Allies and opponents: up to 40 million losses of life, according to the most recent tallies (Korol, 1996: 418, 424), and a correspondingly huge-scale reversal of the advances made during the Five Year Plans, altogether dwarfing the self-inflicted wounds of the collectivization of the peasants and purges of the Communist Party, and dealing the Soviet Union blows from which it would never recover (Harrison, 1996: 172). For all the assertion of its superpower in the Khrushchev years sustained by early successes in the space race, the USSR was in nearly every respect far behind its rival the USA. Perhaps its only clear advantage was dominance of the 'heartland' of Eurasia, to use the geopolitical concept introduced before the First World War and now encouraging post-Second World War US strategists to propose 'containment', 'rollback' and even 'first strike'. Doomsday was avoided, however narrowly, during the Cuban missile crisis and other critical moments, but, undoubtedly, the Cold War made a major contribution to the figuratively earth-shattering events of 1989 and 1991.

However, the collapse of Soviet control over the countries of East-Central Europe did not deter Gorbachev (1988: 180–1) from talking of the common European home, and there is indeed a case for a thorough reappraisal of the relationship between post-Soviet Russia and the rest of the continent. We will return to this topic after an examination of the impact on the Soviet Union, its satellites and the rest of Europe of the early process of globalization.

Globalization

Arguably, the world has always been one. If this be so, globalization is the growing realization of a fact rather than an actual process in itself. To illustrate this line of thought, let us take the Russian word *mir*: three letters, and three meanings. In the first place, it is the commune, the centre of existence for Russian peasants through many centuries. Secondly, it is the whole world, the commune writ large, so to speak. Last but not least, it is peace, an apparent reflection of the security felt by peasants living together. Hence the old Soviet slogan, *mir miru* – peace to the world, rarely if ever granted in our own time and not often to be found before. But we can follow Edward Keenan in his pursuit of 'Russian political culture' via the reconstruction of the outlook of the Russian peasants, in medieval times and since (Keenan, 1986). Their world has no finite shape, but tends to come to an end with the horizon of their physical vision. This will include a broad swathe of the sky as well as a narrower perimeter down to earth. Not surprisingly, therefore, their biggest ideas are ethereal: for example, spirits inhabit the trees around the commune as well as its huts. A primitive cosmography, perhaps, but harmonious, and with its own kind of globalization, worthy of preservation, even of recapture, as a reminder that the world exists beyond human beings. But, of course, while there have been many (and remain at least a few) counterparts to the Russian peasants throughout the continent, the biggest such reminder for many Europeans would be their more formal religion, almost exclusively Christianity. (Whether or not Islam can be considered a European religion remains a moot point: certainly, many Muslims have lived in Europe, and even more do so now. The position of the other major formal religions is even more problematic in this regard. Possibly religions know no terrestrial frontiers.)

In a secular manner, its most self-assertive inhabitants did not realize the full dimensions of planet Earth until the voyages of discovery and exploration of the period around 1492, and even then the continents of Australasia and Antarctica awaited incorporation into the European understanding, not to mention large parts of the continents already identified. But, to repeat, because we did not know that it was there does not mean that it was not in fact there. There was one world beyond the perception of our ancestors, as we, their descendants, now all know.

However, globalization in its normal use is a term applied to a process of the recent past. If we insist upon the argument that it is perception as well as reality, the best starting point is Hiroshima. The dropping of the atomic bomb confirmed with an awful intensity the view of a fragile globe already suggested by the Second World War that it brought to an end. Arguably, this was also the 'first shot' in the Cold War, which led to an ever more intensive arms race illustrated by vast comprehensive maps adorning the walls of command centres in the USA and the USSR (with more emphasis than before on transpolar routes), and also brought about a full realization by the person in the street that human life could well be brought to an end not only within the boundaries of the two superpowers, but everywhere (Alperovitz, 1995; Henrikson, 1975; LaFeber, 1997: 24–5). More hopeful promoters of globalization were spin-offs of the Cold War and the ensuing space race, satellite television, the personal computer and e-mail, to give but three examples.

Supporters of President Reagan would maintain that his energetic support for the 'Star Wars' of the Strategic Defense Initiative was another, ultimately benign consequence of the Cold War, since the Soviet realization that it could not compete made a major contribution to the collapse of Soviet power. On the other hand, the 'astronomical' expenditure on the SDI and other Cold War projects threw not only the Soviet but also many other economies into disarray. Of course, there has been, and remains, a quasi-Keynesian aspect to the investment of trillions of dollars, pounds, francs and other currencies on armaments. No doubt, the Truman Doctrine and Marshall Plan of 1947 primed the pump of US capitalism as well as helping to save much of Europe from Communism. Thus bolstered up, the United Kingdom and France could pretend to acquire their own 'independent' deterrents, and invest in some of their own industries as they did so. But such expenditure is capital rather than labour intensive: it has made a few people rich and given rather more a job, but done little to tackle the more widespread problem of unemployment which has beset all Western economies in the later stages of the Cold War and after, especially since the decline of traditional heavy industries such as coal and steel.

As for the Soviet economy, it never recovered from the destruction of the Second World War and was thrown into further disarray by the strains of the Cold War. To a considerable extent, the collapse of the Soviet bloc and then of the USSR itself was also brought about by its isolation from the world economy and failure to adapt quickly enough to the demands of the third industrial revolution (the technological, following the first of manufacturing, coal and iron of the late eighteenth–early nineteenth century and the second of mass production, oil and steel of the late nineteenth–early twentieth century) (Maier, 1991).

But the globalizing impact of the Cold War was more than strategic and economic: it was also ideological. While the USA updated Wilsonism and the old West European empires attempted to come to terms with 'decolonization', the USSR needed to re-examine its own 'Marxism-Leninism'. This was a more difficult task than might first appear: on the face of it, the Russian Revolution had been accompanied by a set of ideas, scientific, progressive and global. On the other hand, from the very beginning, Soviet ideology contained a considerable ingredient of Russian patriotism, against the chauvinistic excesses of which Lenin considered it necessary to issue a number of warnings (Figes, 1996: 696–700).

Stalin, as already mentioned, defined Leninism as Soviet revolutionary drive plus American efficiency. As the Five Year Plans gathered speed, he also found it necessary to develop Lenin's concept of 'socialism in one country' and a new kind of Soviet patriotism at the same time as warning of the likelihood of a further intervention. This duly arrived with the Second World War, after which Stalin attempted to come to grips with the Cold War situation in such works as *Economic Problems of Socialism in the USSR*, arguing in 1952 that the Soviet Union should rebuild and extend its strength as the capitalist powers tore themselves to pieces in internecine rivalry (Stalin, 1952: 37–41). The Khrushchev era brought the assertion of super-power and the development of the 'peaceful coexistence', not necessarily undermined by Nikita Sergeevich's most famous utterance 'We will bury you'. For what he had in mind here was not so much a military victory as the ultimate triumph of Communism as a system over its rival capitalism. At about this time, the dissident view of the convergence of the two systems was advanced by Andrei Sakharov (Bailey, 1990: 256–8). Officially, Soviet policy remained 'peaceful coexistence' through its last decades, even though the 'Brezhnev Doctrine' insisted on the right to intervene in the internal affairs of the countries of Eastern Europe in response to any external threat. But no doctrine could prevent the collapse of the Soviet 'empire' abroad in 1989 and at home in 1991. Whether or not this comprehensive doctrine spelled 'the end of ideology', however, is a moot point to be discussed in the next section.

Before that, we need to turn our attention to another significant aspect of globalization involving the Soviet Union and the Eastern bloc, and caught in the title of an alarming book, *The Coming Plague: Newly Emerging Diseases in a World out of Balance*, first published in 1994. To take the example of AIDS, this too was caught up in the Cold War with the assertion of the KGB that the syndrome was the consequence of a CIA plot. Meanwhile, at a London summit on the subject in 1988, the Soviet Minister of Health insisted that the Slavic populace had been rendered immune by its genetic superiority! Lower-level ignorance contributed to an upsurge in AIDS among those sexually celebrating the fall of the Berlin Wall in 1989 (Garrett, 1995: 382, 476, 500). Generally speaking, the removal of the Iron Curtain meant the penetration of a *cordon sanitaire*, riddled all the more quickly through the insufficiency of such necessities as condoms and syringes. However benign many of its features, freedom had also come to mean a dangerous licence, encouraging the international commerce in narcotics as well as the arms trade. Equally terrifying was a poisonous force that had never needed to bother with frontiers, the nuclear power unleashed by the Chernobyl nuclear accident of 1986. Along with apprehension concerning the condition of other power stations as well as the nuclear strike force on land and at sea, this was a powerful reminder that the world had become an interdependent community.

The 'global village' of mass communication no doubt made a contribution to the collapse of Communism as 'The Voice of America' was heard in the remotest corners of Siberia, and the delights of the consumer cornucopia were viewed in those places that could be reached by TV. From 1989 onwards, such stations as CNN both recorded and encouraged change. Moreover, even the more traditional printed culture was not immune to wider influences. For example, with the arrival of the 'market economy', the Russian language received such terms as *biznesmen* and *biznesmenka*. Political innovation brought in *reiting* and *press-konferents*. And in a learned journal, one could find the enunciation of new sciences such as *alternativistika* and *globalistika*.

Post-Soviet Russia and Europe

What *are* the alternatives, and how do they relate to globalization? There undoubtedly exists a globalized economy, but along with it are to be found many local economies. Five years after the dissolution of the USSR, there seem to be more of the latter than of the former. Indeed, Russia seems to consist of a number of 'market economies' rather than one, the now familiar kiosks and street peddlers providing the most familiar face of small-scale retail commerce. Large-scale activity may be found in what is left of the military-industrial complex and in energy 'companies', some still closely linked to the state while others are more privatized. Foreign multinationals have done what they can to make deals for the extraction, refining and transport of oil and gas, but, frustrated and baffled by the volatile political and management situation, have opted to concentrate on the deceptively

more tractable circumstances of other ex-Soviet republics such as Kazakhstan, Turkmenistan and, especially, Azerbaijan. As far as the more
traditional economy is concerned, the old Russian attitude towards the land
persists, with no acceptance of wholesale privatization.

Such conservatism has implications for the political scene, where there are
definite appearances of debates, votes and the other appurtenances of
democracy, but many of the aspects of the re-election as President of Boris
Yeltsin and events since can do nothing but encourage scepticism, even
when measured against the far from perfect conducting of the presidential
election in the USA. Indeed, there is a latter-day force in the strictures against
the parliamentary system of the adviser to the last tsar, Konstantin Pobedonostsev. Considering 'The Great Falsehood of Our Time' to be 'the principle of
the sovereignty of the people, the principle that all power issues from the
people', Konstantin Pobedonostsev (1965: 32) wrote:

> The people loses all importance for its representative, until the time arrives
> when it is to be played upon again; the false and flattering and lying phrases
> are lavished as before; some are suborned by bribery, others by threats – the
> long chain of manoeuvres spun which forms an invariable factor of Parlia-
> mentarism. Yet this electoral farce continues to deceive humanity, and to be
> regarded as an institution which crowns the edifice of State. Poor humanity!
> (ibid.: 36)

The old saying, democracy is the worst system of government apart from all
the others, is under severe strain in Russia. Could it be that the traditional
political culture of the *mir*, geared more to collective responsibility than
individual choice, is likely to reassert itself in a more conspicuous manner?
Moreover, around the world, there are violations of the democratic order
ranging from cynical lip-service to flagrant infringements, altogether obliging us to doubt whether we have yet seen 'the end of history'. The Chinese
approach may yet hold greater sway in world politics than the Western
liberal alternative.

World politics encourages geopolitics, always by definition global, and yet
within its broad framework there has been a tendency to concentrate on the
heartland of Eurasia, and adjacent waterways, especially the Atlantic, which
was reinforced during the early years of the Cold War. Already, however,
some amendment was necessary to the 'classic' English-language formulations of Mackinder and Mahan, not least because of the growing influence of
the Pacific and then Indian oceans, but also because of the added new
dimension of the air, which gave unprecedented significance to the Northern
transpolar route, and then of outer space, which not only encouraged new
departures for strategic thinking such as SDI but also accelerated the
realization of the process of globalization. Who could see photographs taken
from space and not accept that it is indeed a small world, and that processes

on Earth as well as in the sky are making it so day by day? In other words, the geopolitical approach, like any other, is obliged to become more completely and more objectively global.

In a mundane, everyday manner, will local cultures be able to preserve their external characteristics, even their essence inviolate? To be sure, Samuel P. Huntington (1996) has advanced the argument that the twenty-first century will be marked by a clash of civilizations. But the Coca-Colonization has not ceased, and pop music has become even more pervasive since the day that John Lennon observed that the Beatles were more famous than Jesus Christ. Since then, too, the enormous spread of computer-speak has given emphasis to the emerging universality of the English language. Moreover, if papers in microbiological journals are no longer published in such a *Weltsprache* as German, will not minor tongues inevitably be cut out (Schröder, 1995: 31)?

Meanwhile, the problems of neologism are far from confined to *franglais* alone. In recent Russian writing on the social sciences and humanities, imported words at times threaten to overwhelm the domestic language. Simultaneously, one can be pleased to learn of the infiltration of *bikhevior-istskie metodiki* and regret that no more appropriate way can be found of adopting behavioural methodology. But let us return to the new sciences already introduced above – *alternativistika* and *globalistika*, especially as discussed by historians. How are Russians professionally concerned with the past adapting their world view to the pressures of the present?

We will concentrate on two approaches, neither of them constituting a school as rigorous as the Marxist-Leninist (itself sometimes more flexible than was normally assumed) but both distinctive enough to be placed in opposition to each other. Without too much distortion, one approach can be labelled 'formation' and the other 'civilization': the former is partly the heir to all-embracing Marxism-Leninism, often explicitly so, while the latter looks for heterogeneous alternatives. Yet it would be going too far to call 'forma-tion' scientific and 'civilization' artistic, for both are reactions to the following intimation:

> in the Russian historical tradition, the striving for historical synthesis is constantly fed by the intuitive feeling of the overall 'unity' of the world, intrinsically inherent in our national culture. This thoroughly suppresses the development by us of historical relativism, denying the possibility of a general basis for the comparative study of cultures and civilisations. 'The Russian spirit is characterised by the aspiration for wholeness and all-embracing totality, towards the ultimate and highest value in fundamentals.' So wrote the eminent philosopher of 'the silver age' S. L. Frank. (*Tsivilizatsii*, 1995: 6)

Thus, from the medieval chronicles to the development through the nineteenth century by N. M. Karamzin, S. M. Solov'ev and V. O. Kliuchevsky, the 'Russian historical tradition' is far from the empiricism of the British and American, although it does bear closer comparison with the French *science* and the German *Wissenschaft* (Dukes, 1996: 57–8, 157–9). Moreover, a close comparison can be made between the 'historical sociology' expounded by Kliuchevsky and the Marxist-Leninism of his Soviet successors: the common aim has been an approach characterized by its *zakonomernost*, or 'regularity of law'. A famous debate in the early 1960s between an American scholar and two Soviet colleagues centred on this concept, which still governs the work of many post-Soviet scholars today (Gefter and Mal'kov, 1966–67). However, while Russia remains 'pluralist', a number of approaches may be adopted, including the empiricist. At least some colleagues from over there have welcomed the opportunity to remain aloof from all grand schemes, to concentrate on 'concrete' history.

And so, to repeat and emphasize the point, there are no 'schools' since 1991 as there were before: 'formation' and 'civilization' are tendencies, sometimes overlapping, by no means constantly antithetical. On the one hand, emphasis is given to universal processes, often in the tradition of Marx, but with at least some mention of his predecessors and successors. There has been one suggestion that Marx was wrong about a number of problems, for example that of the commune, and that all of his doctrine that is still valid was taken from other sources, including Adam Smith and Adam Ferguson of the Scottish Enlightenment. Equally, there has been another suggestion that Marx was far too Eurocentric in his approach, which was saved from parochialism by Lenin. On the whole, 'formation' appears to accept the eighteenth-century argument that there are stages through which human development as a whole must pass, and to incline towards the nineteenth-century Westerner tradition (Ovsiannikov, 1995: 83). On the other hand, the focus is on Russia, its 'uniqueness', and the uniqueness of other cultures within a broad range of civilizations. To some extent, the line of filiation here stems from the Romantic and Slavophile movements of the nineteenth century, and can lead (although it does not always lead) to a nationalist, even an extreme nationalist, position. Both tendencies may be said to have sprung from concerns with Russia's relationship to Europe, and to the world as a whole.

The work of two writers, neither of them a professional historian, will be briefly discussed in illustration of the two approaches. In his 'Farewell to Marx', the sociologist Vsevolod Vilchek sets out to demonstrate the 'logical *zakonomernost*' of the development of 'non-classical' societies (in the sense of not following normal lines of development), one of them – Russia – in particular. He posits five stages of production – primitive, slave, feudal, industrial (capitalist) and post-industrial (communist) – paralleled by five kinds of knowledge – pre-mythological, mythological, canonical (subjective-collective), scientific (individual and objective) and post-scientific (problematic). He adds a further series of five modes of social communication – pre-oral, oral, written, printed and post-printed – combining with the others to constitute the bare bones of his formation theory. Within this framework, Vilchek defines Russia as an 'autocolony', rejecting as analogies Pinochet's Chile, post-World War Two Germany and the countries of Eastern Europe and China because of the failure to take advantage of appropriate opportunities presented in 1987–88. Gorbachev drew back from the brink, fearing a chaos and collapse which his hesitation only made more certain. Here (without suggesting Nero or any other personal counterpart of Gorbachev), Vilchek finds a resemblance to a literally classical society – ancient Rome – which might grow if the CIS develops into the States of Eurasia (Akhiezer, 1994; Vilchek, 1993).

Eurasia is less the patch of the sociologist Vsevolod Vilchek than of the self-proclaimed genius Lev Gumilëv, whose fertile imagination sometimes ran away with him. Watching the play of sunlight in an isolation cell as others prepared for the celebration of Stalin's seventieth birthday, Gumilëv began to develop his basic idea of 'impassionedness' (*passionarnost*) or superfluous energy. Coupled with the concept of the 'noosphere', that is, the biosphere modified by human ingenuity adopted from Vladimir Vernadsky, impassionedness led on to a theory of ethnogenesis. In Gumilëv's view, an ethnos was a group distinguishable from another by a typical pattern of behaviour, and sometimes combining with other such groups in a super-ethnos such as the Graeco-Roman, the Byzantine, the Arab, the Ottoman, the West European, the Chinese, the Old-Turkish, the Mongol and the Great Russian. While the affinity that could be found within a superethnos was lacking in the relations between one superethnos and another, according to Gumilëv, Great Russia was able to prosper because it could move away from the Byzantine superethnos and resist the West European because of its long symbiosis with the nomads of the steppe. So, far from being an unbearable yoke, the Mongol invasions presented an opportunity for beneficial alliance. Although the approach of Gumilëv defies typification, it can perhaps be labelled neo-Eurasian civilizationist (Naarden, 1996; compare Nekrasov, 1995 and Trepavlov, 1995).

But perhaps the most important approach under the heading of 'civilization' is the Orthodox Christian, intimately connected with distinctive qualities of Russianness, for example *sobornost* – literally 'conciliarism', but more a kind of collectivity or togetherness:

Its roots are very deep and firm, and have peculiarities making it attractive for Russians. They come from popular meetings of remote times – the epochs of prehistoric clans and tribes, 'military democracy', the popular *veche* in Novgorod and Pskov (on a regular basis from the twelfth to the fifteenth centuries, since they were assembled in republics, even if feudal, oligarchical), in other towns – the centres of principalities (they were summoned in extreme circumstances, at the time of popular revolts, for example, in so far as authority was constituted not by republican organs but by monarchical princes and their advisers). The traditions continued to live in both peasant and urban communes, Cossack circles (*rady*), soldier and musketeer councils (*sovety*) (elected from regiments, for example, during the course of the Moscow uprising of 1682). (Buganov, 1996: 87)

These popular bodies elected their own leaders and representatives into the nineteenth century, and beyond. Arguably, the spirit of *sobornost*, and of other essential Russian characteristics, is still alive today, not only in its secular tradition but also as fostered by the Orthodox Church, not to mention Buddhism and Islam.

This briefest of summaries cannot hint at the variety of arguments, but a further simple indication can be given by adding another couple of newly created sciences, *sinergetika* and *virtualistika*, to the *alternativistika* and *globalistika* already mentioned above. These are all imports, obviously, but there is at least one with largely indigenous origins. This is *zemliachestvo*, which seeks to capture the essential oneness of life on earth through the reassertion of its ancient roots in folklore and religion, and is defined by one of its adherents as follows:

> Zemlya is the earth – Zemlyanin is the global, natural, authentic characteristic of all human beings. Every person is naturally Zemlyanin at birth. It is a remarkable aspect of the Russian language that it manifests this intuitive, communal conception that our collective humanity is grounded in, and united by, a passion for a common global consciousness. (Gostev and Tucker, 1995: i–ix)

Zemliachestvo proceeds from the thesis that the relations of a person with the world are understood only through 'a synthesis of modern psychologies and sciences with ancient philosophies and arts'. Much of the synthesis is unconventional: for example, one of its components is 'a "deep" psychological analysis of interaction between the phenomena of consciousness–unconsciousness and the human (psychic) potentialities of fields of knowledge', while history is taken to be 'the projection of the result of struggle between provident and demonic forces, i.e. what is occurring in our reality depends on events which are happening in certain spiritual/metaphysical worlds' (ibid.: 1–51).

At the same time, 'East–West relations are considered as the condition of permanent dialogue between the left and right hemispheres of mankind's global brain'. West is often combined with North and South with East, since 'the realization of Western social homeostasis' occurred mostly in the North, and its Eastern equivalent in the South. The characteristics of Western sociohomeostasis are:

- intensive, yet controlled social and intellectual dynamics
- apparent democratic participation and freedom of personality and individualism
- tendencies towards socioeconomic progress, political manipulation and power
- technologically driven activity (manipulation) towards the managing of nature and the environment

The characteristics of Eastern socio-homeostasis are:

- minimal and monotonous social dynamics, mostly cyclical, with deliberate social repetition
- centralization of social life conceptualized as serviceability to a state over and above the individual
- tendencies to maintain a stability of social environment without concern for the danger of stagnation
- an orientation towards preserving and not intervening in the physical environment
- engendering of a totalitarian political structure and maintenance of a state-administrative distribution of property, communality, and so on

The process of history demonstrates a continuous West/North – East/South macro-interaction, the latest stage of which has been movement from the former to the latter in the shape of technological revolution. Generally: 'These geo-cultural migrations have transferred significant spiritual values, which seem to be seminal in the psychic and social preparation of preconditions for a global revolution of consciousness of our common humanities.' And today, 'we are witnessing the beginning of an integral world outlook formation, based on the creation of global ethics as a system of unified humanistic principles, determining a norm of behaviour for people'.

Russia could play an important part in this development, according to the *zemliachestvo* argument, not only as a bridge between East and West, but also as the creator of a new type of socio-homeostasis consisting of a new level of harmony between individual and society/state and a new type of highly spiritual personality (founded on traditional collective unconsciousness). Discovering its Eurasian essence, Russia, as a country of the female symbol, will conduct relations with the USA, a country of the male symbol, on which the harmony of the planet will depend. Globalization indeed!

References

Akhiezer, A. S. (1994) Samobytnost Rossii kak nauchnaia problema, in Rossiia – raskolotaia tsivilizatsiia?, *Otechestvennaia istoriia*, **4–5**, 3–45.

Alperovitz, Gar (1995) *The Decision to Use the Atomic Bomb and the Architecture of an American Myth*. London: HarperCollins.

Bailey, George (1990) *The Making of Andrei Sakharov*. London: Penguin.

Buganov, V. I. (1996) Razmyshleniia o sovremennoi otechestvennoi istoricheskoi nauke, *Novaia i noveishaia istoriia*, **1**, 77–87.

Burbank, Jane (1986) *Intelligentsia and Revolution: Russian Views of Bolshevism*. Oxford: Oxford University Press.

Crosby, Alfred W. (1994) *Ecological Imperialism: The Biological Expansion of Europe, 900–1900*. Cambridge: Cambridge University Press.

Crummey, Robert O. (1987) *The Formation of Muscovy, 1304–1613*. London: Longman.

Dukes, Paul (1990) *The Making of Russian Absolutism, 1613–1801*. London: Longman.

Dukes, Paul (1996) *World Order in History: Russia and the West*. London: Routledge.

Febvre, Lucien, in collaboration with Bataillon, Lionel (1925) *A Geographical Introduction to History*. London: Kegan Paul & Co.

Figes, Orlando (1996) *A People's Tragedy: The Russian Revolution, 1891–1924*. London: Jonathan Cape.

Franklin, Simon and Shepard, Jonathan (1996) *The Emergence of Rus, 750–1200*. London: Longman.

Garrett, Laurie (1994) *The Coming Plague: Newly Emerging Diseases in a World out of Balance*. London: Penguin [1995 edn].

Gefter, M. Ia. and Mal'kov, V. L. (1966–7) Reply to an American scholar, *Soviet Studies in History*, **5**, 3–23.

Gorbachev, Mikhail (1988) *Perestroika: New Thinking for Our Country and the World*. New York: Harper & Row.

Gostev, Andrei A. and Tucker, J. C. (1995) *Zemlyanin-1: The Emerging Global Citizen: Essays on the Evolution of Human Consciousness*. Moscow–San Francisco: Russian Academy of Sciences, Institute of Psychology and others.

Harrison, Mark (1996) *Accounting for War: Soviet Production, Employment, and the Defence Burden, 1940–1945*. Cambridge: Cambridge University Press.

Henrikson, Alan K. (1975) The map as an 'idea': the role of cartographic imagery during the Second World War, *The American Cartographer*, **2**, 19–53.

Hughes, Lindsey (1997) *Birth of an Empire: Russia in the Reign of Peter the Great, 1682–1725*. London: Yale University Press.

Huntington, Samuel P. (1996) *The Clash of Civilisations and the Remaking of World Order*. New York: Simon & Schuster.

Keenan, Edward L. (1986) Muscovite political folkways, *Russian Review*, **45**, 115–181.

Korol, V. E. (1996) The price of victory: myths and reality, *Slavic Military Studies*, **9**, 417–26.

LaFeber, Walter (1997) *America, Russia and the Cold War, 1945–1996*. New York: McGraw-Hill.

Naarden, Bruno (1996) 'I am a genius, but no more than that.' Lev Gumilëv (1912–1992), ethnogenesis, the Russian past and world history, *Jahrbücher für Geschichte Osteuropas*, **44**, 54–82.

Nekrasov, Alexander M. (1995) Medieval Russian culture and the East, *Coexistence*, **32**, 3–7.

Obolensky, Dimitri (1971) *Byzantium and the Slavs*. London: Longman.

Ovsiannikov, V. I. (1995) V poiskakh novykh podkhodov k istoricheskim issledova-niiam, in K. V. Khvostova, Metodologicheskie poiski v sovremennoi istoricheskoi nauke, *Novaia i noveishaia istoriia*, **3**, 79–99.

Pobedonostsev, K. (1965) *Reflections of a Russian Statesman*. Ann Arbor, MI: Michigan University Press.

Schröder, Konrad (1995) Languages, in Monica Shelley and Margaret Winck (eds), *Aspects of European Cultural Diversity*. London: Routledge.

Scott, William (1996) Cook, France and the savages, in Paul Dukes (ed.), *Frontiers of European Culture*. Lewiston, NY: Edwin Mellen.

Stalin, J. V. (1952) *Economic Problems of Socialism in the USSR*. Moscow: Foreign Languages.

Stalin, J. V. (1970) *The Foundations of Leninism*. Peking: Foreign Languages.

Trepavlov, Vadim V. (1995) Eastern influences: the Turkic nobility in medieval Russia, *Coexistence*, **32**, 9–16.

Tsivilizatsii (1995), **3**.

Venturi, Franco (1952) *Roots of Revolution*. London: Weidenfeld & Nicolson.

Vilchek, V. M. (1993) *Proshchanie s Marksom*. Moscow: Progress-Kultura.

White, James D. (1996) *Karl Marx and the Intellectual Origins of Dialectical Materialism*. London: Macmillan.

Further reading

Alaev, L. B. (1996) Gde tonko – tam I porvalos!, in G. N. Sevostianov, Metodolo-gicheskie poiski v sovremennoi istoricheskoi nauke, *Novaia i noveishaia istoriia*, **3**, 75–90.

[Kennan, George F.] 'Mr. X.' (1947) The sources of Soviet conduct, *Foreign Affairs*, **25**, 566–582.

Maier, Charles (1991) The collapse of Communism: approaches for a future history, *History Workshop*, **31**, 34–59.

7

Human Rights, Global Ethics and Globalization

NIGEL DOWER

In this chapter I wish to defend the idea of global ethics and the central place of human rights within it. By invoking and defending a distinction between theory and social reality, I hope to show that appropriate theories of global ethics and human rights can be defended without reference to and independent of globalization, but that globalization can both aid as well as impede the development of appropriate global values as a social reality – that is, values embodied in institutions and practices.

Global ethics

Nature and scope of global ethics

Before we look at human rights discourse we need to locate it within the wider framework of global ethics. By a global ethic I mean one which asserts that there are certain universal values (understood as goods, rights, virtues and/or duties), such as the universal value of liberty or the universal right to life, and certain global responsibilities in respect of those values, i.e. the global scope or extent of our duties, for example, duties to promote or protect values anywhere, such as the duty of individuals or governments in the North to give aid to alleviate poverty in the South. There are two sources of interest in global ethics which have emerged in the latter half of the twentieth century (though ideas about global ethics go back to classical thought): the idea of the global citizenship of individuals, and the claim that the foreign policy of states ought to be guided by ethical considerations and not merely the pursuit of power and national interests.

On the one hand, there has been an increasing recognition that individuals have responsibilities towards human beings in general, not merely towards members of their own societies. The appalling extent of absolute poverty and the widening gap between rich and poor countries, the negative impacts on the environment both of affluence based on industrialization and of rapidly increasing populations, the violations of human rights especially in

Apartheid South Africa, have all challenged the informed individual to do something. Because the world has been becoming a global village, with more information about other parts of the world, and with greater capacity for effective action at a distance, a global civil society, expressed through the development of people's organizations which are international in identity, has been emerging.

Parallel to this is an increasing interest in the ethical issues directly connected with the foreign policy of nation-states. After the Second World War, there was for a variety of reasons a reaction against the 'idealism' that had led to the ill-fated League of Nations, and for a long time foreign policy was analysed and understood in terms of 'realism' which ignored ethical norms. However, the Cold War and the nuclear arms race, which maintained an imperfect security through the threat of nuclear holocaust and failed to prevent many wars in the rest of the world, along with other concerns mentioned above – world poverty, environmental devastation, Apartheid – have invited a return to serious reflection on ethical issues in international relations, and hence an increasing interest in what is called 'normative international relations' theory. There have in fact been, ever since the origins of the international system, three broad approaches to normative issues:

1. The *Sceptical Realist (Anarchist, Hobbesian)* basically asserts the irrelevance of ethics and values to international relations. Relations between states are essentially driven by power and national self-interest, international conventions are not really 'moral' rules at all, and the appeal to the moral language of justice or human rights is a smokescreen.

2. The *Internationalist (Grotian)* claims that moral rules do apply to the conduct of states (though they are not always followed), but that these moral rules have become established as a 'morality of states'. The Peace of Westphalia (1648) established or at least formalized a new international system, and the underlying goal of the 'society of states' is the maintenance of the society of states itself as a stable order – hence the centrality of the rights of sovereignty.

3. The *Cosmopolitan (Universalist, Kantian, Idealist)* also asserts that there is a morality governing international relations, but it is a morality embracing the whole of mankind in one global community; it thus transcends national boundaries, and provides goals and aspirations which may well go beyond either current state practice or indeed what an internationalist 'morality of states' may require. There are many forms of cosmopolitanism, including Human Rights theories. Some of these will be mentioned later.

The relationships between these three need not concern us here (Beitz,

1979; Bull, 1977), except to note that both the internationalist and the cosmopolitan put forward a form of global ethic as a theory and have reasons for supporting a form of global ethic as a social reality.

Global ethics: empirical and theoretical claims

We are now in a position to identify more carefully the distinction between theory and social reality, by noting the ambiguity in the claim that 'there is a world ethic'. In one sense it is an empirical claim: there is in the world a set of ethical norms and values, accepted by all and generally acted on, embedded in law, institutions, culture and established rules. Put as strongly as this, the answer is of course 'no, there is no such thing'. Indeed if there were, then globalization, for good or ill, would certainly have done its job thoroughly! On the other hand, if we relaxed our criteria for what we are looking for, we would be in a rather different position. Suppose we characterize a global ethic as 'a set of norms and values, shared by adherents in many different parts of the world, and seen by their adherents as global/universal and expressed in common institutions or agreed goals'. Then, it is clear that not only is there a global ethic – there are a number of global ethics.

The morality of states is one such global ethic, as is the common moral framework underlying the global free market – the latter perhaps the most influential global ethic there is at the moment. Members of churches also share in a global ethic, as do members of international organizations such as the Scouts, Greenpeace, Amnesty International and so on. Where the goals and values of different groups converge, there are possibilities for further sharing of values, through agreement, negotiation and co-operation. Clearly the general processes of globalization are contributing towards the development of global ethics in the plural. We might say it is a contribution to the globalization of ethics, that is the tendency for more and more actors to think globally and to become part of networks of actors sharing certain global values, though not necessarily the same values.

Do we want there to be a general convergence of values such that one day there will be one dominant 'global ethic', accepted by almost everyone? And if so, do we want human rights, or certain human rights, to be central to that one global ethic? This question of course takes us away from the empirical, descriptive approach on to the theoretical approach. Does our ethical theory require that ideally everyone share the same global ethic? Should they share the ethic which our theory asserts?

Any cosmopolitan theory in a sense requires general acceptance of the values specified in the theory, for without general acceptance of them, they will not be generally acted on. Hence we have the importance of the development of appropriate institutions, culture and practice, in relation to which globalization is highly relevant. Yet, as I shall argue, there are good reasons why a cosmopolitan theory need not require that everyone should accept the same values or beliefs.

Diverse theories, common principles

We should acknowledge that there is a very wide range of theoretical approaches. A brief account of some of these positions will serve two purposes: first, to flesh out a number of 'cosmopolitan' theories in order to show more fully what a global ethic is, and second, to use this survey to further the argument that we need to distinguish between diverse sources and common principles (see Nardin and Mapel, 1992 for a useful survey of positions).

Some of these approaches, particularly in the recent Western tradition, are essentially secular ethical theories, theories of morality which are not dependent upon religious or theological premises: thus for instance, Utilitarianism, which has as its foundation the 'greatest happiness principle' (or more generally the principle of maximizing good), Kant's ethical theory, which stresses the categorical imperative of respecting the rational agency in all human beings, and human rights theories which take as their starting point that all human beings *qua* human beings have rights, are all examples of such cosmopolitan theories, and will be discussed more fully below. Other approaches include the use of the social contract approach: Charles Beitz (1979), for instance, takes the fundamental insight of Rawls's well-known *A Theory of Justice* (1971), that principles of justice are justified as those which would be chosen by people in an 'original position' of impartiality, and extends it to the global sphere, by treating the whole world as one society in which principles of justice apply. Natural law theories, as found in writers such as Aquinas, Suarez and Vitoria, which stress the idea of certain laws pertaining to human well-being inherent in human nature and discoverable by reason, have historically informed much thought about human beings in the *civitas maxima* (the 'greatest community'), and hence much thought about international relations.

Other theories are specifically religious in origin, whether based on differing interpretations of mainstream religions such as Christianity, Islam or Buddhism, or on certain kinds of ecological ethic, which are religious at least in the sense of presupposing a world view (a way of looking at nature, the planet, etc.) very different from the typical human-centred world views in the secular tradition. Most mainstream religious thinkers will see a kind of unity in humankind and therefore an ethical call to care for human beings anywhere, though their theology or underlying metaphysical theory about reality may be quite different. (Christianity and Buddhism, for instance, may differ quite fundamentally about the role and relevance of a transcendent creator God in the scheme of things and values.) Ecological theories which are distinct from ethical theories (which merely concern themselves with human well-being present and future) tend to assume a kind of ethical relationship which humans have with the natural world and other living things, which, because it is not mediated by or dependent on convention or social traditions, is implicitly if not explicitly global in scope.

Two things are immediately apparent when we look at this range of theories. First, it is extremely unlikely that there would ever be a situation in which everyone, or even the vast majority of human beings, would accept the same theory, nor is it at all clear that it is either desirable in itself, or necessary for the emergence of a common ethical framework sufficient for human co-operation. Second, despite all these variations between 'isms' (and indeed within 'isms'), there is nevertheless immense scope for convergences in terms of the values and principles which are to be accepted and acted on. Such convergence will constitute an agreed world ethic, and insofar as it takes the form of publicly embodied rules and practices, will be a 'global ethic' in the 'social reality' sense, which each theorist will have reason to sustain as embodying the principles which the theory enjoins her or him to advocate as a shared set of principles. Of course, as I noted earlier, different convergences may emerge, so there may be several global ethics which develop. The distinctions I have been making are perfectly illustrated by the case of human rights.

Human rights: the basic issues

A theoretical claim

Most theories of human rights have the following general characteristics: certain claims are made about all human beings, *qua* human beings. These claims are made on the basis of some theory about universal elements of human well-being, that is, about what is inherent in human nature (Locke, following the earlier 'natural law' tradition of Aquinas), based on the implications of reason and agency (Finnis, 1980; Gewirth, 1978). Corresponding to the possession of these rights are certain obligations or duties on the part of other human beings to respect or protect these rights. That human beings possess these rights does not depend on whether, as a matter of fact, these rights are accepted by others generally, embedded in law, custom or convention. (Someone who like Wilberforce believed that slavery was wrong or that a human being had a right not to be enslaved would not think his claim falsified by the fact that most people did not believe this or that the practice of slavery was all around him.)

If human rights do not depend for their existence on such facts about social reality, then, *a fortiori*, they do not depend on facts about global social reality. Claims about the rights of man long predated attempts to build such rights into international declarations. If human rights discourse has become not only a firmly established part of our international law (declarations, covenants, etc.) but also the public culture of statesmen, diplomats and the media; if human rights discourse has become part of the internalized moral thinking or habits of moral thought of a very large number of people throughout the world, then these changes, as part of the wider process of globalization, are no doubt important for the greater realization of human rights. But they are neither here nor there so far as the theory of human rights is concerned. The existence of human rights predates processes of globalization and is unaffected by whatever processes are taking place.

Social reality

On the other hand, there is another sense in which the processes of globalization are crucial to claims about the existence of human rights. One aspect of globalization is the development of the global economy – transnational companies, complex international trading agreements, global markets, the spread to all parts of the world of a certain 'free market' culture, the wider impacts on the global environment of activities within any country – made possible in part through developments in global communications, transport systems and technologies generally. But the latter developments have also facilitated other changes, particularly in the way people 'think' beyond the boundaries of their own societies, whether through the Internet, mass communications, or INGOs (international non-governmental organizations). Although we can, and many do, consider what we do in a global context but still with a view to what will benefit our own country or society (or benefit ourselves as members of it), increasingly, and as part of the process of globalization, loyalties go beyond the nation-state, and people's identities broaden beyond membership of their 'own' society, so that a person's interests are in what benefits wider wholes (or what benefits oneself as a member of wider wholes, such as a transnational, an INGO, or simply as a 'world citizen').

This process is relevant to human rights in the following way. If the claim that human rights exist is a claim that certain conditions or states of human beings are acknowledged by a significant number of agents to be things to which human beings have 'rights' as human beings, that these human rights are embedded in law, domestic and international, that thinking in human rights terms has been internalized into the culture of politicians and international diplomats, then the facts of globalization are very relevant to whether human rights exist, and if so, what they are. In this sense, it may be said that human rights exist now whereas they did not a hundred years ago, or that they are better established now than fifty years ago.

It is worth noting that while ideas about moral rights common to all human beings, whether referred to as natural rights, the 'rights of man' or, more recently, 'human rights', go back several centuries, the emergence of human rights as setting global standards, against which, for instance, the behaviour of governments towards their own citizens can be measured, is a relatively recent development, generally associated with the immediate aftermath of the Second World War. The Nuremberg trials (1945–46), in which individuals were tried for 'crimes against humanity', reflected and reinforced the growing opposition to the traditional principles of international law which did not see individual human beings as the proper subjects of international law, since what happened within national boundaries was entirely an internal matter (and if an individual acted on behalf of his country in a war he was protected by that fact). In 1948 the *Universal Declaration of Human Rights* was passed in the General Assembly of the United Nations. This set out in thirty articles various 'rights and freedoms' to which everyone was equally entitled. As a declaration it did not have the status of binding international law but provided in effect a common moral ideal to aspire to. In 1966 two covenants specifying in more details the rights in the *Declaration* were accepted which, once ratified by sufficient governments, became binding in international law (though problems of enforcement still exist in a world of independent sovereign states). The *Covenant on Civil and Political Rights* deals, as the title suggest, with those rights we have to freedom of speech, assembly and religion, freedom to participate in political activity, freedom from attack, the right to due legal process. The *Covenant on Economic, Social and Cultural Rights* emphasized the rights we have to economic well-being, to subsistence, to work, to housing, to education, to medical care, and generally to conditions in society which enable us to achieve our well-being. Although, theoretically, the international community accepted the whole range of rights so specified, in practice different countries and groups of countries emphasized some at the expense of others. This was particularly striking in the Cold War era when the liberal democracies emphasized liberty rights, that is, rights to be free from certain forms of interference (by other citizens or the state itself) and the communist bloc emphasized the socio-economic rights which were more in the nature of rights to receive certain benefits from the state. In the same post-war period many other attempts have been made to codify rights, both multilaterally through the UN system (e.g. the *Convention on the Rights of the Child* (1989)) and regionally (like the *European Convention* in 1950) and through individual countries building into their constitutions bills of rights which asserted in domestic law the same human rights asserted internationally (Donnelly, 1993).

Human rights: theoretical source and shared values

Where does that leave the discourse about human rights? It should help to explain how it is possible for human rights to be the expression of a particular ethical theory, but at the same time be part of what is out there in the social world, a set of norms agreed on by a significant number of actors and embodied in public institutions and shared practices. What now needs clarification is how it is possible for a theorist, who puts forward an ethical theory which is not a rights-based one, to support an agreed set of norms which are formulated in human rights terms and which may become part of the public culture.

So far as international consensus is concerned, what matters about human rights discourse is the recognition that certain key features of human well-being matter, and matter universally – subsistence, security, liberty, community, etc. – and that we have duties, which are in principle global in scope – to protect and promote these, so far as international consensus is concerned. What does not matter is the theory out of which these values are supported.

J. L. Mackie (1984) once argued, in an impressive article called 'Can there be a right-based moral theory?', that, if one contrasted a rights-based theory with a goal-based theory and a duty-based theory, the case for the first emerged out of a recognition of the inadequacy of the other two. He first makes the general point, of relevance to what follows, that any ethical theory will make reference to 'items of all three kinds, goals, duties, and rights, or, equivalently, about what is good as an end, about what is obligatory, or about what ought or ought not to be done ... about what people are entitled to have or receive or do' (Mackie, 1984: 169). Theorists will tend to see one of three elements as basic and the other two as derived from it.

What are the problems about regarding duties or goals as basic? A duty-based theory without reference to the good which the duty was meant to promote would be sterile, since there is nothing commendable about doing duty for duty's sake. On the other hand a goal-based theory which simply saw good as something to be maximized would be open to the standard objection to 'utilitarianism' that in maximizing the good, one will sometimes sacrifice the individual's well-being. For instance, a person's privacy, her or his interest in not being deceived, even her or his life might be sacrificed in the public interest or for the greater good of all; and if we regard this as wrong it is natural to say that that person has a right to privacy, non-deception or life which ought not to be sacrificed simply because more overall good to others will ensue. A rights-based theory at least makes sense of the intuition just indicated, because it emphasizes that it is individual humans who matter.

Mackie is surely right about this, but it seems to me that this insight is one that can be and is incorporated, as he recognized himself, into ethical theories far more diverse than the ones which announce themselves as human rights theories.

Take two well-known theories – Utilitarianism and Kantianism, both clearly global in scope. It is well known that Bentham dismissed natural rights as 'nonsense on stilts', and that Utilitarianism as a general theory is not founded on postulating in human nature anything like a right, but rather certain natural facts like the desire for pleasure as the basis of the good. On the other hand, the development of a set of rights and duties specifying how we are to treat one another in all normal circumstances can be supported on utilitarian grounds as leading to the greatest good. One of the features of so-called 'rule-utilitarianism' is that it stresses the 'utility' of rules which are well established and generally followed. But Utilitarianism can also support what may be called the 'internalizing' of this rule-following into habits of thought, producing what R. M. Hare (1981) calls the 'intuitive' level of moral thought. That is, normal moral development involves individuals forming a conscience which, in almost all normal circumstances, delivers clear, authoritative or 'intuitive' judgements about what ought to be done (without the individual having to calculate the overall consequences). Acknowledging and respecting the rights of others is part of that intuitive response. However, at another 'reflective' level one can see that the justification for the operation of that intuitive level of moral thought is that it almost always leads to the best overall results. It is also worth noting that the logic of 'rights' even appears, *sotto voce*, in the theory itself, since the remark of Bentham quoted by Mill, 'everyone to count for one, no one more than one', looks remarkably like an entitlement/rights principle at the heart of the theory's methodology (Mill, 1861).

If it is remarked that Utilitarianism must allow the occasional violation of a person's 'right', this has to be accepted, but does not take away the propriety of talking of rights. If the only rights were absolute rights, we would have very few rights and very few rights theories, and if such a condition were insisted on, most of international discourse on human rights would be clearly out of order. It is worth noting that in the public arena, rights are things which are *promoted* as well as respected, and inevitably it is the whole system of rights which has to be taken into account in decision-making. In any case, for most socio-economic rights, where resources are very limited relative to what is needed, there are bound to be trade-offs and choices between equally appropriate claims.

Kant's ethical theory is not generally thought of as a 'rights' theory either, and some Kantians, such as O'Neill, would wish to contrast the Kantian approach with the human rights approach (O'Neill, 1986). Kant's theory is centred on the central principle of duty, the 'categorical imperative' seen as the demand of practical reason. This categorical imperative is expressed in a number of formulations, the two most well-known being: 'Act only on that maxim through which you can at the same time will that it should become a universal law' (Kant, 1948: 88) and 'Act in such a way that you always treat humanity, whether in yourself or in the person of any other, never simply as a means but always at the same time as an end' (Kant, 1948: 96). These formulations stress two fundamental features of moral thought. First, we should apply the principle of universalizability: if one action is right or wrong, then any other action of the same kind is right or wrong. Second, we should respect all other persons equally as autonomous beings and as sources of value which we need to take into account when we act; thus it is wrong to exploit or use others simply as means to our own ends, which is precisely what we do if, for instance, we deceive or coerce them.

Although Kant's theory is not presented as a rights-based theory, it is easy to see how his theory maps on to human rights thinking, both in regard to universalizability and with regard to respect for persons, since the idea that all fellow human beings should be treated in a certain way, in virtue of their equal status as rational agents, comes very close to a rights thesis. It certainly locates the idea of rights, if not at the foundation of the theory, at least fairly close to the foundations. After all, two key features of rights thinking are the claims that all human beings are to be treated in the same way in respect of features of their common humanity (i.e. a thesis of universalizability) and that the interests of human beings are to be respected and not sacrificed as a mere means towards either the private good of another or the public good of others. It is worth adding that the whole apparatus of rights is made much more of in Kant's political theory, where the respect for the rights of others is central to treating them as autonomous pursuers of their own ends, and Kant was in fact very sympathetic to the ethical aspirations behind the republican revolutions of his time in France and America which were inspired by the 'rights of man'.

This discussion of Utilitarianism and Kantianism is not intended to obscure or undermine the distinctiveness of theories, noted earlier, whose leading edge is, as it were, the assertion of something inherent in human nature – an expression of the natural law, rights known by the light of reason, or what is inherent in our capacity for reason and action. But it is to suggest that many other ethical theories of a 'global' nature can certainly support a consensus of ethical values and norms couched in 'human rights', which can be agreed upon as a basis for concerted action. Indeed as a matter

of fact, 'human rights' discourse is one of the most well-established internationally agreed ethical discourses in existence.

I hope at least to have shown how a wide variety of theories can all support
a framework of human rights norms, and how, internal to each theory's
commitment to see such norms spread, there is reason to support this shared
framework, and indeed support the various mechanisms whereby such
values are publicly embodied and shared at a global level. Insofar as the
process of globalization supports these developments, then globalization
contributes towards the more effective expression of human rights.

Principle and applications

Globalization makes a difference to what obligations in respect to human
rights we have in practice, but not in principle. As an initial and over-simple
statement of the contrast, let us note, following Shue, that in principle
human rights are the 'minimum demand of all humanity on all humanity',
and that the demands they make can be summarized as three *types* of duty:
the duty not to deprive others of their rights, the duty to protect from
standard threats of deprivation, and the duty to come to the aid of those
deprived of their rights (Shue, 1980). Shue also argues that we should accept
as socially basic, as presupposed in the pursuing of whatever other goals we
may have, three such rights – the right to subsistence, the right to security
and the right to liberty. All these claims represent a framework in principle
for thinking about rights and their corresponding duties. Globalization does
not affect this framework at all.

Globalization may, however, make certain forms of duty appropriate
which were not appropriate before. These duties may be appropriate either
because they become possible or because they become morally overriding.
They may become possible whereas before they were impossible; global
communications may make us aware of tragedies to which we can react, but
about which we did not know before, and global technologies make distant
actions possible or realistic which were not before. Certain duties may
become appropriate because they become morally overriding in a way they
were not before. The existence of a human rights convention to which one's
country subscribes makes it necessary to observe rights one might not
otherwise have felt obliged to observe, or public moral outrage, itself
informed by awareness of and support for international standards, may
pressure a government into protesting against a human rights violation in
another country, which it would not have done in the absence of that moral
outrage. It has often been an excuse or defence of lame foreign policy over
human rights issues that too much is at risk in terms of international peace
and co-operation. How far this inactivity was in the past justified is

debatable, but certainly the strengthening of international conventions and of public conscience alters the ethical framework within which particular decisions whether or not to intervene for the sake of human rights are taken.

Clearly, a holder of a human rights theory (and indeed more generally a global ethic) which asserts how ideally we ought to treat one another will want to create the conditions in which, within the constraints of decision-making in the real world, those ideals will be realized more fully. Since the existence of human rights in the 'social reality' sense will, on the whole, make it easier for decisions to protect or promote human rights in fact to be taken (and taken justifiably), then human rights theorists have every reason to work towards creating those conditions. The process of globalization will be important for the development of those conditions. As we shall see, not all forms of globalization are necessarily favourable to the realization of human rights, so practical choices will have to be made, insofar as the process of globalization can be influenced by conscious human choice. So it follows that a human rights theorist has every reason to be very interested in the ways globalization helps or hinders the effective realization of the rights which his theory postulates. Still the theory itself does not stand or fall on any claims about globalization itself.

Globalization as a threat to human rights

But the relationship between human rights and globalization is not altogether a happy one. There are in fact a number of respects in which globalization can be said to be threatening to human rights in a variety of ways.

Development, poverty and diversity

I shall focus on the impacts which globalization is having on 'development', particularly development in countries in the South. Initially it may be thought that globalization contributes very positively towards processes of development. The development of the global economy is very much premised on stimulating the economic growth of poorer countries, both as providers of resources and labour and also as part of expanding consumer markets. That is, although the key economic actors – multinational companies and the like – aim at profit and wealth for the First World, the increasing inclusion of the Third World is an essential part of the process. There is a question, which I note here but do not deal with, as to whether poorer countries do in fact benefit properly in conventional economic terms or rather lose out in terms of unequal economic power between rich countries and transnational companies and themselves.

But my main concern here is with two more specific types of effects on poorer countries – on the one hand the impoverishment of the very poor who are often marginalized and made poorer as other parts of the economies of Third World countries are drawn into the global economy, and on the other hand the destruction of traditional cultures among those who are drawn into that economy and its practices. Though the ethical problems are somewhat different in the two cases, they are linked because they are effects of the same broad processes of modern development. In fact there is a kind of 'out of the frying pan into the fire' logic to the situation. Although this is an over-simplification, one might say: either the poor in the South are drawn into the global economy, in which case there is the danger of the destruction of local culture, or the poor are not, in which case they are in danger of being economically impoverished and marginalized.

There are two features of the global economy which are pervasive and dominant – the ethics of the (relatively unregulated) market place and the model of the good life based on the free individual consumer of material goods. These are two aspects of a dominant global ethic, which, whether we like it or not, powerfully inform the actions of economic actors every-where.

The problem with the unregulated free market is that in most poorer countries its effect is to impoverish the poor, no longer protected by tradi-tional communal values and networks of support, and not able to survive properly in the competitive market place. If we suppose that people do have a human right to subsistence or to a reasonable socio-economic way of life, then the impact of the global economy has often been to make things worse and to undermine the capacity of poor people to realize their basic socio-economic rights.

On the other hand, what is also happening is the destruction of traditional culture or what has been called the 'homogenization' of cultures (Sachs, 1992), the flattening of cultural variations in the face of the pervasive model of economic well-being. Although these changes would not take place unless local people in some sense wanted them, this fact does not settle the question whether it is a good or bad thing. (To assume that 'wanting' it settled the matter would be to beg the question, since the adequacy of what people (think they) want is part of the liberal paradigm which is in dispute!) It is for many a deeply worrying feature of the modern world that insufficient value is placed on cultural diversity, both as a value in itself and as a means to well-being in other ways. If then we recognize that people have a right to cultural diversity, what is happening in the name of 'development' is simply under-mining this right.

Whether and to what extent globalization has to have these kinds of effects is another matter. Certainly there is no reason at all why the development of the global economy had to be driven by a libertarian ethic or by policies at national and international levels which pay little attention to issues of 'social justice' or the fair distribution of wealth. Such values could become incorporated into the processes of globalization. On the other hand the 'homogenizing' effects of globalization are more problematic, simply because the very nature of globalization, the increased involvement of local communities and their members in wider networks of communication and exchange of goods, services and ideas, inevitably affects the culture of those affected. Globalization is inevitably in tension with tradition, but it need not be anti-traditional. That is, it need not undermine what is valuable in cultures. But if it is to be sensitive to what is valuable in diverse ways in diverse societies, there needs to be far more sensitivity to the value of diversity than seems to be occurring at the moment.

Are human rights qua expressions of Enlightenment thinking part of the problem?

Is there a conflict between talking of human rights and valuing cultural diversity? It might be thought that the promotion of human rights in the international arena is part of the problem here, precisely because it is part of the globalization process. On this argument globalization itself is a late expression of the idea of the Enlightenment with its confident assertion that there is universal knowledge, including universal values, discoverable by the use of universal reason. Thus the very idea of universal rights may be seen as part of European Enlightenment thinking, and thus both the articulation of these rights in public documents and their promotion throughout the world may be seen as an exercise in 'cultural imperialism'. From the inside it looks as if these values, while universal and accessible to reasonable thinkers anyway, just happen to have been discovered by Europeans from the eighteenth century onwards. To many in the rest of the world who see this from outside the mindset of European thought, these ideas look like the projection of European values themselves on to the rest of the world as well as of the European assumption that universal values are possible or necessary anyway (Dower, 1996).

There is of course always a danger that, if ideas originate in one culture and then spread elsewhere, they still represent culturally specific values which are not really appropriate elsewhere. It may well be that some values or rights presented as universal are rightly to be criticized. But it is a much stronger claim and more disputable to say that the idea of universal rights, or the idea of certain values being common to all human beings, is not genuinely applicable to the world as a whole.

Resistance to the idea of universal values will come from at least two sources, relativism and communitarianism. The ethical relativist takes the fact (which at some level cannot be disputed) that there is cultural diversity and argues that these differences of values are deep and incommensurable, so there is no universal vantage point or common standpoint from which to construct or discover a universal ethical theory. A communitarian argues that values arise out of particular cultures and traditions and may therefore vary from culture to culture, and that since the scope of obligation is grounded in the relationships which constitute the moral community, the idea of global obligations is not properly grounded (Sandel, 1982, and for contrasts to cosmopolitanism, Brown, 1992). Given these two approaches, we need to see human rights as a fiction, like any other proposed set of universal values or norms.

A full-scale rebuttal of these sceptical moves cannot be undertaken here, but we should note the following opening moves in the reply. First, any theory which seriously undermines the possibility of universal global obliga-tions (i.e. obligations of one society or person toward other societies or persons in other societies) undermines all such normative standards, not merely the 'imperialistic' ones that are not liked – standards of respect for, toleration of or support for diversity, as much as standards to do with promoting particular values. Second, if values are validated by general acceptance in a society, this renders such things as moral reform or progress not only difficult but incoherent, since the minorities on the leading edge of change cannot have a coherent ethical position. These first two objections rely on a conception of morality which makes it rest on more complex factors than what happens to be established in any given society. The second pair of objections rather takes on the theorists' own conception of morality and draws different conclusions from it. Third, then, it may be argued that the facts of diversity are exaggerated, and that there is a common core of universal values, values essential to any society being a society at all. These values may have differing local expressions and may exist alongside other cultural values which are genuinely different, but there is a core of common values. Fourth, if moral values depend on the existence of community and shared traditions, the fact is that in the modern world global community does actually exist, albeit in a less developed form than in domestic societies. Indeed the emergence of this global community is part of what globalization is about. Finally, once we distinguish between the value of respecting cultural diversity and the denial of universal value, much of the motivation for fashionable relativist postures disappears.

So, briefly, the problem with theories which deny the possibility of univer-sal values (whether derived from the European tradition or anywhere else) is that if the approach were adopted it would deprive the thinker of any basis for advocating as a principle to be adopted by all cultures the principle of mutual acceptance and respect, since that at least would be a universal principle. My more limited concern here is to defend the claim that a human rights theory need not run foul of the accusation of cultural imperialism. So long as there is included among the basic rights the right to individual and cultural autonomy and the corresponding duty to respect diversity (at least within limits), and indeed the acceptance that how basic rights are interpreted and expressed is to some extent contextually sensitive, the value of diversity can be preserved within a human rights framework. It can then go alongside the continued commitment (which is threatened by relativism) to a global framework of obligation to support the realization of rights throughout the world. (This twin commitment is what I have elsewhere called 'diversity with solidarity'.)

Conclusion

Arguably, the general thrust of globalization is sustainable economic development and the development of the world as a whole into an efficient network of consumers. Yet, although the main features of globalization have more to do with the development of the global economy, there is little doubt that another aspect of globalization has been the recognition of the impact of human activity on the environment as global in scale, and therefore the need for responses at a global level. The tendency to 'think globally' is part of globalization, but 'thinking globally' is itself a process which may become more mature as time goes on. By the process of maturation I mean the transformation of consciousness and identity which will accompany the realization that we really are – and we don't just intellectually (or for moral reasons that appeal to the head alone) say that we are – global citizens who are as much concerned about the world as about our own country or local neighbourhood. The world can become a 'global neighbourhood' (to quote from the title of a recent book written by the Commission on Global Governance (1995)). Many things point in the direction of this development, not least the expansion of international NGOs, dedicated to global ideals of many kinds, and the informal networking of millions of individuals through the Internet and global communications. If that process of maturation occurs, then the categories of global thinking could become less dominated by economic, institutional and political considerations, and more influenced by ethical, spiritual and ecological considerations about the 'whole' of which we are a part. If that is so, then human rights values and ecological values will between them constitute the twin pillars of a global ethic which will turn globalization into a proper expression of human enlightenment.

References

Beitz, C. R. (1979) *Political Theory and International Relations*. Princeton, NJ: Princeton University Press.

Brown, C. R. (1992) *International Relations Theory: New Normative Approaches*. London: Harvester.

Bull, H. (1977) *The Anarchical Society*. London: Macmillan.

Commission on Global Governance (1995) *Our Global Neighbourhood*. Oxford: Oxford University Press.

Donnelly, J. (1993) *International Human Rights*. Oxford: Westview Press.

Dower, N. (1996) Europe and the globalization of ethics, in P. Dukes (ed.), *The Frontier of European Culture*. Lampeter: Edwin Mellen Press.

Finnis, J. (1980) *Natural Law and Natural Rights*. Oxford: Clarendon Press.

Gewirth, A. (1978) *Reason and Morality*. Chicago: University of Chicago Press.

Hare, R. M. (1981) *Moral Thinking*. Oxford: Clarendon Press.

Kant, I. (1785) *Groundwork of the Metaphysics of Morals*; trans. H. Paton (1948) under title *The Moral Law*. London: Hutchinson.

Mackie, J. L. (1984) Can there be a right-based moral theory?, in J. Waldron (ed.) (1984) *Theory of Rights*. Oxford: Oxford University Press.

Mill, J. S. (1861) *Utilitarianism*, reprinted in M. Warnock (ed.) (1962) *Utilitarianism*. London: Fontana.

Nardin, T. and Mapel, D. R. (1992) *Traditions in International Ethics*. Cambridge: Cambridge University Press.

O'Neill, O. (1986) *The Face of Hunger*. London: Allen & Unwin.

Rawls, J. (1971) *A Theory of Justice*. Oxford: Oxford University Press.

Sachs, W. (ed.) (1992) *The Development Dictionary*. London: Zed Books.

Sandel, M. J. (1982) *Liberalism and the Limits of Justice*. Cambridge: Cambridge University Press.

Shue, H. (1980) *Basic Rights: Subsistence, Affluence and US Foreign Policy*. Princeton, NJ: Princeton University Press.

8

Global Democracy: Ideals and Reality

————

PHILIP RESNICK

In the late twentieth century, a powerful globalizing economic trend thrusts toward the achievement of a market utopia on a global scale. At present, no counter-tendency effectively challenges the globalization thrust. (Cox, 1991: 335)

I

Recently, there has been a spate of writings on the topic of global governance, and with it, global democracy. The Commission on Global Governance, co-chaired by Ingvar Carlsson and Shridath Ramphal, made the following observations in its 1995 Report, *Our Global Neighbourhood*:

> Technological advances have made national frontiers more porous. States retain sovereignty, but governments have suffered an erosion in their authority . . . . The challenges facing the world today . . . demand co-operative efforts to put in place a system of global governance better suited to present circumstances . . . . The emergence of a global civil society is an important precondition of democracy at the global level . . . . More and more people are making connections across borders and developing relationships based on common concerns and issues: the environment, human rights, peace, women's roles and many more. (Report, 1995: 11, 39, 62)

Richard Falk (1995: 254), in his summary presentation of the views of the World Order Models Project, writes as follows:

> What gives promise to the vision of cosmopolitan democracy is the legitimation of democratic ideas of governance on a universal basis, the embodiment of these ideas in human rights as specified in global instruments, the democratic implications of nonviolent approaches to resistance and reform, and most of all, the deeply democratic convictions of transnational initiatives that have begun to construct the alternative paradigm of a global civil society . . . . The cumulative drift has been and remains . . . the deepening and the expansion of democracy in relation to all fields of human endeavour.

David Held (1995: 279) has outlined the short- and long-term objectives of what he calls the cosmopolitan model of democracy. These range from reform of the UN, of the International Court, and the foundation of new co-ordinating economic agencies to the establishment of a global parliament, an interconnected global legal system, and to a permanent shift of a growing proportion of a nation-state's coercive capability to regional and global institutions.

At one level, such writings strike a chord. Observers of the contemporary post-Cold War scene are acutely aware of new global forces that are shaping the world economy, such as the emergence of East Asia as a key economic pole, the formation of new trading blocs in both North and South America, and the restructuring of the economies of Central and Eastern Europe; of a new international division of labour that encompasses the entire globe and gives new salience to the activity of transnational banks and corporations; of new technologies such as robotics that have rendered traditional modes of manufacturing or resource extraction obsolete; of modes of communication from video to television to fax to the Internet that transcend national boundaries. Does it not make sense to start addressing political, no less than economic and cultural, developments in global terms?

The wave of democratization that swept much of Latin America, Eastern Europe, the ex-Soviet Union, parts of East Asia, and South Africa over the past decade has clearly sparked fresh thinking in many quarters. While the triumph of liberal democracy is not inevitable, whatever the claims of some of its major boosters might lead one to believe (Diamond *et al.*, 1989; Di Palma, 1990), we do nonetheless face the prospect of entering the twenty-first century with a majority of the earth's population living under regimes that formally can be termed democratic. This may mean little more than a patina of civilian rule and multi-party competition in a fair number of states; it may imply deeper commitments to institutional checks and balances or to individual human rights in those, predominantly western, countries where a longer-standing democratic culture has taken root.

Even in such countries, however, for example, Japan, Italy, and France, there has been widespread dissatisfaction in recent years with existing institutions and leaders. It has become fashionable to talk about democratic deficits and to highlight the relative inability of national governments in a period dominated by neo-liberalism and state retrenchment to influence and control the key economic variables. In the words of Atul Kohli: 'People can elect whatever government they want in contemporary democratic states. But that does not mean that governments can do whatever they want.'[1] Or as Jean-Paul Fitoussi and Pierre Rosanvallon (1996: 110) observe: 'The law of markets is more powerful than the law of states. The opening up of the world dilutes each country's traditions within an undifferentiated ensemble where no national society is master over its own destiny.'

For certain traditional purposes such as economic protectionism, national industrial development, or even independent foreign policy-making, the nation-state is simply too small to cope effectively with larger global forces. For other purposes such as environmental protection, regionally-based economic activity, or the promotion of participatory democratic decision-making, it is simply too large, too distant from the concerns of locally-based populations and communities. Hence the increased appeal of subnational forms of governance, not only in states divided along linguistic and cultural lines like Canada or Belgium, but in more unitary-type states like Italy.

The last few decades have witnessed important forms of experimentation with regional or continental size arrangements grouping a diversity of states. The most successful has been the European Community/Union. Its political structures stop well short of a formal federal arrangement; yet they do, in embryo, contain the seeds of a supranational community. Other geographical areas, for example North America, the countries of Latin America's southern cone, ASEAN, and the Asian–Pacific Basin, have been the scenes of growing economic integration through free trade arrangements of greater or lesser complexity. While none of these ensembles has gone as far down the road of economic and political union as has Europe, they bear further evidence of the importance that regional economic arrangements and trans-national capital and communications links have come to assume in our age. These regional experiments may prove stepping stones towards even larger-scale experiments with integration in the twenty-first century.

Yet there is the need for extreme caution before we translate such trends into the seamless forces of global political integration. Very serious opposition in both Denmark and France to the Maastricht Treaty in 1992, persistent Euro-scepticism by many in the United Kingdom and elsewhere, and Norway's 'NO' vote in its 1994 referendum on membership in the European Union all underline limits to the process of European integration. There is room for considerable scepticism about the social dimension of European citizenship (O'Leary, 1995) and about its democratic resonance (Tiilikainen, 1995: 38). Hans Ulrich Jessurun d'Oliveira (1995: 76, 84) observes:

> Union citizenship is for the time being nothing more than a new name for a bunch of existing rights, a nice blue ribbon around scattered elements of a general notion of citizenship . . . . Nobody in his or her right mind would use the word citizen to describe the relationship between people and international organizations like GATT. To indicate the position of people under the Maastricht Treaty as citizenship is nearly as gross a misnomer. As an alibi it may please Brussels; whether it changes anything in the sceptical attitude and weak position of the populations of the Member States is, in my view, highly improbable.

The United States, the one remaining superpower in the post-Cold War era, shows little inclination to transfer real power to any multinational authority that it cannot control, or to enhance significantly the powers of the United Nations. Other major states, such as China or India, which represent enormous chunks of the world's population and have recently begun to come into their own, do not seem to be prepared to cede political sovereignty to any degree to supranational authorities.

Nor are the problems of other significant regions of the earth to be wished away by reveries about global democracy. Most of the states of Africa and the Middle East lack internal democratic structures. Some of the most tragic situations that have captured international attention in recent years – Liberia, Rwanda, Somalia, Bosnia – have been ones where effective state authority of any kind has been absent. It is fanciful in the extreme to start evoking global-type democratic institutions with such cases in mind. Nor do the many authoritarian regimes from Nigeria to Iraq to Burma to China to Indonesia show much likelihood of giving way to something liberal-democratic any time soon.

In tackling a topic such as this one, we cannot wish certain hard realities out of existence. This does not mean that we need succumb to the cynicism of the realpolitik school of argument, its disdain for moral imperatives in human affairs, its jejune assumption that might makes right where human nature is concerned and with respect to whatever political prospects may lie ahead. But the proponents of global democracy must not simply take their own desires to be reality.

What then are some of the obstacles to the realization of global democracy? There are a number of headings under which these can be discussed: (1) uneven economic development; (2) diverging political traditions; (3) cultural or ethnic identities; (4) solidarities that are primarily local or national in character.

Uneven economic development

Data suggest that there has been no closing of the gap between the richest and poorer states of the globe: 'As the UN Human Development Report for 1996 notes, total economic wealth in the world (global GDP) is $23 trillion, of which only $5 trillion, or 22 per cent, is accounted for by developing countries, even though they have nearly 80 per cent of the world's population' (Keenan, 1996). According to International Labour Organization figures, 'more than 800 million human beings are now unemployed or underemployed in the world' (Rifkin, 1995: xv). Indeed, something of the same pattern is emerging within western societies – with some 35 million unemployed in the OECD world alone. As Robert Reich, the former American Secretary of Labour, has noted: 'Globalization is in the process of creating in our industrial democracies a sort of underclass of demoralized and impoverished people' (Reich, 1995). According to Richard Barnet of the Institute for Policy Studies in Washington, the average American CEO received 149 times the average factory worker's pay in 1994; furthermore, at least 18 per cent of American workers with full-time jobs earned a salary placing them at or beneath the poverty line (Krumholz, 1996).

If we think back to the Greeks, the origins of democracy are related to concerns about extreme economic inequality. Solon's reform of the original Athenian constitution was linked to lifting the crushing debt load of the Attican peasantry: 'I brought back many to our god-given land / Who had been sold abroad, some wrongfully / Some by due process; others, too, in flight / from pressing debts' (Rodewald, 1974: 60). While equality of economic condition (*isomoiria*) was not the rallying call of the democratic party in the way that *isonomia* (equality before the law) and *isegoria* (equal right to speak in the assembly) were, it is also true that the proponents of democratic ideals in ancient times did believe in some minimal conditions of equality among the citizenry (Ober, 1990; Resnick, 1997: ch. 2). This becomes even more true in the modern representative regimes we associate with the nation-state.

The widening of political citizenship did help set the stage for the welfare state – though not the demise of property rights! – from Bismarck's Germany to other western societies in the twentieth century. T. H. Marshall's enunciation of the civic, the political, and the social elements of citizenship, associated respectively with the eighteenth, the nineteenth and the twentieth centuries, became something of a shibboleth during the heyday of the post-World War Two welfare state and mixed economy (Marshall, 1950; Bulmer and Rees, 1996). Many came to argue that western societies were in the process of extending social citizenship to their populations through universal health care, education, pension benefits, housing subsidies, unemployment insurance and welfare benefits, thereby complementing the juridical and political rights that had been accorded in an earlier day.

Some of this faith has now fallen into disrepute. Fiscal crisis since the 1970s, stagflation, concerns about levels of state expenditure, taxation, and high debt loads have all taken their toll. The rise of monetarism and of neoliberalism have been associated with roll-backs to levels of social entitlement and to the principle of universality in recent years (Minc, 1994; Mishra, 1990). There has been much more difficulty reaching agreement about social charters, for example in Europe (O'Leary, 1995), than regarding the free movement of capital and investment.

More stark yet are the issues facing the underdeveloped world. International labour guidelines need to be developed with respect to child labour or health and safety issues. Much of the South in this regard finds itself in the same situation as did the European lower classes at the beginning of the industrial revolution. Countries lack bargaining power *vis-à-vis* transnational corporations. There is little inclination on the part of governments to regulate their domestic economies too severely, thereby undercutting the attractiveness to outside investors and potential access to export markets. For this would go against the current emphasis on market rationality.

An important part of any battle for global democracy, therefore, must involve an attack on the values of the unregulated market place. The editor of the French publication *Le Monde diplomatique*, Ignacio Ramonet, has been criticizing what he calls 'the single permitted orthodoxy' (*la pensée unique*), that is, market liberalism, in the contemporary world. More recently he has gone on to castigate what he calls the movement to 'globalitarianism', that is, a market-driven version of totalitarian-type thinking about deficits, debts, privatization, etc. (Ramonet, 1997). Creating the conditions for global democracy, I would argue, will involve putting issues of economic and social equality back on to the agenda. It will involve sensitizing public opinion internationally to the extreme inequality of living conditions between North and South. Environmental issues are one focus for debate. Human rights issues are another. Health and social issues are yet another.

At the same time, the very parameters of global economic development further the concentration of wealth and power in the core countries. There has been some widening to include East Asia in recent decades. But whole regions and continents remain at the margins of the global economy. And there are many impediments to the development of a democratic ethos – from urban squalor and organized criminality to the absence of governments that can provide efficient public services and not simply plunder their own population.

For the moment, there is a lack of institutional means at the international level to address the more salient problems. There have been international conferences on all kinds of questions – from the environment to the condition of women to population to the plight of cities – but these have resulted in high-sounding declarations and little more. There have been institutions like the International Monetary Fund or the World Bank that have played an important role in shaping national public policies. Such organizations have been very much under the thumb of the richest and most powerful countries, and have invariably prodded countries in the South to pursue fiscally conservative policies entailing significant cuts to public expenditures and social programmes (George, 1988, 1992). The international situation at the end of the twentieth century resembles that in Rome towards the end of the republic, with a powerful aristocratic class controlling the *comitia centuriata* and Senate (Finley, 1983: 86); or the pre-reform British Parliament or the pre-1918 Prussian Landtag dominated by the upper class. As René Dumont (1991: 9) has observed:

The growing gap between the rich and poor countries is becoming more and more intolerable. If it continues unabated, we could by the middle of the next century have more than ten billion poor on our little planet, facing a billion rich. Such a situation would be politically untenable.

And in the words of José Lutzenberger (1996), former Brazilian Minister of the Environment:

We must realize that all these new free-trade arrangements, NAFTA, GATT and so on, were not made to benefit ordinary people. They were conceived by the powerful for the powerful. Transnational corporations need global markets, not only to get cheap resources from the Third World, but also to destroy within their own countries the social conquests of their workers.

In other words, there is a potential conflict between the proponents of global integration around unlimited capital flows and free trade agreements and those who would give greater weight to human concerns and social needs in the equation. 'Globalitarianism', to repeat Ramonet's term, runs counter to the spirit of global democracy, even if, in a contemporary version of Hegel's cunning of reason, it may help set the stage for an eventual break-through to something more genuinely democratic.

Diverging political traditions

It is difficult to envisage a common democratic space at the global level in the absence of reasonably common democratic traditions at the national one. The European Union, for all its limitations, was not built out of states with both democratic and non-democratic institutions. Indeed, a *sine qua non* for membership was a commitment to democracy. Hence the rather important role which the European Community played in helping the transition to democracy in southern Europe – Greece, Spain and Portugal – in the 1970s. And the lure of membership in the European Union is helping to consolidate democratic institutions in Eastern Europe since the fall of the Wall.

Is democracy possible at the global level in the absence of functioning democratic institutions in the overwhelming majority of states? A forum like the United Nations, even during the Cold War years, was one thing, for its aspiration to universality did not presuppose a commitment to common political institutions among its member states. How comfortable would the proponents of global democracy be with a similar model in constructing some kind of world parliament or world executive? Would it matter if China or Nigeria or Indonesia would not allow their citizens to vote freely for representatives of their choice in such a body? Or if they could only do so under conditions of coercion, media control and the like where only candidates favoured by the regime in power would have any real chance of election? What legitimacy might such an international body have, if its members were a mixture of democratically and less than democratically chosen ones?

The argument could be made that there would be a growing moral imperative for the non-democratic states to conform to the model of the long-established democratic ones – communicating vases of a sort. But the barriers to this happening are many, and there are no guarantees that meaningful multi-candidate competition, or freedom of assembly, or freedom of political organization would become the universal order of the day.

Unequal economic conditions, diverging historical and cultural traditions, the threat of internal subversion or inter-ethnic conflict, the indispensability of a strong hand at the helm, can easily be invoked to justify resistance to such procedures. Xin Chunying, a lawyer at the Chinese Academy of Social Sciences, notes that East Asian governments emphasize the particularity of human rights protection and the priority determined by the specific conditions of each country (Xin Chunying, 1995). Similar claims have been made by Lee Kuan Yew in Singapore. To some degree, these overlap with the arguments that have been advanced by a number of political philosophers in the western world that community may be more important than the individual rights that liberal theory emphasizes (Sandel, 1996; Taylor, 1985: ch. 7); or to put it more boldly that the 'good' ought to trump the 'right' (MacIntyre, 1981). The eminently contestable character of democracy, its very indeterminacy (Lefort, 1986: 25), makes it difficult to imagine easy agreement about the common institutions of global democracy or about its underlying ethos.

Cultural or ethnic identities

Global democracy presupposes some minimal sense of agreement about who the *demos*/people or the many *demoi*/peoples making up the globe are. But among the most acute problems that bedevil the world on the eve of the twenty-first century are those linked to conflicting forms of identity. The most notable of these are nationally, ethnically, religiously or tribally driven. The break-up of multinational federations in the Soviet Union, Czechoslovakia, and Yugoslavia come to mind – the last in particular accompanied by bloody conflict, ethnic cleansing, and the like. Secessionist or autonomist sentiments in Quebec, Scotland, Flanders, Catalonia, the Basque country, Punjab, or Kashmir; the conflicts in Rwanda and Burundi between Tutsis and Hutus; the claims of the Kurds to a homeland of their own; or of the Tibetans; or of the tribal peoples of Burma; or of the indigenous peoples of the Americas all underline just how powerful such forces can be. How does one ensure that those speaking in the name of the people are not doing so to the

exclusion of significant sections of the population who feel culturally or
ethnically apart from their co-citizens?[2]

Then there is religious fundamentalism. At one level, spokesmen for the
great religions of the world preach the virtues of peaceful coexistence, social
justice, tolerance and the like. As Küng and Kuschel (1993: 21, 24–34) have
asserted: 'By a global ethic we mean a fundamental consensus on binding
values, irrevocable standards, and personal attitudes. ... [These would
include] non-violence and respect for life; solidarity and a just economic
order; tolerance of a life of truthfulness; equal rights and partnership
between men and women.' At another level, there are intransigent forces at
work. Members of the Christian Coalition in the United States are generally
intolerant of views that do not match their own; the same is true for Jewish
settlers in the West Bank who embraced someone like Baruch Goldstein,
responsible for the massacre of Muslim worshippers in Hebron; Islamic
fundamentalists in Algeria who wantonly assassinate Catholic clergy; Hindu
fundamentalists in India, destroying mosques and emphasizing the Hindu-
ness of the country. Are the adherents of such beliefs about to throw in their
lot with any version of global governance that is based upon principles of live
and let live?

It will be very difficult to institute some type of global democracy as long as
the passions that sustain extreme nationalism or religious fundamentalism
are running strong. And the legitimacy of existing states – that are themselves acutely divided along religious, tribal or cultural lines – to be the units
that are represented in the UN or some future world parliament will always
be open to attack.

The would-be architects of global democracy will need to come to terms
with the shifting tectonic plates of ethnicity and religious identity. It is all
very well to seek to promote a measure of religious and ethnic pluralism; or
to invoke the UN Declaration of Human Rights of 1948. But minority rights
are not commonly respected in various parts of the world. The boundaries of
states and the identities of peoples do not always conveniently overlap. There
are many more candidates for the status of national community or ethnic
minority in the world in which we live than for that of sovereign state. Global
democracy cannot simply wish these out of existence.

Even within western countries, the nature of representation and of political community is very much open to debate – and not purely along national,
religious or ethnic lines. Recent decades have seen the emergence of forms of
identity politics, speaking to such variables as gender, colour or sexual
orientation. Potent political movements have come to champion the politics
of difference and to challenge the notion of any overriding national community as a result.

This has implications for the quest for global-type democracy. For the splintering of identities that has become the norm for certain political movements and intellectual currents – and this within nation-states – makes it all the more difficult to envisage shared values at a level larger than the nation-state: '[P]ostmodern theorists have emphasized fragmentation against unity, disorder against order, particularism against universalism, syncretism against holism, popular culture against high culture and localism against globalism' (Featherstone, 1995: 73–4). In an era of multiple and conflicting identities, individuals who come to emphasize one particular facet of their identities at the expense of all others may be all the less willing to enter into democratic dialogue with their fellows. Jean Bethke Elshtain (1993: 75) has observed that '[t]o the extent citizens begin to retribalize into ethnic or other "fixed-identity groups", democracy falters. Any possibility for human dialogue, for democratic communication and commonality, vanishes ... . Difference more and more becomes exclusivist.' And Eric Hobsbawm (1996: 43) writes:

> What does identity politics have to do with the Left? The political project of the Left is universalist: it is for all human beings. However we interpret these words, it isn't liberty for shareholders or blacks, but for everybody .... It is not fraternity only for old Etonians or gays, but for everybody. And identity politics is essentially not for everybody but for the members of a specific group only.

To what degree is what passes for postmodernism, that is, the eclipse not only of metanarratives but of common narratives altogether, itself a major impediment to fruitful dialogue across national lines? Since the majority of the proponents of global democracy are usually found on the left, these need to ask themselves where a politics that celebrates differences without limits may lead. It is one thing to affirm the legitimacy of cultural diversity or to underline the less than universalistic character of some of the key values that the post-Enlightenment tradition of the West has fostered. It is quite another to abandon the search for shared or converging values altogether.

Given the incredible concentration and clout of transnational capital, there is a compelling need for those who believe in checks and balances and in countervailing powers to act internationally as well. Masao Miyoshi (1996: 7–6) has argued the following:

> Transnational corporations are unencumbered with nationalist baggage. Their profit motives are unconcealed. They travel, communicate, and transfer people and plants, information and technology, money and resources globally .... In order to exploit the different economic and political conditions among the current nation-states, they ignore borders to their own advantage.

And beyond any purely economic argument, there is a moral and political one. For unless there is some sense of common purpose that links us across national and other lines, there is no likelihood of our forging the type of institutions that would speak to global, as opposed to purely national or regional, interests.

Local and national solidarities

Nonetheless, we need to recognize that international solidarity, all said and done, is a good deal less prevalent than solidarities closer to home. Extreme disasters, such as the famine in Ethiopia in the mid-1980s, may touch a chord – especially when iconic figures of popular music decide to become involved. But generally, a flood or earthquake or tornado or air crash on one's home turf touches public opinion there far more acutely than a similar disaster 10,000 kilometres away. A minimal sense of common interest has arisen in recent years regarding forces that cross national borders, for example, global warming, the destruction of the ozone layer. Yet progress in addressing such questions has been remarkably uneven, and pursued far more successfully at the national than at the international level.

Despite amazing progress in the means of communication, and the fact that non-governmental organizations of all kinds have emerged over the past few decades spanning national boundaries, we are far from that shared solidarity among peoples across the globe that the notion of a world *demos* or world citizenship would evokè. In all candour, we need to recognize that such leaps are not only unlikely in the foreseeable future, but may even cloud our judgement regarding what realistically can be attained.

This implies taking nation-states seriously, despite the current vogue in various circles for non-territorial forms of identity and interaction. (Are we all living on the Internet?) And it means taking, if not nationalism, then at a minimum patriotism, to be an enduring and necessary feature in the building of a global democratic order. Maurizio Viroli, in a provocative essay, has attempted to distinguish between patriotism and nationalism (Viroli, 1995: 58–9, 186). The crucial difference seems to lie in the fact that patriotism, rooted in an earlier version of civic republicanism, is potentially more compatible with a commitment to values of common liberty and welfare that cross national lines than is nationalism, which has often had an ethnically-based component to it. Having roots in a particular country is not incompatible with a sense of cosmopolitanism and open-mindedness towards the inhabitants of other states. We need to foster such a cosmopolitanism; but for most of us this cannot come at the price of denying some primary loyalty to our fellow citizens.

II

This brings me, then, to the second part of this chapter, which will briefly explore what may in fact be possible, in envisaging some form of global democracy in the twenty-first century. Let me examine this under three rubrics: (1) institutional structures; (2) economic, political, and other imperatives; (3) cultural diversity.

Institutional structures

These can range from reform of the United Nations to attempts to lay the basis for a more robust form of bottom-up democracy at the global level. Where the first is concerned, there have been various proposals for reform, for example, a restructured Security Council with permanent membership for countries such as India, Brazil, and perhaps Nigeria (Report, 1995: 240); a World Bank and IMF in which non-Western countries play a larger role (ibid.: 146–9); a new World Central Bank (Human Development Report, 1994: 85); and the establishment of a permanent military command under UN aegis, able to interpose itself effectively in trouble-spots where an international presence is required (Report, 1995: 110–12).

Others would look to a bolstered role for the International Court of Justice at The Hague and for the enforceability of International Human Rights declarations and covenants (Held, 1995: 269, 279). Still others, in their opposition to globalization from above, speak of an enhanced role for global civil society, for example, organizations concerned with the environment, human rights and international development in the global arena (Falk, 1995: chs 6, 7).

And then there are those who engage in more utopian-type exercises, such as mapping the possible structures of a future global parliament and executive authority. The author is one who has tried his hand at this, using the example of Cleisthenes' reform of the Athenian constitution circa 508 BC as a possible model for how we might proceed, if we are concerned with overcoming perhaps the most important divide that stands in the way of any common political solidarity at the international level: that between the rich and poor countries of the world (Resnick, 1997: ch. 1).

In a nutshell, the proposal builds on the fact that Cleisthenes sought to overcome the cleavages between the city of Athens, coastal Attica and the interior by dividing the polis into ten tribes, each with components from the three regions. The principal divisions in our late-twentieth-century world are as much economic as geographical or cultural. So we should seek to establish units at the global level – perhaps ten in all – made up of states drawn from the wealthier, the middle and the poorer categories.

The people of the world would directly elect their representatives to a world parliament. To keep such a body to manageable size, it might be limited to around 500 members, that of the council in ancient Athens. The most populous states, for example, China or India, would clearly have greater representation than tinier states. Yet representation would be through one of the ten global units each with an identical 50 members in the world parliament; hence no single state, however populous or wealthy, would be able to dominate its proceedings.

Following the European Union model, we might also seek to establish a rotating executive charged with the day-to-day administration of world-level affairs for a six-month period. Each of the global-level units in turn would come to play a symbolically important, albeit carefully circumscribed, role. Some harmonization of interests across the divide of North and South would occur within each. All important matters, nonetheless, would need to be referred to the world parliament as a whole. And nation-states would inevitably play a crucial role in its deliberations.

Areas of potential jurisdiction for a global democratic authority might include peace and war; global environmental matters; the provision of developmental aid for infrastructure, education, and health services in the poorest countries; and perhaps the setting of some minimal international labour and social standards. Some financial resources, perhaps along the lines of James Tobin's proposal to tax international foreign exchange trans-actions (Human Development Report, 1994: 70), would come to be vested in this authority. And a World Court with an expanded mandate would play an adjudicative role with regard to its powers and responsibilities.

Writers like Riccardo Petrella have sketched a number of other possibilities for global integration. These range from sustainable global integration around the principle of a global commons, for example, the air, the sea, certain key resources, to an integrated world economy where regionally integrated units like the European Union or NAFTA play a key role, and a unique world integrated market, something which he calls the Gattist model. While he sees the first of these three as the most desirable, he sees the third as the most probable development, though not until some time after the year 2015 (Petrella, 1994: xviii–xx).

Proposals like these may help us to frame the debate about international governance, particularly should the circumstances for broadening and deepening political solidarities at the global level present themselves. But we would be wise to recognize the passionate opposition any transfer of powers to some supranational level of authority would arouse. Progress in such a direction will be extremely measured.

Economic, political and other imperatives

One would hope that it will not require an economic catastrophe, of the sort that rocked the world after 1929, to set the stage for greater political integration at the global level. At the moment, we have an international political economy where global capital is remarkably free to follow its own agenda. This, however, may not remain true indefinitely. The pendulum in these matters tends to swing back and forth from market to regulation and political control (Polanyi, 1957); it is hard to imagine, for example, that there will not be persistent calls for better environmental regulations, child labour laws, minimum wage legislation, in countries now engaged in wholesale industrialization; or that a call for a more equitable division of the fruits of the new technologies or of the international division of labour that has benefited the uppermost echelons of the global economy will not come to be voiced. At the same time, there are incredible demographic pressures being placed on cities throughout the world, on water basins and other resources, on migration patterns, that will have their consequences at the global political level.

If the experience of the European Community/Union is anything to go by, political leadership of the highest order will be required to help lay the foundations for some kind of global political community. The world will need figures of the stature of Jean Monnet, or if one prefers the ancient model, lawgivers like Solon or Cleisthenes.

Almost certainly, functional agreements will precede any full-bodied proposals; and the framework for world democratic governance – whether building on the United Nations or going beyond it – will be limited to those areas of responsibility that cry out for international attention: for example, peace, war, and global security; North–South political and economic relations; global environmental matters; key issues of human rights. Subsidiarity – by which is meant the primary responsibility of national, regional, and local governments for matters which can optimally be dealt with at those levels – is even more valid as a principle here than it has become in the European Union.[3]

The building blocks of any such arrangements will remain states. Parallels with the underpinnings of the Europe of today spring to mind; so too do the ambiguities and uncertainties that European unity presents even to its supporters:

> I think that we need to build a Europe of nations. The sentiment of national allegiance is now a legitimate historical fact that we need to respect – provided we can avoid the terrible adventures that have marked our century. Eventually a supranational Europe? Why not? I would hope so. But I prefer not to make any pronouncements about this; professional experience has taught me that events rarely happen in the manner that we predict. (Le Goff, 1996: 17)

We would be wise to think of global democracy as proceeding in the same bottom-up manner. To expect that the inhabitants of nation-states with long historical traditions or that have recently achieved independence will simply submerge their sense of national identity within a cosmopolitan ensemble is to dream in Technicolor. The only construct that makes sense is that of multiple identities, national for certain purposes, subnational for others, and supranational in those limited areas of activity that require international co-ordination (Heater, 1990: ch. 9).

Cultural diversity

Global democracy must take account of the cultural diversity of humanity:

> The globalization process should be regarded as opening up the sense that now the world is a single place with increased contact becoming unavoidable, we necessarily have greater dialogue between various nation-states, blocs and civilizations: a dialogical space in which we can expect a good deal of disagreement, clashing of perspectives and conflict, not just working together and consensus. (Featherstone, 1995: 102)

This has implications for possible models of democracy that we seek to develop, for example, sources beyond the Western tradition, and for the type of global community that we envisage (Bell, 1996; Tehranian and Tehranian, 1995). For certain purposes we may see transnational cultural patterns emerging, with core values subject to alteration: 'A process of mutual learning can follow, moving towards a "fusion of horizons" in Gadamer's term, where the moral universe of the other becomes less strange. And out of this will come further borrowings and the creation of new hybrid forces' (Taylor, 1996: 20). More optimistic observers may even envisage a universal global ethic, built upon common human entitlements and rights (Nussbaum, 1996; Puchala, 1995).

Realistically, however, we must expect strong resistance to any full-scale homogenization of values. Communities of language, faith and nationality will continue to play a very important role in defining identities into the twenty-first century. Indeed, I would argue that cultural diversity is the *sine qua non* for any non-tyrannical global order we can imagine. Whatever else global democracy incarnates, it cannot be the political or cultural hegemony of any one state or grouping of states. So the best we can hope for is a form of cosmopolitanism that respects the plural character of the peoples of the earth.

Humanity needs ideals. The premise of this chapter has been that it is necessary to begin thinking about a third level of democracy, beyond the polis or the nation-state. For the first time, economic conditions and modes of communication make a more global type of interaction/integration a possibility. And there are compelling demographic, ecological and social reasons to move in such a direction in the coming century.

But we need to be realistic in our thinking. On the one hand, we may be tempted to buy into Rousseau's delineation of human nature in its primordial state as based on a certain sympathy for our fellow human beings and on the desire to not do them harm (Rousseau, 1964). On the other, there is the Hobbesian reading of human nature with its aggressive and self-aggrandizing qualities leading to war (Hobbes, 1968: Book I). Or to put it another way, we have the version of universal peace bequeathed us by such eighteenth-century luminaries as the Abbé St Pierre or Immanuel Kant; and we have the equally compelling observations about hard power interests that the proponents of the realpolitik position from Thucydides down to today proffer.

If global democracy is ever to get off the ground, we must find a way of appealing to the more altruistic side of human nature. But – and this is not a small but – we must simultaneously appeal to a self-preserving instinct, that comes to accept the need for minimal political governance at the global level because the alternatives are simply too bleak. An unregulated global market place will not suffice; nor will the domination of the strongest states or powers; nor will the absence of global authority altogether. These are the imperatives – more than some abstract commitment to global democracy – that will frame the debate in the decades to come.

Notes

1. In a round table discussion at the International Political Science Association World Congress in Berlin, 1994.
2. For an interesting discussion of the problems this can pose, see the Summer 1996 issue of *Dissent*, entitled 'Embattled Minorities Around the Globe'.
3. For a good discussion of the theoretical origins of the concept of subsidiarity, see Millon-Delsol (1992).

Bibliography

Bell, Daniel A. (1996) Minority rights: on the importance of local knowledge, *Dissent*, Summer, 36–41.

Bulmer, Martin and Rees, Anthony (eds) (1996) *Citizenship Today: The Contemporary Relevance of T. H. Marshall*. London: UCL Press.

Cox, Robert (1991) The global political, economic, and social choice, in Daniel Drache and Muric Gertler (eds), *The New Era of Global Competition*. Montreal: McGill/Queen's University Press.

Diamond, L., Linz, J. and Lipset, M. (eds) (1989) *Democracy in Developing Countries*, 4 vols. London: Adamantine Press.

Di Palma, Giuseppe (1990) *To Craft Democracies*. Berkeley, CA: University of California Press.

d'Oliveira, Hans Ulrich Jessurun (1995), Union citizenship: pie in the sky, in A. Rosas and E. Antola (eds), *A Citizens' Europe*. London: Sage, pp. 58–84.

Dumont, René (1991) *Démocratie pour l'Afrique*. Paris: Seuil.

Elshtain, Jean Bethke (1993) *Democracy on Trial*. Concord: Anansi.

Falk, Richard (1995) *On Humane Governance: Toward a New Global Politics*. Cambridge: Polity Press.

Featherstone, Mike (1995) *Undoing Culture: Globalization, Postmodernism and Identity*. London: Sage.

Finley, Moses (1983) *Politics in the Ancient World*. Cambridge: Cambridge University Press.

Fitoussi, Jean-Paul and Rosanvallon, Pierre (1996) *Le Nouvel Age des inégalités*. Paris: Seuil.

George, Susan (1988) *A Fate Worse than Debt*. New York: Grove Press.

George, Susan (1992) *The Debt Boomerang: How Third World Debt Harms Us All*. London: Pluto Press.

Heater, Derek (1990) *Citizenship: The Civic Ideal in World History, Politics, and Education*. London: Longman.

Held, David (1995) *Democracy and the Global Order*. Cambridge: Polity Press.

Hobbes, Thomas (1968) *Leviathan*. Harmondsworth: Penguin.

Hobsbawm, Eric (1996) Identity politics and the Left, *New Left Review*, **217**, May–June.

Human Development Report (1994) United Nations. New York: Oxford University Press.

Keenan, Victor (1996) Highway robbery by the super-rich, *Guardian Weekly*, 28 July.

Krumholz, Mark (1996) Taking on the multinationals. Internet paper.

Küng, Hans and Kuschel, Karl-Josef (eds) (1993) *A Global Ethic: The Declaration of the Parliament of the World's Religions*. New York: Continuum.

Lefort, Claude (1986) *Essais sur la politique, XIXe–XXe siècles*. Paris: Seuil.

Le Goff, Jacques (1996) *L'histoire*, juillet–août.

Lutzenberger, José (1996) Re-thinking progress, *New Internationalist*, **278**, April.

MacIntyre, Alasdair (1981) *After Virtue*. Notre Dame, IN: University of Notre Dame Press.

Marshall, T. H. (1950) *Citizenship and Social Class and Other Essays*. Cambridge: Cambridge University Press.

Millon-Delsol, Chantal (1992) *L'État subsidaire: Ingérence et non-ingérence de l'État: le principe de subsidarité aux fondements de l'histoire européenne*. Paris: Presses Universitaires de France.

Minc, Alain (ed.) (1994) *La France de l'An 2000*. Paris: Éditions Odile-Jacob.

Mishra, Ramesh (1990) *The Welfare State in Capitalist Society*. Toronto.

Miyoshi, Masao (1996) A borderless world? From colonialism to transnationalism and the decline of the nation-state, in R. Wilson and W. Dissanayake (eds) *Global/ Local*. Durham, NC: Duke University Press, 78–106.

Nussbaum, Martha (1996) Patriotism and cosmopolitanism, in Joshua Cohen (ed.), *For Love of Country: Debating the Limits of Patriotism*. Boston: Beacon Press.

Ober, Josiah (1990) *Mass and Elite in Democratic Athens*. Princeton, NJ: Princeton University Press.

O'Leary, Siofra (1995) The social dimension of community citizenship, in A. Rosas and E. Antola (eds), *A Citizens' Europe*. London: Sage, pp. 156–181.

Petrella, Ricardo (1994) A new world in the making, in U. Muldur and R. Petrella (eds), *The European Community and the Globalization of Technology and the Economy*. Brussels: 1994, pp. ix–xx.

Polanyi, Karl (1957) *The Great Transformation*. Boston, MA: Beacon.

Puchala, Donald (1995) The ethics of globalism. Academic Council of the UN System, John Holmes Memorial Lecture 3.

Ramonet, Ignacio (1997) Régimes globalitaires, *Le Monde diplomatique*, January.

Reich, Robert (1995) in *US News and World Report*, 6 February.

Report of the Commission on Global Governance (1995) *Our Global Neighbourhood*. New York: Oxford University Press.

Resnick, Philip (1997) *Twenty-First Century Democracy*. Montreal: McGill Queen's University Press.

Rifkin, Jeremy (1995) *The End of Work: The Decline of the Global Work Force and the Dawn of the Post-Market Era*. New York: Putnam.

Rodewald, Cosmo (ed.) (1974) *Democracy: Ideas and Realities*. London: Dent.

Rousseau, Jean-Jacques (1964) *Discourse on the Origin of Inequality*, ed. Roger Masters. New York: St Martin's Press.

Sandel, Michael (1996) *Democracy's Discontent: America in Search of a Public Philosophy*. Cambridge, MA: Harvard University Press.

Taylor, Charles (1985) *Philosophy and the Human Sciences: Philosophical Papers II*. Cambridge, MA: Cambridge University Press.

Taylor, Charles (1996) A world consensus on human rights? *Dissent*, Summer.

Tehranian, M. and Tehranian, K. (1995) The recurrent suspicion: democratization in a global perspective, in Philip Lee (ed.) *The Democratization of Communication*. Cardiff: University of Wales Press, pp. 38–74.

Tiilikainen, Teija (1995) The problem of democracy in the European Union, in A. Rosas and E. Antola (eds) *A Citizens' Europe*. London: Sage, pp. 19–38.

Viroli, Maurizio (1995) *For Love of Country: An Essay on Patriotism and Nationalism*. Oxford: Clarendon Press.

Xin Chunying (1995) The growth of East Asia and its impact on human rights, cited in Bell (1996).

9

Globalization and Governance: A Historical Perspective

CRAIG N. MURPHY

This chapter places the current era of 'globalization' in its historical context first by outlining a general perspective on the process and then by discussing four earlier, similar periods in the histories of Germany and the United Kingdom. This second part of the chapter reports on the European half of a comparative exploration of 'Gramscian' hypotheses about the governance problems associated with globalization in four regions of relatively equal size: the United Kingdom, Germany, the northeastern part of the United States, and the northeastern part of Japan. Of the approximately 80 regions of the world with current populations of 60 to 90 million, these are the only four that have been both the political and the economic centres of what Volker Bornschier (1995) identifies as the societal models that have exerted 'substantial adaptive pressure upon other societal models', meaning that other societies have been 'forced to incorporate the [model's] economically and politically superior institutions if they did not want to risk being outdone by the competition for core position'.

Arguably, Europe is still in the position to generate a societal model that can exert 'adaptive pressure' on the rest of the world, but it can only do so within limits imposed by the historical trajectory of capitalist industrial society. This chapter is an attempt to lay out some of those limits, especially those associated with processes of increasing economic scale hinted at by the popular concept of 'globalization'.

Ways of understanding globalization

Thomas Biersteker (1994) provides a useful operationalization of 'globalization' as the strategic reorientation of governance institutions toward what Overbeek and van der Pijl (1993: 7) call a larger 'paradigmatic scale of operation'. Thus, the key signs of globalization over the last fifteen years include the reorientation of business from inter-OECD to global markets and the growing focus on issues of international competitiveness by governments at all levels, including the most powerful global-level intergovernmental agencies, the IMF and the World Bank.

This way of looking at globalization recognizes that 'governance', the coherence and stability provided to societies by conscious, goal-oriented administrative action, is an aggregate of strategic actions taken by a host of forces. Effective systems of governance are characterized by the compatibility and relative coherence of the various strategies of the different social forces that contribute to social stability (Rosenau, 1995). Using the slightly different language of Antonio Gramsci, effective governance involves the compatible functioning of the ensemble of institutions within a 'historical bloc'.

A focus on the globalizing strategies of all the various actors that contribute to governance encourages us to think about the incoherence and lack of compatibility among the current strategies of firms, states, international institutions and popular social forces. Biersteker emphasizes the increasing social inequality that is likely to arise from the essentially defensive globalizing strategies of so many of today's firms, whose emphasis is on cost-cutting and the shedding of long-term commitments to employees and suppliers. The current liberal fundamentalist orientation of the international institutions reinforces such strategies, as do the competitiveness policies of the many governments that have come to conclude that their country or region must 'export or die'. As Philip Cerny (1995) argues, 'The main focus of this "competition state" in the world ... is the proactive promotion of economic activities, whether at home or abroad, which will make firms and sectors located within the territory of the state competitive in international markets, rather than the state being directly responsible for market *outcomes* which guarantee the welfare of its citizens'.

To the extent to which rapid growth and rapid capital accumulation are essential to the stability of capitalist societies, it is problematic that the current mix of globalizing strategies has not been able to return industrialized countries to the higher growth rates of the 1950s and 1960s. To understand why this mix of strategies has failed we need to consider a second perspective. 'Globalization' can also be understood as the *actual* process of increasing the paradigmatic scale of leading industries, that is, the process of increasing the size of the market and, through it, the division of labour associated with those industries that contribute the most to industrial growth. 'Globalization' is the aggregate economic outcome towards which Biersteker's changes in strategies point. Paradoxically, it is an outcome that is unlikely to be achieved with the current mix of strategies.

To go back to Biersteker's level of strategies we might argue that periodically governments, capitalists and labour have simultaneously seemed to recognize the logic of Adam Smith's argument that 'the division of labour' (meaning, for Smith, more than anything else the complexity and labour-saving character of industrial processes) is 'limited by the extent of the market'. The periodic reorientation of strategies towards that goal has assured that the paradigmatic scale of industrial economies has grown in a step-wise fashion ever since the Industrial Revolution. Each new step-wise increase in the size of the markets served by the leading industries has also been associated with the transition from one industrial era to the next, a change, as Smith would have expected, in the complexity and labour-saving characteristic of the industrial processes in the leading industries.

Each new era has also meant a change in the leading industries themselves. Economies as small as those of the north of England, New England or Belgium were all big enough for the development of the early industrial economies of the cotton mills. More extensive, 'national' economies were needed for the mid-nineteenth-century Railway Age. The new lead industries of the turn-of-the-century Second Industrial Revolution grew within the larger market areas of extended nation-states: the British Empire of the 'new' imperialism, the 'German' market area that had been expanded to and beyond continental Europe through the economic integration encouraged by the Public International Unions, and the international market area centred on the United States. The more complex industrial processes of the mid-twentieth-century Automobile Age or Jet Age required the larger market area of the 'Free World' as a whole (Bornschier, 1995; Murphy, 1994; Overbeek and van der Pijl, 1993).

Governments and intergovernmental organizations could create the opportunities at the beginning of each of these eras simply by following the dictates of Smith's liberal theory and removing barriers to trade and investment in new industries. Businesses then had to seize those opportunities. The new leading industries of each era have been created 'first movers' who made the large fixed investments needed to achieve the potential technical economies of scale in production and 'economies of scope' from joint production and distribution allowed by the market areas governments had opened (Chandler, 1990: 17–34). Moreover, new models of labour–management relation responding to 'the ideological and technical problems that appear whenever changes in scale and complexity of the firm, the international competitive environment, or working-class unrest challenge current practices' have always been central to the successful strategies of first-mover firms (Guillén, 1994: 1). As they became generalized, the new labour–management models have become part of larger, long-term societal compacts worked out with popular social forces.

The current 'globalizing' strategies of so many firms are not directed to long-term, large-scale investment in new processes of production and new economies of scope. Instead, they are defensive, cost-cutting strategies designed either to jump into new markets for old products before others do, or to find new, cheaper, and often less permanent sources of materials and talent to be used in the fields where the firm has already developed a strength. Firms that have taken the longer view, especially those in the newer information-based industries, nonetheless are apt to follow strategies that are incoherent with those of states, international institutions and popular social forces (Kobrin, 1995). In sum, while many firms, governments and key international institutions all have begun to follow strategies oriented toward a larger paradigmatic scale of operation, it is doubtful whether this will trigger a new, high-growth industrial age, a 'Third Industrial Revolution' or an 'Information Age'.

Studies of earlier transitions from one industrial era to the next can tell us something about the prospects for the current age. Analysts of economic long waves see similarities between the last fifteen years of incoherent globalization and the economic downturns and troughs that preceded the take-offs of the Railway Age (which began in the 1840s), the Second Industrial Revolution (beginning in the mid-1890s), and the Automobile Age (beginning in the 1940s) (Goldstein, 1988).

During each of those troughs 'conservative' policies and eventually quite 'parochial' ones emanated from the governments of major industrialized countries (Namenwirth, 1973; Sterman, 1992; Weber, 1981). Such policies also emerged from the international organizations in which the industrial powers played a key role. Those policies were oriented towards protecting financial markets and competing with other states in a world of what appeared, at the time, to be diminishing opportunities. Similarly, some long wave analysts see the defensive globalizing policies of firms – their downsizing, their push for 'flexibility', their attempts to gain every bit of potential profit from currently-developed technologies and existing plants – as another endogenous consequence of the long wave trough. The defensiveness of these policies is fundamental; the connection of some to globalization merely incidental. Some defensive firms find new sources of labour and materials, and new markets for old products, abroad. Others do not. But both strategies are simply reactions to economic forces outside the firms' control; they do not represent progress toward a fundamentally new industrial era.

World-systems analysis and the larger literature on the political-economic competition among industrial powers provides additional insight about the importance of governance strategies in accelerating and defining new industrial eras. Thus, for example, Richard Rubinson (1978: 40–5) argues for the usefulness of seeing each industrial take-off as the consequence of interregional competition for the long-term investment of capital accumulated in the last era of industrial growth, much of which sits in short-term, nonindustrial investments throughout the trough. In that sense, Germany and the northern United States (regions that first began to become major industrial centres in the Railway Age) were 'winners' in the competition for much of the capital that was accumulated in the English Industrial Revolution, much of which had been invested in more speculative ventures in the somewhat illusory economic 'good years' that dotted the 1820s and 1830s.

Volker Bornschier (1995) adds that one characteristic of each of the successive groups of regional 'winners' has been the greater social inclusiveness of their 'social models' as compared to those of the leading industrial regions of the preceding eras, an observation he links to the political battles that typified the entire industrial core during the transition. Thus, Railway Age industrial societies typically adopted a 'liberal' social model, following the liberal uprisings of 1830–48. The Second Industrial Revolution was typified by 'class-polarized' societies, but ones which took their form after the expansion of participation and the extension of compulsory education in the 1880s. And, of course, the post-war capitalist industrial societies were typically even more inclusive with re-allocative market economies and strong welfare states.

Analysts of the more recent industrial competition among core powers, including Hart (1992) and Simon Reich (1990), have made the further argument that there may be a sort of historical drag of the less-inclusive societal models in regions that were earlier winners. This would help explain why some governments have difficulty developing what some imagine would be the most successful, self-interested globalizing strategies. Thus, the United Kingdom and the United States (to different extents, or to the same extent at different times) 'remain ideologically opposed to, and institutionally incapable of, discriminatory economic policies' that may typify the more successful twentieth-century 'competitiveness' strategies (Reich, 1990: 34–8).

Other scholars have attempted to develop an even more integrated understanding of the role of government, corporate, and *popular strategies* in the transition from one industrial era to the next (Cox, 1987; Gill, 1990; Murphy, 1994; van der Pijl, 1984, 1994), an understanding grounded in Antonio Gramsci's rich historical political sociology and in Karl Polanyi's (1957) thought-provoking history of the industrial era. Some of this literature describes what can be called a 'build, thrive, clash, grab, hoard' cycle (Murphy, 1994: 26–45, 261).

The *build* phase is characterized by the formation of a new historical bloc, reflected in a mix of governance strategies of firms, states, international institutions, and popular social forces which result in relatively large fixed investments in the new leading industries. This leads to a period of relative prosperity (*thrive*), also characterized by the mitigation of the social conflicts inherent to capitalist industrialism. This period, along with the build phase, may be characterized by a Gramscian form of 'hegemony'.

The end of this period is apt to be marked by a kind of 'high cosmopolitanism', a widespread willingness of governments to risk resources in new liberal internationalist projects. This is the phase in which the first of the new market-expanding international institutions that become relevant to the *next* phase of industrial growth have been established: the International Telegraph Union of 1865, which helped create the infrastructure of the 'extended national' markets of Second Industrial Revolution take-off in the 1890s, the Radiotelegraph Union of 1906, which helped link the intercontinental markets of the Automobile and Jet Age, and INTELSAT of 1965, a provider of the key infrastructure for today's anticipated Information Age (Murphy, 1994: 6).

However, almost simultaneously with this high cosmopolitanism, some of the inherent conflicts re-emerge: conflicts with labour, conflicts with those on the periphery of the privileged capitalist core, conflicts between different industrial centres of the core, and conflicts with other social models governing parts of the world economy. These *clashes* mark the beginning of a long period of reduced prosperity, the next phase of which begins with the reassertion of capitalist power in a profit-*grab*bing mode that may include cost-cutting globalization. As Henk Overbeek (1990: 28) argues, this period is one in which productive capital is in crisis and the 'concept of money capital', liberal fundamentalism, ' "presents itself" as the obvious, rational solution'. Governments adopt cost-cutting policies and begin to focus on issues of international competitiveness, and the institutions responsible for the stability of the international financial system begin to impose liberal fundamentalist policies on states that are increasingly desperate for such international or transnational support.

The scholars who borrow from Gramsci argue that while this phase of reassertion by capital, especially by financial capital, may be marked by significant economic activity, much of it is apt to be speculative, and of little lasting importance. Moreover, when speculative bubbles burst, the habit of under-investment in production is apt to continue, leading to the stagnation of the *hoard* phase of even more defensive strategies and greater political parochialism – the phase that many Gramscians, like many world-systems and long wave analysts, fear the world economy has now entered.

In slightly different ways Robert W. Cox (1992), Kees van der Pijl (1990, 1994) and I (Murphy, 1994) have described the transitions that take place at this point as involving the second half of what Polanyi (1957) called the 'double movement' against the extreme market logic of the liberal fundamentalism that becomes so predominant in the 'grab' phase. That movement involves the intellectual leadership of 'experts in government' or the 'cadre class', men and women who have often been *critical* liberals who partially accept the Smithian logic, but who also see a larger role for government. Van der Pijl sees them, in the twentieth century, as most typically found among the core supporters and officials of social democratic parties. These intellectual leaders have marshalled both political leaders and industrial leaders (most often, of the new potential leading sectors) in what Gramsci called 'passive revolutions', comprehensive reformist projects that, nonetheless, require no 'fundamental reordering of social relations' (Forgacs, 1988: 428).

One of the most distinctive aspects of the Gramscian accounts of both nineteenth- and twentieth-century transitions has been the argument that these passive revolutions have been supported by international institutions. Transnational and intergovernmental bodies have not just played a role in the 'internationalization' of the economically coercive aspects of state power (i.e. the role of international financial institutions at the beginning of each transition). In the 'build' part of the cycle international institutions have promoted new, less defensive strategies for both firms and states, the kind of strategies that can contribute to an effective governance mix.

The earlier transitions in the United Kingdom and Germany

The paragraphs above give a global perspective on a process whose local histories can be interpreted quite differently. What follows is a brief discussion of the evidence of past moments of 'globalization' in Europe's two major industrial centres. It is intended both to illustrate the pattern identified and to highlight the significant deviations that have occurred.

The First Industrial Revolution: grounds for questioning the argument

Britain's industrial take-off occurred from about 1795 to 1815, the years when 'power looms became general' (Flamant and Singer-Kérel, 1968: 13). The end of the country's previous rapid growth period corresponded to what a number of world-systems scholars consider to be Britain's victory in a hegemonic struggle with France. This was *not* a moment of 'high cosmopolitanism', but rather of the mercantilist policies that early liberal economists later would decry. Nevertheless, the mid-eighteenth-century boom did end with the eruption of conflicts on Britain's periphery, in the American colonies (Agnew, 1987: 34), followed by a conservative political turn that reinforced traditional, if not 'capitalist', power. After defeat by the Americans, William Pitt the Younger took office bent on sinking Britain's unprecedented national debt, which had been created by the war. He initially supported the profit-grabbing policies of the Indian monopoly (so decried by Adam Smith) and instituted defensive policies to break the Indian cloth industry and prevent the export of textile manufacturing know-how. He continued the imposition of seemingly draconian policies of fiscal responsibility on governments on the periphery of England – Ireland, Scotland, and the remaining colonies (Overbeek, 1990: 36–41; Polanyi, 1957: 136; Reilly, 1979).

Two events triggered the change in Pitt's strategies that allowed the Industrial Revolution take-off: the French Revolution and the 'climatic' bread riots of 1795 when the popular masses 'stiffened by the Jacobin consciousness of a minority' attempted to force the 'old moral economy against the free market' (Thompson, 1963: 63–7). Overbeek (1990: 39; compare Flamant and Singer-Kérel, 1968: 13) concludes: 'The French Revolution provided an effective shield behind which English manufacturers were able to prosper. The upper classes closed ranks .... The Napoleonic Wars and the consequent protection from continental competition allowed English industrial capital to expand rapidly and turn England into the workshop of the world.'

Relations with the hands employed in that workshop were largely influenced by the system put into place in 1795 when the threat of the Jacobin contagion seemed the greatest: the Speenhamland system of poor relief. Its authors (ecclesiastical/civil authorities who were certainly neither 'liberal' nor 'expert' in any modern sense) saw it as a generous attempt to reinstitute part of the societal contract that had been so disrupted by the new economic system. Although Speenhamland ultimately proved a disaster for the British masses, Polanyi (1957: 93) argues that it may have prevented starvation throughout much of England, and certainly weakened the revolutionary movements.

Nonetheless, only historical apologists for Pitt (e.g. Reilly, 1979) speak of the post-1795 government strategy as one marked by greater inclusiveness. E. P. Thompson (1963: 63, 429) describes a strategy highlighted by violent reaction, including Pitt's 'assault' on the groups pushing for constitutional reform, his suspension of Habeas Corpus in the face of the popular threat, and the brutal suppression of the United Irishmen's rebellion of 1798, which marked the beginning of the imposition of the disastrous early nineteenth-century system that gave the island's poor the least relief from the market logic that was taking hold throughout the increasingly united kingdoms.

The war economy that nurtured the English Industrial Revolution *did not* encourage companies to invest in equity enhancing new systems of production. In large part, as Thompson (1963: 463) argues, this was due to the incentive for exploitation created by the Irish policy, which created so many 'ready recruits for Satan's mills'. Not surprisingly, as Polanyi (1957: 78) points out, the debate among historians about the possible improvements industrialism brought to working-class life is a debate about data on the period after the abolition of the Speenhamland in 1834.

Into the Railway Age: greater confirmation

Events that more closely correspond to the Gramscian model mark the beginning of the second industrial era that followed the conservative years when Speenhamland was abolished. The pattern tends to hold not only in the United Kingdom, but also in Germany.

At the end of the Napoleonic Wars, and near the end of the English Industrial Revolution boom, Germany witnessed an outburst of 'high cosmopolitanism', including Friedrich List's first successful movements for inter-German free trade areas (Bundestag, 1989: 65; Henderson, 1959: 16, 35, 68; Grübler and Nakicenovic, 1991: 314; Rubinson, 1978: 46). In Britain the post-war decade witnessed less change in industrial policy, although analysts note a clear evolution away from wartime protection and towards the liberalism that would characterize the hegemonic power at the middle of the century (Overbeek, 1990: 37–8).

However, Britain shared with Germany a sharp increase in popular agitation in the decades after the defeat of the French. 'Thousands of disbanded soldiers and sailors returned to find unemployment in their villages' (Thompson, 1963: 603). The Belgian and French Revolutions of 1830 inspired new democratic movements in Britain and throughout the German states. Thompson (1963: 671) contends that in 1819 and again in 1832 revolution was possible 'because the Government was isolated and there were sharp differences within the ruling class'. But British conservative forces found unity in the programme to abolish Speenhamland and institute a wider free market in labour (amid arguments about the growing problem of new competitors abroad) while, in most states, German conservatives were able to keep the democratic agenda subservient to the push for industrial development; in both nations the typical depression-era arguments about the need to respond to international competition found favour (Bundestag, 1989: 65; Henderson, 1959: 39; Polanyi, 1957: 78).

The depression-era agitation of the poor reached its height between 1844 and 1848 and culminated in passive revolutions represented by the Ten Hours Act in Britain (1847) and the economic policies initiated by the revolutionary Frankfurt parliament of 1848, which continued to have an impact on Germany even after reaction set in to undo the political liberalizations enacted. In both countries the reformist programmes that brought together bourgeois and aristocratic forces came in response to the fundamentally new, *national* scale of popular movements, the Chartist democratic movement and the Owenite socialists in Britain and, in Germany, the myriad 'spillover' 'international' socialist and labour movements whose seeds could be found in specific industrial regions, especially among the machine-breaking Silesian weavers whose strikes reached their peak in the years of greatest hardship from 1844 to 1847 (Henderson, 1959: 148, 193, 227–31; Overbeek, 1990: 45; Polanyi, 1957: 166–7; Rubinson, 1978: 48; Thompson, 1963: 821).

The British and German intellectual leaders whose ideas underlay the passive revolutions of the late 1840s exemplify the kind of 'cadre class' 'critical liberals' pointed to by Gramscians. They embraced some aspects of market society, but rejected others. For example, in arguing for the anti-market, welfare-oriented Ten Hours Bill, Thomas Macaulay scoffed at what he considered the protectionist logic of the arguments about international competitiveness advanced by industrialists who defended longer hours. It was absurd to imagine that German firms with longer hours would benefit because they would leave the German working class to be an unproductive 'race of degenerate dwarfs' (Henderson, 1959: 148–9). Similarly, List, whose vision of national economy was only fully embraced in the late 1840s, was both an anti-market critic of liberalism (as he is usually caricatured in today's international political economy literature) and one of the most loyal adherents to Smith's argument that division of labour is limited by the extent of the market (Murphy, 1994: 62–8).

Germany gained from the securing of a physically larger market area after the revolution and reaction of 1848 left the German states and their continental neighbours with more secure, more unified social orders. William O. Henderson (1959: 147–8, 230–1) contends that the trade liberalizations which immediately followed had a much greater impact on investment decisions than the initial German liberalizations of the 1820s (the early German customs unions). Arguably, this was due to the mixture of carrots and sticks that the new government strategies provided. On the one hand, they enforced a level of inter-firm competition that encouraged something of the same kind of individualistic, success-oriented business strategies that developed at the same time in the United States (Guillén, 1994: 92). On the other hand, in Germany, as in the USA, governments provided much of the investment capital for the railway boom (Bundestag, 1989: 66; Henderson, 1959: 14).

German states did not, however, do as well as the Americans in encouraging social equity. Henderson (1959: 149, 242) comments that Macaulay's characterization of the abysmal conditions of German workers (quoted earlier) was somewhat valid when it was made and remained so for many years, despite improvements that began in the mid-1850s with the first of Prussia's precedent-setting 'welfare state' policies abolishing most child labour and requiring public schooling until age 14.

The fact that Prussian policies were not immediately generalized throughout the country reflects one final point which needs to be emphasized about this period: at the point at which both Germany and the United States first rose to global prominence as industrial powers, neither country was united under a strong central government. In this sense, strategies that contributed to the industrial era by the German Customs Union, the North German Federation, and even the federal government in Washington (Deudney,

1995) are indicators of the possible contributions that intergovernmental institutions would play in later periods. In both countries the existence of trans-regional popular movements help explain the continuing influence of the relatively weak central institutions on industrial change.

Entering the Second Industrial Revolution: continuing the pattern

Similarly, in both regions the transition to the next industrial era followed a similar path, beginning with the consolidation of greater power at the centre. Britain's path diverged, owing to the greater centrality of imperialism in its late nineteenth-century passive revolution.

In both the northeastern United States and Germany the Railway Age ended in clashes with less industrialized regions within the 'nation' – the American Civil War and Prussia's three wars: the nation-unifying war with Denmark over the latter's German territories (1862), the Austro-Prussian War (1866) which assured that the less industrialized, multi-national empire would remain outside the national system, and the Franco-Prussian War (1870), in which the German states won control of what were perceived as culturally 'German' territories that had been part of France (Agnew, 1987: 445–7; Henderson, 1959: 304–5; Rubinson, 1978: 56–60). Both Germany and the United States experienced short-lived post-war economic booms encouraged, in large part, by the deeper political unification of national market areas that had already been unified by an 'international' rail and telegraph system before the wars of the 1860s (Agnew, 1987: 49; Berghahn, 1994: 3). But the economic policies of the post-war governments in both countries suffered from too great a dominance by capitalist interests: the institution of 'government by, for, and of businessmen' in the United States (Agnew, 1987: 47) and what one prominent German historian called 'the [post-war] epidemic of unleashed greed for money making' in Germany (Bundestag, 1989: 175). In both countries, the late 1870s, 1880s, and early 1890s were marked by depression, downward pressure on wages, repressive policies in the defeated territories, and even greater capitalist hoarding after the bursting of speculative bubbles.

In both countries, rapid, consistent economic growth fuelled by large-scale investment in the new industries of the Second Industrial Revolution began only after a reformist turn in the policies of the national government. Those passive revolutions, in turn, were in part triggered by a transformation in the form of political organization by labour and by other segments of the popular masses.

In Germany the first key element of government policy protection of agriculture was put into effect in response to demands of elite farming interests during the grabbing and hoarding of the late 1870s and 1880s.

Nonetheless, Polanyi (1957: 185) is probably correct in saying that the policy benefited the rural masses as well. This was the first element of what historians have traditionally understood as the Prussian–Industrialist compact of 'social imperialism' that allowed Germany's unprecedented economic growth at the turn of the century (Reich, 1990: 12; Rubinson, 1978: 51–4). Prussian landowners gained protection and Prussian control of the state. Industrialists would later, in the 1890s, gain the extensions of the welfare state that would assure industrial peace, as well as the big military contracts (which only began to appear in 1898).

This traditional view underplays the importance of the growing political role of German labour. Prior to the repeal of the draconian anti-socialist laws, in 1890, Germany's shared culture, relatively small size, and newly created national labour market had already led to the emergence of a powerful labour movement. The movement, and its socialist political party, also stood at the centre of a 'globalizing' labour movement, the Second International, whose territory of greatest organization strength was nearly congruent with that of the European market area created by the early Public International Unions. After labour internationalism grew in the late 1880s and early 1890s, German government leaders attempted, in Gramsci's words, to 'decapitate' the German movement via the political and economic reforms of the early 1890s.

To a great extent, the German government was successful. Second Industrial Revolution German socialists, having been brought into the political process, worked with the government to create the expanded German welfare state (Berghahn, 1994: 247–51; Bundestag, 1989: 175). They also worked with industrialists to assure that German firms were really the first to embrace the principles of 'systematic management' which were so central to achieving the economies of scope and scale associated with the Second Industrial Revolution (Chandler, 1990: 393–41; Guillén, 1994: 93–5). Most of them were firms that embraced an export-oriented economic policy from the mid-1890s onward (Berghahn, 1994: 123; Borchardt, 1991: 9–12). They gained relatively little from the German government's increasing turn toward an illiberal imperialism. In fact, the major German 'first movers' in the key Second Industrial Revolution – electrical and chemical industries – relied much more on the inter-imperial private market cemented by the late nineteenth-century international organization system, the Public International Unions (Murphy, 1994: 126–7).

An additional role was played by international institutions in the Second Industrial Revolution in both Germany and the United States. The civil servants, social reformers and social analysts who took the lead in creating the proto-welfare state policies of the 1890s found mutual support through the international organizations concerned with social welfare that were part of the Public International Unions. In Germany this was especially clear; after all, most of the first international labour and social rights conventions had been sponsored by the Kaiser in the early 1890s when he was flirting with the idea of finding his role in history as the protector of the workers (Murphy, 1994: 60, 70).

The United Kingdom played a much less active role than either the USA or Germany in the late nineteenth-century wave of innovation in international organization. In the 1880s depths of the 'long wave trough' the British government did play a central role in establishing commissions for Turkey and other debtor nations that were designed to protect the international financial markets (Polanyi, 1957: 15). But in most other fields British leadership was absent. This lack of intergovernmental innovation was of a piece with the marginal and relatively slow changes in all the strategies that contributed to governance in the Britain of the Second Industrial Revolution. Arguably, Britain's late nineteenth-century passive revolution began earlier than the similar developments in Germany and the United States. Overbeek (1990: 47–52) contends that the surge of Irish nationalism in the 1870s (triggered, in large part, by the effects of the depression), and the recurrent fear of growing unity between the Irish struggle and the labour struggle, strengthened a 'social imperialist' political and economic project that defined the country's business and government strategies for the next fifty years. Government looked to the rapid development of Britain's new overseas empire as the source of rising real wages and new migration opportunities for the poor. As a result, the most successful British firms of the period were those tied to the import of colonial goods, or those, such as Unilever, that operated within the empire at both ends of the commodity chain turning African palm oil into soaps sold in Bombay as well as Birmingham (Chandler, 1990: 378). The dominant management strategy of the period, emphasizing low fixed investment and high profitability, really required little of the shift to systematic or scientific management that characterized the most successful German and American firms (Guillén, 1994: 211; cf. Veblen, 1966: 117–22).

Britain's smoother and earlier shift into a workable late nineteenth-century political economy had its downside. Overbeek (among others) traces Britain's 'hegemonic decline' to the late nineteenth-century decisions to emphasize the advantages of imperial business rather than to compete head to head with the Germans and Americans in the newer industries. Certainly, Britain's turn-of-the-century social order was somewhat more vulnerable to internal conflict than the other two. George Dangerfield (1961: 217–21) argues that the crisis that ended that social order began much earlier than the First World War, in 1910, as industrial wages began to drop in the 'attack of Capital upon Labour' that anti-imperialist critical liberals had predicted would be the necessary consequence of an imperial system that did not invest in high wages and high productivity at home. As Dangerfield (1961: 402) points out, a planned general strike of 1914 that might well have united all three groups that were in a growing, militant conflict against the British social order – labour, Irish nationalists, and suffragists – was only averted by the outbreak of the war.

Into the Automobile Age: a moment of militarism, then the pattern returns

During the First World War the development sequences of Germany, the United Kingdom and the United States became linked. It is, in fact, the linked experience of these three countries from 1914 onward that has provided most of the evidence for the wide-angle lens picture of globalization and governance strategies that Gramscians have developed. Not surprisingly, the picture tends to stay the same as we move down to the level of core regions. The First World War marked an early stage in a long period of conflicts linked to the industrial development of the prior growth era. Fundamentally, the conflict was one of overlap and clash of industrial economies – conflicts over markets where their industries competed to sell their goods, conflicts over access to resources-providing peripheries, and conflicts reinforced by arms races fuelled, in part, by competitive industrial policies. In the inter-war years, when the conflicts were held in abeyance even if they were not resolved, the reassertion of capitalist power led to a brief period of economic growth (whose beginning and end differed slightly in different countries) as well as the re-emergence into prominence of the class conflicts that had been submerged by war. The 'casino capitalism' of the 1920s proved ephemeral and the New York stock market crash ushered in a period of relatively parochial government economic policies, especially those expressed through international and transnational financial institutions which were, in Polanyi's (1957: 233) words, willing to sacrifice 'free governments' in 'vain deflationary efforts' that did not restore the 'free markets' that their liberal fundamentalist advocates felt they were protecting. Instead:

> A cellular process was introduced into human society . . . the frantic efforts to protect the external value of the currency as a medium of exchange drove the peoples, against their will, into an autarkic economy. The whole arsenal of restrictive trade measures, which formed a radical departure from traditional economics, was actually the outcome of conservative free trade purposes. (Polanyi, 1957: 24–7)

The states that first thrived in this situation were those the least hampered by liberal institutions that did not fit the new order:

> Thus Germany, once defeated, was in a position to recognize the hidden

shortcomings of the nineteenth century order, and to employ this knowledge to speed the destruction of that order. A kind of sinister intellectual superiority accrued to those of her statesmen in the thirties who turned their minds to the task of disruption, which often extended to the development of new methods of finance, trade, war, and social organization, in the course of their attempt to force matters into the trend of their policies. (Polanyi, 1957: 29)

Germany and northeast Japan moved out of the Great Depression much more quickly than the UK and the northeastern USA, in part because the illiberal regimes quickly embraced national champions and the newest systems of scientific management (Gordon, 1991: 271; Hart, 1992: 58, 201; Johnson, 1982: 29; Reich, 1990: 61, 200, 278).

Yet Polanyi is correct in arguing that liberal states rapidly learned to shift away from the market, although in Britain's case the move away from liberal fundamentalism – which began as the country went off the gold standard in 1932 – initially only led to a re-establishment of the empire-oriented industrial policy with little of the 'social' benefits of the turn-of-the-century version of the same policy (Overbeek, 1990: 63, 81). Nonetheless, British firms began to adopt a new 'human relations' orientation to management, which became part of the successful post-war strategy mix (Guillén, 1994: 220–2).

Despite similar moves away from the market that characterized the historical bloc formed in the United States before the Second World War, the continuing commitment of the US government, business and labour to some of the principles of liberalism helps explain the ultimate triumph of the American model over the social models of its militarist wartime adversaries. The German and Japanese paradigms involved a privileged economic core and an exploited periphery. In both cases the size of the privileged core was restricted by nationality of lead nation; their models had no room for co-operation with other capitalist industrial states. The outward orientation of the American model, a consequence (in part) of the growing significance of the country's large 'international' business community, committed the US government to the promotion of the principles of its own domestic historical bloc on to other core regions. Thus, the American victory led to the promotion of mass production and mass consumption, systematic management and human relations, and anti-communist unions and popular parties, to all parts of the industrialized capitalist world. (In most cases, this was done with the help of international institutions.)

In the defeated nations the political part of this formula led to the elimination of the older, militarist forces. It allowed social democratic and conservative liberal parties (which had arisen at the same time as the militarist forces) to dominate the national political system after the war (Fukutake, 1989: 78; Gordon, 1991: 340; van der Pijl, 1994: 174–5). At the level of the firm the American policy buttressed the commitment of West German firms to scientific management and encouraged the borrowing of the latest technologies and management methods which was so characteristic of Japanese companies in the 1950s and early 1960s (Chandler, 1990: 617; Guillén, 1994: 126). Relative to the popular classes, the American policy helped return German labour to the privileged position it enjoyed before the Nazis' rise (Hart, 1992: 182–8).

Some observers even argue that victorious Britain did not fare as well. Had the country been defeated, it might have had the 'benefit' of the forcible removal of the unproductive characteristics of the old social imperial industrial order (Olson, 1982: 76; Overbeek, 1990: 112). There are at least two difficulties with this conclusion. First, the USA actually did play a role in undermining the imperialist forces within Britain, for example during the Suez Crisis (Overbeek, 1990: 99–100). Second, contrary to the views of some authors, the Americans did not break up all the combinations of vested interests within West Germany and Japan; rather, they supported a coherent mix of strategies of labour, business and government in each country, based on what was historically possible. Thus, for example, in both states the actual result was somewhat less 'liberal' than what may have been desired by some American intellectual leaders, although the mix may, as a consequence, have been more effective (cf. Reich, 1990: 61).

In any event, in Britain, as much as in West Germany and Japan, the post-war policy mix led to rapid and massive investment especially by the leading firms of the 'Automobile Age'. Initially, everywhere, much of that investment was American, and it was spurred by the Marshall Plan and the stability engineered in Japan and western Europe by other aspects of the victors' interventions in the market. Along with that investment came the post-war 'Golden Years' of relatively widespread prosperity.

Waiting for a passive revolution?

West German writers are apt to argue that the first cracks in the post-war historical bloc appear in the disenchantment with materialist culture and student protests of the late 1960s (Bundestag, 1989: 415–19). In Britain they were the economic crises faced by the Wilson and Heath governments at the beginning of the 1970s (Overbeek, 1990: 133). Whatever the initial triggers, the oil crisis of 1973 became a key break throughout the OECD. Adjustment to the crisis occurred at different rates in the different regions, but in each case it resulted in a 'neo-liberal' shift in governmental economic policy and the increasing prominence of financial capital. What can the earlier transitions tell us about when and how this slow-growth era will end?

First, and perhaps most significantly, most of the earlier transitions have been directly associated with 'passive revolutions', reformist changes in government and business strategy that have taken place only after a 'successful' strategic political reorientation by at least some popular social forces (at home or abroad). 'Success' in this case is manifest simply by increased fears on the part of the privileged that a more radical transformation might be possible. Thus, the first lesson might be that some strategic reorientation on the part of socialist, labour and other mass-oriented movements will be essential before the 'need' for reformed business and government strategies is recognized.

A number of the cases suggest that the most appropriate change in popular strategies would involve their own 'globalization'. The reorientation of mass movements to a national level helps explain the Railway Age transitions in Germany and the United States and the Second Industrial Revolution transition in Japan. The threat of a truly unified 'Irish nationalist–British labour' movement contributed to the politics of British social imperialism. The centrality of German socialists in the increasingly significant Second International helped trigger the simultaneous transition on the continent. Fears of the Third International played into the Automobile Age transition in all four regions. Today, in Europe, the development of a continent-wide popular movement is probably an essential precondition for the European-wide reformist changes in government and business strategy that would make the next industrial age possible.

Yet it is also clear from the earlier cases that it was not just the 'globalization' of popular strategies that engendered the reformist responses – it was the substantial fear of an unacceptable social transformation engendered by the *success* of some of those strategies that made the difference. That is why changes in popular strategy that took place *abroad* were also vitally important.

The actual 'industrial labour' of the economy administered by the core regions is found not only some distance within other core regions – it is also found, increasingly, in the rapidly growing semi-periphery. William I. Robinson's (1996) study of the recent wave of 'democratization' around the world could be read as suggesting that the successful transformation of popular strategies – the key to the next industrial cycle – has already begun to take place through the wave of radical popular democracy movements throughout the semi-periphery in 1980s and early 1990s. Moreover, Robinson's analysis points to the beginning of a sort of 'passive revolution' that has come in response, for that is how he understands the Western and, especially, the US policy of promoting the more limited democratic transitions that have taken place in so many countries over the last ten years. As Gramscians would expect, the international organization system has played a central role in this process. Secretary General Boutros-Ghali (1995) makes a strong case that it has become *the* central function of the United Nations.

One significant question for future research concerns the degree to which the promotion of what Robinson calls 'low intensity' democracy in the rapidly industrializing semi-periphery has led transnational firms to make the kind of large-scale, equity-enhancing investment in new industries that has been associated with the 'build' phase of previous industrial cycles. I am sceptical. Certainly there is no sign of any lessening of neo-liberal fundamentalism in Western Europe, the United States, or Japan as a result of the recent (partial) victories of democracy movements in Eastern Europe and the Third World. Nonetheless, if large scale investments have begun to take place in the rapidly industrializing world it may mean that the incoherence of Europe's current business, government and labour 'globalization' strategies will matter little in the long run. Instead of exerting 'adaptive pressure' on the societal models of the rest of the world, Europe would join the rest of the world in being subject to the pressure of more productive, profit-enhancing social models developed elsewhere.

Acknowledgements

I am grateful to Robert Cox, Stephen Gill, Henk Overbeek, Herman Schwartz, and Kees van der Pijl for comments on an earlier version of a longer paper reporting research on all four cases.

References

Agnew, J. (1987) *The United States in the World-Economy: A Regional Geography.* Cambridge: Cambridge University Press.

Berghahn, V. R. (1994) *Imperial Germany, 1871–1914: Economy, Society, Culture, and Politics.* Providence, RI: Berghahn Books.

Biersteker, T. J. (1994) Globalization as a mode of operation: conceptual changes within firms, states, and international institutions. Watson Institute for International Studies, Brown University, Providence, RI, June.

Borchardt, K. (1991) *Perspectives on Modern German Economic History and Policy.* Cambridge: Cambridge University Press.

Bornschier, V. (1995) West European unification and the future structure of the core, in C. K. Chase-Dunn and V. Bornschier (eds), *The Future of Hegemonic Rivalry.* Baltimore, MD: Johns Hopkins University.

Boutros-Ghali, Boutros (1995) Democracy: a newly recognized imperative, *Global Governance*, **1**, 1–13.

Bundestag (1989) *Questions on German History: Ideas, Forces, Decisions – From 1800 to the Present.* Bonn: Bundestag Publications Section.

Cerny, P. G. (1995) Globalization and the changing logic of collective action, *International Organization*, **49**.

Chandler, A. D., Jr with T. Hikino (1990) *Scale and Scope: The Dynamics of Industrial Capitalism*. Cambridge, MA: Harvard University Press.

Cox, R. W. (1987) *Production, Power, and World Order*. New York: Columbia University Press.

Cox, R. W. (1992) The United Nations, globalization, and democracy. The 1992 John W. Holmes Memorial Lecture. Providence, RI: Academic Council on the United Nations System.

Dangerfield, G. (1961) *The Strange Death of Liberal England: 1910–1914*. New York: Capricorn Books.

Deudney, D. (1995) The Philadelphia system: sovereignty, arms control, and balance of power in the American states-union, circa 1787–1861, *International Organization*, **49**, 191–228.

Flamant, M. and Singer-Kérel, J. (1968) *Modern Economic Crises and Recessions*. New York: Harper Colophon Books.

Forgacs, D. (ed.) (1988) *An Antonio Gramsci Reader*. New York: Schocken Books.

Fukutake, T. (1989) *The Japanese Social Structure: Its Evolution in the Modern Century*. Tokyo: University of Tokyo Press.

Gill, S. (1990) *American Hegemony and the Trilateral Commission*. Cambridge: Cambridge University Press.

Goldstein, J. (1988) *Long Cycles: Prosperity and War in the Modern Age*. New Haven, CT: Yale University Press.

Gordon, A. (1991) *Labour and Imperial Democracy in Prewar Japan*. Berkeley, CA: University of California Press.

Grübler, A. and Nakicenovic, N. (1991) Long waves, technological diffusion, and substitution, *Review*, **14**, 313–42.

Guillén, M. F. (1994) *Models of Management: Work, Authority, and Organization in Comparative Perspective*. Chicago: University of Chicago Press.

Hart, J. A. (1992) *Rival Capitalists: International Competitiveness in the United States, Japan, and Western Europe*. Ithaca, NY: Cornell University Press.

Henderson, W. O. (1959) *The Zollverein*, 2nd edn. Chicago: Quadrangle Books.

Johnson, C. (1982) *MITI and the Japanese Economic Miracle: The Growth of Industrial Policy 1925–1975*. Stanford, CA: Stanford University Press.

Kobrin, S. J. (1995) *Beyond Symmetry: State Sovereignty in a Networked Global Economy*. Department of Management, The Wharton School, University of Pennsylvania, Philadelphia, June.

Murphy, C. N. (1994) *International Organization and Industrial Change: Global Governance since 1850*. Cambridge: Polity Press.

Namenwirth, Z. (1973) The wheels of time and the interdependence of value change, *Journal of Interdisciplinary History*, **3**, 649–83.

Olson, M. (1982) *The Rise and Decline of Nations: Stagflation and Social Rigidities*. New Haven, CT: Yale University Press.

Overbeek, H. (1990) *Global Capitalism and National Decline: The Thatcher Decade in Perspective*. London: Unwin Hyman.

Overbeek, H. and van der Pijl, K. (1993) Restructuring capital and restructuring hegemony: neo-liberalism and the unmaking of the post-war order, in Henk Overbeek (ed.), *Restructuring Hegemony in the Global Political Economy: The Rise of Transnational Neoliberalism*. London: Routledge.

Polanyi, K. (1957) *The Great Transformation: The Political and Economic Origin of Our Time*. Boston, MA: Beacon Press.

Reich, S. (1990) *The Fruits of Fascism: Postwar Prosperity in Historical Perspective*. Ithaca, NY: Cornell University Press.

Reilly, R. (1979) *William Pitt the Younger*. New York: G. P. Putnam's Sons.

Robinson, W. I. (1996) *Promoting Polyarchy: Globalization and US Intervention, Hegemony, and Democracy in the Twenty-first Century*. Cambridge: Cambridge University Press.

Rosenau, J. N. (1995) Governance in the twenty-first century, *Global Governance*, **1**, 13–44.

Rubinson, R. (1978) Political transformation in Germany and the United States, in B. H. Kaplan (ed.), *Social Change in the Capitalist World Economy*. Beverly Hills: Sage.

Sterman, J. D. (1992) *Long Wave Decline and the Politics of Depression*. Systems Dynamics Group, Sloan School of Management, Massachusetts Institute of Technology, Cambridge, MA, October.

Thompson, E. P. (1963) *The Making of the English Working Class*. New York: Pantheon Books.

van der Pijl, K. (1984) *The Making of an Atlantic Ruling Class*. London: Verso.

van der Pijl, K. (1990) Socialisation and social democracy in the state system, in W. Koole, M. Krätke, H. Overbeek, R. Schildmeijer and K. van der Pijl (eds), *After the Crisis: Political Regulation and the Capitalist Crisis*. Department of International Relations, University of Amsterdam, March.

van der Pijl, K. (1994) The Reich resurrected? Continuity and change in German expansion, in R. P. Palan and B. Gills (eds), *Transcending the State–Global Divide: A Neostructuralist Agenda in International Relations*. Boulder, CO: Lynne Rienner Publishers.

Veblen, T. (1966) *Imperial Germany and the Industrial Revolution*. Ann Arbor, MI: Ann Arbor Paperbacks.

Weber, R. (1981) Society and economy in the Western world system, *Social Forces*, **59**, 1130–48.

Further reading

Fligstein, N. (1990) *The Transformation of Corporate Control*. Cambridge, MA: Harvard University Press.

Reinsch, P. S. (1911) *The Public International Unions*. Boston, MA: Ginn.

Rosenberg, N. (1994) *Exploring the Black Box: Technology, Economics, and History*. New York: Cambridge University Press.

Sterman, J. D. and Mosekilde, E. (1994) Business cycles and long waves: a behavioral disequilibrium perspective, in Willi Semmler (ed.), *Business Cycles: Theory and Empirical Methods*. Boston, MA: Kluwer Academic Publishers.

10

European Integration and Globalization

GEORGE ROSS

Globalization and the beginnings of European integration

A half century has passed since modern European integration began. In the aftermath of the Second World War, European nations sought workable formulas for new co-operation, and eventually six among them – Italy, France, West Germany, Belgium, The Netherlands and tiny Luxembourg – agreed on the 1957 Treaty of Rome that established the European Economic Community (now the European Union, EU).[1] Much lay behind this search, including a genuine desire to prevent Europe from regressing to bloody warfare. Yet the origins of European integration may best be seen in the light of globalizing tendencies at work at the time, even if the word was not used at the time.

Three globalizing processes and the new Europe

Arguably the most important influence on the coming of European integration was the emergence of the United States as an economic superpower. Initially the Americans seemed more concerned with setting up a viable 'globalized' trading regime than with regional integration. US leadership thus reconstructed the capitalist world's financial operations in the Bretton Woods system, involving US commitment to make the dollar a global reserve currency backed by a fixed gold standard. It also was decisive in founding a World Bank and the International Monetary Fund to grant individual trading nations the financial leeway to run occasional international payments deficits and to police the system in the interests of balanced international accounts. The General Agreement on Tariffs and Trade (GATT), a multilateral organization to promote free trade, also came from this period.

The Europeans, flat broke after the war, needed to rebuild but they had little to trade and no money to pay for what they bought. The Americans very quickly got involved in the loan business. The coming of the Marshall

Plan in 1947 formalized and elaborated the American role as financier of European recovery, making billions of dollars available for the reconstruction of European economies, provided mainly that the Europeans co-ordinated plans for putting the money to good use. Only Western Europeans signed on, however. The USSR and its satellite countries, who were invited, refused to participate. The Plan also prodded the Europeans to greater regional economic co-operation through the Organization for European Economic Cooperation (OEEC).[2] In general, the Europeans used Marshall Plan aid in ways that suited their national goals. But America's globalizing purposes had to be heeded.

The outbreak of Cold War, the systematic confrontation between the United States and the Soviet Union, coincided with the Marshall Plan and involved a second, different process of 'globalizing', this one geo-strategic.[3] Cold War mobilization and rearmament formed the background for European integration. The biggest step was taken by the USA itself when it committed huge new resources for the most massive peacetime military build-up in its history. The USA then promoted and largely paid for European nations to follow through the formation of the North Atlantic Alliance, founded in 1949. American troops and matériel were stationed strategically throughout Europe under a unified North Atlantic Treaty Organization (NATO) command structure. In essence, the security environment within which European integration began had become a global one dominated by superpower rivalry in general, and, from the point of view of future EU members, specifically by American power. Put another way, the bulk of European national military capacity was pooled into new transnational arrangements over which Europeans themselves had but minimal control, a loss of sovereignty that happened long before recent economic globalization.

The 1950 Schuman Plan, which led to the European Coal and Steel Community (ECSC), the first breakthrough to integration, was an indirect product of this new and globalizing economic, political and security setting. The immediate ideas came from the fertile brain of Jean Monnet, but the constraints which made producing such ideas necessary – American pressure to resolve outstanding post-war economic and political differences between the French and the Germans and thus normalize the new Germany and allow it to participate in European defence in the Cold War context – were global. In the immediate wake of ECSC success, advocates of integration decided to promote the 'Monnet method' of sectoral integration with supranational ambitions in other areas, failing in the beginning, most spectacularly with the European Defence Community (EDC).[4] Energy returned quickly, however, under the leadership of the Belgian Paul-Henri Spaak, with Monnet in the background. The Spaak Report of April 1956 suggested 'a European common market ... [leading to] a vast zone with a common economic policy'.

The two Treaties of Rome in 1957 officially founded the European Economic Community (EEC) and Euratom (the European Atomic Energy Authority). Underlying the success were deals between France and Germany, themselves undergirded by the logics of the Cold War. A common market was at the core of the new EU to remove barriers to trade and establish rules for promoting trading relationships among member states. It would also create a common commercial policy towards third countries and abolish 'obstacles to freedom of movement for persons, services and capital' among member states. Its other general objectives included common policies in agriculture, transport, a 'system ensuring that competition in the common market is not distorted', and procedures for co-ordinating economic policy and controlling balance of payments disequilibria. There were also a European Social Fund and a European Investment Bank to promote the development of less developed regions and 'association of the overseas countries and territories'. Member states would be obligated to harmonize their legal systems on common market matters.

The initial period of implementation of the Rome Treaty revealed yet a third form of globalization, the transnational diffusion of an American model of consumerism and mass production. Europeans began to taste the joys of cars, household appliances, seaside vacations and television. Fordist manufacturing was the driving force, usually in large 'national champion' companies. By the 1960s average growth in EU member states was an impressive 5+ per cent per year and trade among them grew even more rapidly than economic growth itself.[5]

Paradoxical globalization and national specificity

This third form of globalization was paradoxical, however. For the period of the great post-war boom, from 1950 to 1974, the diffusion of the American model helped reconfigure European *national* developmental models, along with a solidification of democratic institutions, new commitments to social justice and the redistribution of wealth.[6] Where did European integration fit, then? These national islands of new Fordist consumerism were highly interdependent. Economically, each traded more and more with the others. Integration decisively helped increase such trade. Politically the Germans needed Europe to rebuild self-respect and credibility after the Nazi era. Others needed Europe to keep the Germans in place. Everyone needed the United States for military help in the context of Cold War, and the United States wanted the Europeans to co-ordinate.

This confluence of globalizing and nationalizing trends meant that European integration and national goals coexisted with difficulty. The EU's designers had clearly nourished hopes that the integrationist activists they were letting loose in Brussels, particularly at the European Commission, would rapidly 'Europeanize' more and more activities. They also counted on functional linkages between policy areas to create a snowball towards greater integration. National leaders, promoting their own national models, had little desire to see the EU's mandate enlarged, however. The problems crystallized as the new EU carried out the busy schedule of activities prescribed by the Rome Treaty. Constructing the customs union went well, the EU negotiated for its members in the General Agreement on Tariffs and Trade (GATT) and certain other processes were smooth. Dealing with matters which could interfere in the internal business of member states was more of a problem, however. In particular regulatory issues like competition policy, social protection and regional development presented challenges. Setting up the Common Agricultural Policy (CAP) was perhaps most complicated.

The treaties had proposed that after January 1966, the Council of Ministers would be able to decide certain matters by qualified majority, implying that a nation might be outvoted. This was anathema to President Charles de Gaulle of France, who forced everyone into the so-called 'Luxembourg Compromise' of January 1966. After this point unanimity became the EU decision-making rule for nearly two decades. De Gaulle spoke not only for France. Most member state governments were at the epicentre of national economic and social regulatory mechanisms and in a period when national trajectories in macroeconomic, industrial and social policy were successful there was little real demand for a major transfer of regulatory activities to a supranational level. EU institutional and policy development thus stalled after the mid-1960s at about the level which its member states needed. The Common Market became a handmaiden to continental Europe's post-war boom, a useful tool for certain purposes, but unwelcome in other areas. The further Europeanization of economic processes that the Rome Treaty had originally proposed, the movement of capital, for example, was not on the cards, since it would have undercut the key components of the different national models.

In the early 1970s, after the first, 'Common Market' phase of implementing the Rome Treaty was completed, European idealism re-emerged. Leaders thus set out plans to 'widen' the EU by including the British, Danish, Irish and Norwegians and to 'deepen' it by giving the Community larger budgetary powers, foreign policy co-ordination and Economic and Monetary Union (EMU). The EU enlarged from six to nine members in 1973 (the Norwegians voted against in a national referendum). There were ambitious new plans in regional development (through the creation of the European Regional

Development Fund) and social policy as well. The world around Europe was changing, however, leading to policy divergence between key member states. The French, still determined to minimize EU supranationality, disagreed with the Germans about Economic and Monetary Union. *Détente* in the Cold War renewed debate about foreign policy issues. Most importantly, enlargement to Britain was troublesome. The British quickly became chronic EU nay-sayers, particularly on budgetary matters. Monetary policy also became a troubling issue, traceable to a sea-change in the post-war order, the collapse of the American-administered Bretton Woods monetary system.[7] The new financial world brought fluctuating, often volatile, exchange rates which made EU members more vulnerable. The EU first agreed in 1972 to establish a currency 'snake' – an arrangement to keep EU currencies within 2.5 per cent of one another within a broader 'tunnel' of exchange values. The snake disappeared in the fallout from the 1973 oil shock. The oil price rise fed an already inflationary environment, causing prices to jump rapidly. Efforts to fine-tune this problem contributed to the perplexing policy environment of 'stagflation' – simultaneous inflation and sluggish growth.

This was a turning point in Europe's post-war history. The boom was ending, growth levels declined and unemployment began to grow. From this point European economies would have great difficulty sustaining near-full employment, maintaining spending on social programmes and keeping their public finances in order. When EU member states initially improvised on old themes to cope, usually assuming that the new conditions were transitory, it made matters worse. Productivity, profit margins and investment levels declined and European industry began to lose competitive advantage. Europe's 1970s failures were constructed of the same national materials as earlier successes. The 1960s had deepened tendencies toward inflexible labour markets, inflation and statist economic management, creating patterns that shaped responses in the 1970s. Organized labour had a clear interest in protecting jobs and post-war reforms in industrial relations and social policy. The political left, whose strength was based largely on labour, had its own stake in post-war strategies. Capital had depended upon the national state for favours, protection and subsidies. Finally, state managers had their own interests to advance. Political structures and coalitions at the coming of the crisis therefore led national governments virtually everywhere towards accentuation of the specifically national developmental strategies that earlier had worked so successfully.

Proactivity or an accidental approach to globalization? The EU to Maastricht

By the end of the 1970s, EU members had begun to *need* 'more Europe'. Convinced, however, that the national development strategies which had worked so well during the post-war boom could be revitalized, most member states did not *want* more Europe. Policy divergence grew. International trade expanded less rapidly than it had and intra-EC trade expansion virtually stopped. The 'Common Market', the EU's first stage, ultimately rose and fell as an instrument of a capitalist 'Europe of States'. Accounting for the renewal of European integration which came next constitutes an intriguing puzzle. Many in the globalization debate claim that it should be explained in terms of globalization – European nations returned to integration because changes in their international surroundings obliged them to. Another answer, one which I find more adequate, is that European nations, reacting to the collapse of their earlier efforts to conciliate national political economies with a more open trade setting through the Common Market, renewed European integration to cope with this collapse. In the process they probably promoted globalization rather more than responding to it.

'1992' and the return of European integration

First, however, we should review the story. In the mid-1980s an extraordinary turnaround began. The return of energetic European integration was part of a new strategy to de-emphasize the role of national states in economic life and create a regional economic bloc structured around a liberated single European market. The shift involved first of all an admission by European elites that post-war national models could no longer be sustained. The key moment came when France, which with Germany took the lead, abandoned its post-1981 strategy of 'social democracy in one country' in spring 1983. In the first half of 1984, under the French Presidency of the Council of Ministers, the dimensions of France's shift to a 'Europe option' became clearer. At Fontainebleau in spring 1984 Mitterrand began to untie the EU's knots, in particular the chronic dispute over the 'British Check'. This made fruitful discussion possible in other areas, in particular enlarging the Community to Portugal and Spain. Jacques Delors, a former French Minister of Finances, was appointed President of the European Commission.

It was the Delors European Commission which devised the new EU agenda in its 1985 White Paper on Completing the Internal Market. This, the '1992' programme, was a list of 279 measures to unify the EU's largely separate national markets into an 'area without internal boundaries in which the free movement of goods, persons, services and capital is ensured'.[8] The White Paper also included a timetable which scheduled the sequencing of legislation over two consecutive Commission terms (eight years), hence '1992'. The European Council of June 1985 then agreed to call an 'intergovernmental conference' (IGC) which resulted in treaty changes called the Single European Act (SEA) which linked completing the Single Market to a change in EC decision-making procedures involving 'qualified majority' decisions in most White Paper areas and an extension of the amending powers of the European Parliament.[9] It also proposed an extended list of areas in which the EU could act, including regional development policy ('economic and social cohesion'), research and technological development, and the environment.

'1992' was a quick political success. Business liked it and this helped change a morose climate. Governments in the poorer parts of the EC/EU liked it because of the SEA's promise for increased development aid. Public opinion was benignly positive at first, largely because the Single Market policies were cost-free in the short run (since they would take considerable time to be legislated and come into effect and only then be felt). Organized labour, already taking a huge beating, was unhappier, worrying about the 'social dumping' implications of '1992', but the Delors Commission tried hard to placate its anxieties. The most important source of support for the new Single Market policies, however, was good economic luck. At about the point when awareness emerged that something new was happening in Brussels, European economies started to turn up, investment and business confidence rose. This was as much coincidence as cause and effect, but Europe's new activism could then be associated with a renewal of growth, prosperity and job creation.

The '1992' programme brought a number of ambitious complementary programmes, facilitated by the newly promising setting created by Single Market enthusiasm. The first, perhaps most significant, came in the 'Delors Budgetary Package' of 1987.[10] The 'reform of the Structural Funds', in part a payoff to new Spanish and Portuguese EU members, brought significant commitment to redistribution between richer and poorer member states. Resources would be co-ordinated on a set of prior objectives, the budget for regional aid was to be doubled over the period through 1992, when it would amount to 25 per cent of Community spending and the use of these funds would be planned, mainly by the Commission.[11]

Proposals for Economic and Monetary Union (EMU) came next, in 1987. EMU, to include a common monetary policy, a powerful European Central Bank and a single European currency, was advertised as the logical culmination of the Single Market. Without EMU, currency fluctuations and monetary policy divergence could cause instability and tempt member states to back away from single market commitments. The new campaign began in 1987 with the commissioning of the Delors Report, which, when submitted in 1989, proposed a three-stage path toward EMU plus a new Inter-governmental Conference to redo the EU treaty to fit in EMU. The deeper logic of the EMU plan was political. Pooling monetary and portions of economic policy sovereignty would necessitate supranational control over a wide range of economic matters. The single currency, when it came, would completely remove the tool of currency revaluation from national policy makers.

Up to this point the overwhelming logic of the renewal of European integration was 'market building', the elimination of barriers to trade and competition by deregulation and liberalization. Efforts made by various actors, in particular the Delors Commission, to promote 'spillover' into areas of market re-regulation at European level were relatively limited, with the one important exception of the reform of the structural funds. In particular, hopes that the redistributive effects of the new Single Market would facilitate new initiatives in Euro-level social policy fell rather flat. The May 1989 'Community Charter of Fundamental Social Rights', or Social Charter, was a 'solemn commitment' on the part of member states – only eleven, given furious British opposition – to a set of wage-earner rights based on unfulfilled social promises the Community's treaty base already contained. The Commission quickly produced an action programme to implement it but unanimity decision rules meant that little beyond workplace health and safety proposals, decided by qualified majority, could get through. The Single European Act also included a new Article 118B stating that 'the Commission shall endeavour to develop the dialogue between management and labour at European level which could, if the two sides consider it desirable, lead to relations based on agreement'. The 'social dialogue' which followed did not produce many concrete results, however.

By 1991, the Maastricht negotiating year, the renewal of European integration had reached fever pitch. The Commission was producing unprecedented amounts of legislation to implement the '1992' programme, implementing the reform of regional policy and trying to innovate in social policy areas. The GATT Uruguay Round talks were reaching a critical point and the EU and the United States were staring one another down about the international trade effects of the CAP.[12] The Community also had to respond to the end of the Cold War and German unification. Last, but not least, the member states had committed themselves to two new Intergovernmental Conferences to change the EU treaties. The climax came with the controversial Maastricht Treaty.[13]

At Maastricht, getting a deal on EMU was relatively easy because the 1989 Delors Report had set out a programme which the talks followed. Even the sticking points were predictable. The Germans, asked to give up the deutsch-mark, wanted EMU to provide iron-clad guarantees about price stability and financial responsibility. The British opposed EMU. The Spanish wanted commitment to more North–South redistribution. These hurdles were all overcome. Discussions on 'political union', held separately, were another story. The idea of talking about political union – a common foreign and security policy, greater democratization of the Community, more efficient institutions and coherence in monetary, economic and political action – had emerged only in spring 1990. This gave very little time to make the careful preparations needed to make interstate negotiations orderly.

The Maastricht negotiations brought out classic disagreements about the desirable nature of European integration between 'federalists' and 'inter-governmentalists' and between member states which wanted European integration in the political area and those which preferred minimalism. The proposed 'common foreign and security policy' divided 'Atlanticists' insisting upon the pre-eminence of NATO from those who desired independent European positions. How the EU might be given greater 'democratic legiti-macy' was murky as well. The Germans wanted to give more power to the European Parliament. Others, including the French, wanted greater involve-ment for national parliaments. Finally, there were chronic differences between North and South over development help – the South wanted more and the North did not want to pay.

The final Maastricht document (135 pages, 17 'Protocols', various addenda and 33 separate declarations) was difficult even for insiders to read. It was also problematic in a 'constitutional' sense, since it divided up essential matters among three 'pillars', each with different decision rules. Its substance was the most problematic matter of all, however. EMU would mean that member states would no longer control their currencies and monetary policies. Europe, or rather Europe's proposed new central banking system, would gain much of what the member states lost. Even before full EMU came they would no longer be able to adjust the value of their currencies, run large deficits, allow high levels of inflation and build up large debts, all techniques that had traditionally been useful to cushion domestic economies against changes coming from outside. The range of macro-economic management instruments available to national states would be narrowed to direct taxation policies (indirect taxation being part of the Single Market and hence also guided from European levels). The political union results were less clear. What Maastricht said and what it led to were certain to be different since much of the treaty was vague and 'evolutive', an EU word for vague and open-ended. The CFSP provisions left almost everything to future politicking. The defence area was an empty shell fraught with future disagreements. The ultimate meanings of other Maastricht provisions, the clauses on 'European citizenship', for example, or the 'third pillar' on justice and internal affairs, were virtually impossible to foresee.

Globalization and renewed European integration: a false correlation?

It is all too facile to argue from the present back to the mid-1980s and claim that renewed European integration was in response to globalization. In fact, the record shows that this is far from true. It is important to ask first about the motives of key European actors during this period. Did they think that they were responding to globalization? Or, alternatively, did they perceive themselves as anticipating globalizing trends proactively?

Jacques Delors, President of the European Commission, was clearly one such leader, and in this period he was wont to announce that rapid new European integration was a matter of 'survival or decline'. Without it Europe would soon be swamped by the Americans and the Japanese.[14] The discourse which Delors most often used was significant. Completing the Single Market, EMU and the rest were, to Delors, proactive efforts to prepare Europe to respond effectively to changes in the transnational setting, but not to globalization as currently defined. Delors perceived the dangers facing Europe as coming from the other regions of the 'Triad', primarily in terms of a growing disparity in competitiveness. To him Europe's economic perform-ance was falling more and more behind other advanced capitalist regions.[15] Renewing European integration was an appropriate response. Creating a Single European Market could set up an internally open European regional economy in which business and other actors would gain economies of scale, broader strategic vision and greater competitive challenge. The hope was that in consequence they would abandon parochial national outlooks and adopt new European identities and relationships. EMU was needed, first of all, because the Single Market would be precarious without it. In addition, it could help diminish Europe's vulnerability to inflation and monetary insta-bility created by American inability and/or unwillingness to anchor the international monetary system.

There is considerable evidence that much of large European business shared Delors' perspectives. The other leading political actors had additional geostrategic motives, particularly the Franco-German 'couple'. French Presi-dent François Mitterrand had strong domestic and foreign political reasons for pushing for more Europe. In need of a new strategy to substitute for the failure of his 1981 socialist programme, he decided that renewed European integration, particularly if it worked economically, might be useful. More Europe had the added advantage for Mitterrand of being an ideal way to 'exogenize' reforms that would be explosive if attempted purely within the French domestic scene. Mitterrand also believed that new Europeanization could lead to French centrality in the EU, giving France an international weight – *grandeur?* – beyond its objective capacities. The Germans could not lead, given their history. The British did not believe in Europe. Beyond this, Mitterrand had come of age in the years around World War Two and it was personally very important to him – and traditionally important to French diplomacy – to deepen the commitment of the Germans to the EU and keep them out of the continental mischief that had caused such trouble in the past. This particular concern became even more urgent as the Cold War ended. Finally, reinforced European integration might ultimately help France achieve its traditional Gaullist dream of a Europe freed from American domination.[16]

The German leader, Helmut Kohl, shared Mitterrand's goal of grounding Germany in EU Europe, both because he understood Germany's past and because Europe promised to provide political cover for growing German economic power that was needed to moderate anti-German feelings. Ultimately, however, Germany wanted more and better markets for its goods. British Prime Minister Margaret Thatcher, who ultimately lost out to the Franco-German couple, initially saw the Single Market as one route toward the deregulated quasi-free-trade zone of her Britannic dreams. Other key European leaders had their own domestic, geopolitical and economic interests. The Spanish and Portuguese saw Europe as an anchor for democratization, as a tool to change their economies and as a source of investment capital. The Italians, strongly European in most circumstances, shared many of these purposes. What was most interesting in all this, however, was that renewing European integration to confront some kind of abstract globalization was rarely considered at all.

There are no clear cases that globalization *per se* had priority, however globalization might be defined, in this list of leadership and elite preferences. To be sure, this cannot be taken to mean that globalizing changes played no role in structuring these preferences. But the review does demonstrate, at the very least, that leadership preferences and purposes in the renewal of European integration were many and varied. Globalization issues, when present, were usually combined with other priorities and concerns. At the very least, therefore, it is not particularly useful to draw causal arrows between globalizing processes as independent variables and new Europeanization. More important, the fact cannot be disregarded that the arrows run in the opposite direction from any theory of globalization as independent variable. Renewed European integration, in other words, might have had an important effect in promoting new globalization.

Finally, whatever the varying motives of central actors, what they *did* in responding to processes of difficult-to-decode change was profoundly 'path-dependent'. Despite the demoralization of the 'Eurosclerosis' years, deep

European commitments, institutions, ways of problem-solving and customs already existed. 'Europeanizing' important matters was a habit for European elites built upon significant sunk costs. Thus, given new stimuli in the early 1980s, key European leaders did not really have an abstract choice between 'going it alone' nationally or going forward to 'more Europe'. More Europe provided a much more familiar and compelling course of action. This meant, however, that whatever the reasons for new elite actions – globalization or other – strong incentives towards European integrationist responses existed. The constraints created by this path dependency therefore biased European responses to economic change in central ways.

Path-dependent incentives existed in the choice of concrete policies. Completing the Single Market and EMU had been first broached much earlier (at the Hague Summit in 1969, in fact) as ways of carrying out the 'finalities' of the Rome Treaties after the first, Common Market, phase had been completed. Moreover, they had been discussed to the point of 'solemn commitment' before being shelved. When new circumstances emerged in the Eurosclerosis period of the later 1970s and early 1980s these already legitimated options, whose contents were already sketched, were there to invoke as precedents to follow. Thus when it became possible politically to renew European integration it was these options, rather than starting anew, which were chosen. The ideas, shapes and logics behind what happened in the later 1980s had thus been set out long before anyone had reflected about globalization.

Globalization in one region: the terrible 1990s

The renewal of European integration should thus not be seen as either a reactive or proactive response to perceived 'globalization', at least in the popular sense that the term globalization is now used. Much of what happened after the mid-1980s was meant to resolve problems that had little directly to do with globalization. Moreover, the precise forms of European integration which occurred in this period derived from path-dependent incentives whose logics had been set out long before globalization was a serious concern. These reflections lead to an intriguing, and seemingly perverse, query. Might it be that rather than responding to globalization, the renewal of European integration in the 1980s was significant in hastening globalization's coming? The possibility is worth exploring.

Does European integration promote globalization?

Everyone agrees that enhanced international trade liberalization is one essential component of globalization. That the Single Market programme sought the particular liberalization of financial operations (the end of exchange controls, restrictions on capital movements, the creation of single markets for insurance and banks, etc.) can easily be interpreted as a contributing factor to the rapid intensification of transnational financial flows that is now apparent. Here there is obviously a chicken-and-egg problem, because it might just as easily be argued that financial liberalization in Europe was caused by these flows. Nonetheless, financial liberalization was clearly embedded in the Single Market idea, in the famous 'four freedoms of movement', of goods, services, labour and capital, consecrated as the EU's purpose long before the term globalization became current. Whichever view one adopts, however, that Europe liberalized rather than maintained both internal and international restrictions is highly significant to the explosion of financial dealings we see in the 1990s.

One of the claims most often made for globalization is that it has led to a marked diminution in national policy capacities. Proponents of strong globalization theses most often see the central causal arrows as flowing from autonomous international changes into national contexts. Globalization is the independent variable, in other words, national contexts the intermediate variable, and specific losses in national policy capacities the consequences. Where doubt is permitted, at least for Europe, is in explaining why this has occurred. Take, first of all, one of the most significant losses of national capacity in the economic and monetary policy realms. The current setting for all capitalist societies is one where major constraints exist compelling any country to pursue price stability and avoid public deficits and indebtedness. In this area it may well be possible to speak of a new transnational anti-inflationary monetary 'regime' which has replaced its Keynesian predecessor. The causes of this regime may not be globalization *per se*, however. Renewed European integration made decisive contributions to its elaboration, which occurred in specific policy decisions by particular actors.

The US Federal Reserve, the Reagan Administration and the new British Conservative government all turned to deflationary policies in 1979–80, together causing a huge recession. These decisions aligned the Americans and the British with the Germans, with their own long-standing commitment to price stability. All of this made French Socialist plans after 1981 much more difficult to pursue, leading to the policy shifts of 1983–84. It was at this point that French President Mitterrand decided to implement his new 'Europe option'. French commitment to price stability, judged a necessary complement to the Europe option (alignment of the franc and the DM were deemed important for establishing the credibility of other French European initiatives), created general policy alignment.

It was the institutionalization of this alignment in European monetary policy which turned a set of discrete policy choices into a regime. The EU further institutionalized the regime in its plans for EMU and, later, the 'convergence criteria' for creating EMU which constrained all potential EMU members to control inflation, debt, deficits, currency valuation and interests within very strict limits. The importance of all this for levels of employment in Europe needs also to be underlined. No doubt declining competitiveness and a certain degree (perhaps smaller than generally believed) of employment loss to parts of the developing world explain part of the growth in EU unemployment levels which, incidentally, coincided with renewed European integration. Constraints on rigid price stability and budget balancing account for a large part. Moreover, the creation of a regime was an important element in transferring veto power over economic policy to international financial markets.

The Single Market itself also contributed powerfully to removing capacities from EU states, as it was meant to do. The '1992' programme moved a wide range of policy prerogatives from national to European level while simultaneously 'marketizing' many of the same realms of policy. EU member states thus not only lost policy levers which had been central in the national development models that preceded the '1992' programme, but also these policy areas were largely removed from political determination altogether as they were Europeanized. The marketizing bias of EU treaties and prevailing diplomatic circumstances clearly limited any substantial relocation of regulatory activity to EU level. Studying the fate of the efforts made by the Delors Commissions and their member state supporters to broaden the EU's mandate into market regulating activities in social, regional, environmental and industrial policy is revelatory. Despite considerable goodwill the results turned out to be thin indeed.[17] From the point of view of European citizens, therefore, renewed European integration meant declining ability to constrain and shape markets to promote desirable public goals in social and industrial relations policies, for example. Moreover, the new setting created additional incentives for business to promote labour market and social policy deregulation in the interests of the 'flexibility' needed to cope.

Intentional globalization on one small continent?

We have established that renewed European integration was a complex construction which flowed from multiple motives in response to a variety of pressing problems. It is hard to credit any strong version of globalization as the independent variable, or even as a powerful variable at all. Despite this, the EU is rapidly looking like an exercise in 'anticipatory globalization in one region'. What does this mean? Globalization is supposed to be a process which subordinates nations and their peoples to irresistible market flows beyond their control. In consequence these nations lose earlier capacities to shape economic life and their citizens lose considerable political power – democratic power? – to decide desirable outcomes, particularly distributive outcomes. Whether global trends have done this or not in general, and this remains an open question, the Single Market has simulated it for citizens of EU nations. These nations can no longer regulate economic exchanges within the Single Market. Indeed, given the marketization of most regulatory decisions, there is no one who can do this.

The implementation of Economic and Monetary Union, scheduled to begin on 1 January 1999, will greatly accentuate what has already happened. Decisions, taken largely on German insistence, at the Dublin European Council in December 1996 will extend the stringent Maastricht convergence criteria (in a 'stability and growth pact') well into the next century. Strong guidance and police mechanisms to enforce price stability and budgetary stringency will be backed by the threat of very large sanctions (penalties to miscreant nations of up to 0.5 per cent of GDP are possible).

All this means that the great pressures on governments to pursue rigid price stability and balance budgets, which have been closely correlated with rising unemployment in the 1990s, will be continued. EMU and the coming of the single currency will in themselves remove any possibility of national governments adjusting to changed economic circumstances through the traditional monetary techniques of currency revaluation and interest rate shifts. This means that adjustments will have to be accomplished through changing price and wage levels and manipulating state spending, largely in social protection areas. The implications are clear. EMU will act to exert strong pressures on European nations to 'Americanize' their labour markets and welfare states.

Conclusions: the price of precocious globalization?

A social scientist named Karl Marx projected the 'heavy tendencies' of globalization 150 years ago. It would therefore be foolish indeed for us to deny that globalization is of consequence for modern European integration. But, as the invocation of Marx indicates, globalization must be seen as a long-term affair, beginning with the voyages of exploration, continuing with colonization and mercantilism, progressing through imperialism and neo-colonialism to the present period when financial globalization is a fact, when transnational corporations do see large areas of the planet as their territory, when advanced capitalism has spread well beyond the North American and European regions where it began and when new regions of the world have been integrated into its labour and product markets. Moreover, it would stand to reason, to Marx at least, that globalization could not be seen as simply a process in which autonomous economic flows almost magically become 'global' from having earlier been 'national'. Capitalism had global dimensions, from its earliest points. Quite as important, capitalist globalization occurred, and continues to occur, because specific actors seek to resolve important strategic dilemmas by choices which move them outside earlier geographic parameters. What we now label as globalization may well be the unintended product of strategic choices meant to confront problems which had little or nothing to do with globalization.

At its origins European integration was meant to resolve European regional problems, not to promote globalization. Yet its creation was strongly conditioned by processes of globalization at work long before the concept was used in popular discourse, among them the reconfiguration of great power politics into a bipolar-planetary mode, the reconfiguration of the capitalist world's monetary and financial system to reflect US power and the success of American-style Fordist consumerism as a model for Europe and others to emulate. The irony in early European integration was that Europeanization, in the context of these globalizing processes, created a setting of strongly self-contained national political economies which moved from success to success for more than two decades. When 'crisis' arrived in the 1970s, brought less by globalization than by the discrete acts of oil producers and American administrations, European integration plunged into a dismal, and potentially disaggregating, *sauve qui peut* cycle in which EU members responded by accentuating national strategies at the price of increasing policy divergence in the EU more broadly. The renewal of European integration in the 1980s was caused less by globalization than by strategic choices by key European actors to accelerate integration rather than to continue these discrete national strategies. These choices were constructed around path-dependent constraints left by the earlier period of European integration before globalization was in the current vocabulary. The results, however, look today very much as if European leaders were trying to simulate globalization within the EU – whether or not it actually existed anywhere else. Whatever we make of this, it is clear that the largely unintended consequences of decisions to deepen European integration after 1985 have promoted globalization.

The problem is that these recent stages in the globalization process, whatever their causes, have encouraged massive hyperbole. All manner of claims have been made about the ineluctable decline of the nation-state, completely footloose capitalism and the rapid disappearance of national margins of manoeuvre in economic matters. The image we have used to illustrate this hyperbole is one in which a 'global economy', floating free above continents, acts as an unrestrained and all-powerful independent variable obliging nations, peoples and individuals to respond. That significant change underlies these claims is clear, although it is doubtful, first of all, that reality corresponds to the rhetoric and, next, that causality is as simple as the rhetoric claims. There is another disturbing side to the globalization discourse. It is clearly tainted with interests when it is not directly 'interested'. Capital and conservative elites routinely use it to undercut the popular gains – the welfare state, civility in industrial relations, high wages – of the 'Golden Age' after the war. That social scientists should have bought into this rhetoric, often without serious examination, should lead us to doubt their claims to scientific detachment.

Another deep question is in order. Who can now know whether the forward movement of European integration taken in the last fifteen years of the twentieth century will turn out ultimately to have been an inadvertently proactive response to globalizing trends? In other words, even if the renewal of European integration was largely not to confront new indices of globalization, will it turn out to have been an appropriate response to globalization despite this? All we know now is that for a variety of reasons European leaders have pursued a course of action which has simulated what globalization is claimed to be doing everywhere, within the continental boundaries of the EU. Elite European actors have created huge structural constraints on what European governments can do, and these constraints seem certain to grow considerably in the near future. Other things being equal, European national governments have sacrificed many of their capacities to shape market flows, monetary policy and budgets. To what extent the effects of an EU Single Market, EMU and the projected Euro will sap and perhaps even reconfigure the 'European model of society' with its humane welfare states, civilized industrial relations procedures and negotiated settlements between groups remains to be seen. It is clear that new European integration has comforted the interests which would like to see change in all these areas. These interests disagree, however, on what kind of change should occur – reform or dismantling. It has become clear, as well, that the populations of Europe's nations do not particularly want what their leaders have designed for them. Were the Single Market and EMU now submitted to referenda across the EU there can be little doubt that they would be rejected.

Inadvertent globalization in one region has dispossessed European peoples of many of the democratic prerogatives to which they had become accustomed, and to which many had been initiated, in the period after World War Two. It is no longer possible to influence the allocation of resources and the shape of distribution through public decisions nationally as it once was. The making of many of these fundamental social choices has been shifted from politics altogether, to the market. Others have remained 'public' but have been moved into delegated undemocratic decision arenas. EMU institutions and processes are illustrative of this. Central bankers, only very lightly constrained by politicians, will control policy areas vital to the welfare of ordinary Europeans. It is worth adding that many of the decisions which have gone into the construction of this new order were also made on the outer margins of democratic legitimacy, as has almost always been the case in the history of European integration. European national leaders opted for new Europeanization *in camera*, through diplomacy, using the extensive executive powers reserved to them in foreign affairs to change Europe fundamentally and, in many cases, also to 'exogenize' processes of change which they never could have implemented in their domestic political arenas. Moreover, to the extent to which the European Commission, whatever its good intentions, has pushed new Europeanization forward through the long-consecrated 'Monnet method' of promoting integration by stealth, convinced that it was doing good for European peoples behind their backs, similar remarks are in order.

European integration has most often been defended as a set of techniques to allow different European peoples, each with strong identities, to live together in peace. Centuries of bloody warfare attested to the need for this. Yet recent European integration has gone beyond its original purpose of knitting different nations together in tapestries of mutual exchange and confidence towards removing the control of important matters from the hands of the European peoples themselves. However much the world has changed in recent decades, it is undeniable that these peoples still maintain strong national identities and desires to shape their own national fates. It would be ironic indeed were European integration's simulation of globalization in one corner of one continent to lead to a re-stimulation of these identities and the rekindling of old and best-buried animosities. The various manifestations of intolerant populisms that one sees across the continent are probably less the issue than what is likely to occur as EMU comes into existence and ordinary Europeans are called upon to sacrifice even more than they already have on the altar of Europe. There may eventually be a very large bill to pay.

Notes

1. The European Union came into being when the Maastricht Treaty was ratified in November 1993. 'Europe' (the politics and institutions of European integration) was called the EEC (European Economic Community) or, colloquially, the 'Common Market' until the 1980s, when it became the EC (European Community). I shall use EU throughout, except when explicitly discussing the earliest years, but the reader should be aware of the anachronism.
2. On the general circumstances surrounding the Marshall Plan see Alan Milward, *The Reconstruction of Western Europe, 1945–1951* (London: Methuen, 1984).
3. The best general study on American influences on European integration is Peter

Duignan and L. H. Gann, *The United States and the New Europe* (Oxford: Oxford University Press, 1994).

4. On Monnet's role, François Duchene's recent *Jean Monnet, First Statesman of Interdependence* (New York: Norton, 1994) is indispensable.

5. Loukas Tsoukalis, *The New European Economy*, 2nd edn (London: Oxford University Press, 1993). Chapter 2 reviews these early years.

6. On this 'golden age' see Andrew Glyn and Alain Lipietz's excellent first chapter in Stephen Marglin and Juliet Schor (eds), *The Golden Age of Capitalism* (Oxford: Oxford University Press, 1990).

7. Here is an illustration, if one is needed, that globalization can be evanescent.

8. Delors describes the ways in which he decided upon the single market approach in his preface to Paolo Cecchini, *The European Challenge* (Aldershot: Wildwood House, 1988).

9. Only the most sensitive matters – fiscal policy, border controls concerning the movement of people and workers' rights – remained under unanimity rules.

10. The Delors package proposed an enlarged Community budget which would give the Commission more budgetary latitude and avoid annual money fights. It also proposed small changes in the CAP to keep chronic budgetary squabbles over agriculture off the table.

11. The structural fund priority objectives included aid to less developed regions in the EU (largely in the South), reconversion of deindustrialized areas, programmes to overcome long-term unemployment, help to enter the labour market for unemployed young people and, finally, development and structural adjustment aid in rural areas.

12. On the GATT Uruguay Round negotiations, which ended in 1993, see Hugo Paemen and Alexandra Bensk, *From Gatt to the Uruguay Round* (Leuven: Leuven University Press, 1995). Hugo Paemen was the EU's head GATT negotiator.

13. For a description of Maastricht from the Commission's vantage point see George Ross, *Jacques Delors and European Integration* (Cambridge: Polity Press, 1995), chs 3–6.

14. The 'triadic' analysis recurred frequently in Delors's speeches. For examples, see Jacques Delors, *Le Nouveau concert européen* (Paris: Odile Jacob, 1991).

15. As noted by the European Commission in its 1993 *White Paper on Growth, Competitiveness and Employment* in the prior two decades, 'our competitive position in relation to the USA and Japan has worsened as regards ... employment, our shares of export markets, R+D and innovation and its incorporation into goods brought to the market [and] the development of new products'. In absolute terms Europe continued to have a surplus with the rest of the world, but its growing tendency to import more and export less was telling (as was the particular relative bias of this trade away from cutting-edge products). This tendency was particularly clear *vis-à-vis* countries classified by Eurostat as 'developing' (with 1985 always as index 100, imports were 129 and exports 103 in 1980 as against 143 and 89 in 1990). See European Commission, *White Paper on Growth, Competitiveness, Employment: The Challenges and Ways Forward into the 21st Century* (Luxembourg: EC Commission, 1993), p. 9. The discussion of comparative advantage by industrial sector in the OECD Jobs Study (Paris: OECD, 1994) confirms the Commission's contentions (see Part 1, Table 4.2, p. 132).

16. A great deal of information about the actions of both Mitterrand and Kohl can be found in the three volumes by Pierre Favier and Michel Martin-Roland, *La Décennie Mitterrand* (Paris: Editions du Seuil; Volume 1: 1990, Volume 2: 1991, Volume 3: 1996). Another precious source is Hubert Védrine, *Les Mondes de François Mitterrand, à l'Elysée* (Paris: Fayard, 1996). Margaret Thatcher's memoirs, *The Downing Street Years*, are likewise invaluable.

17. On this topic see Stephan Leibfried and Paul Pierson (eds), *Social Europe* (Washington: Brookings, 1996), particularly the chapters by Martin Rhodes, Wolfgang Streeck and George Ross and the editors' conclusions.

11

Is There a Society Called Euro?

MICHAEL MANN

Introduction

In recent years and in certain respects Europe, at least in the sense of Western Europe, has been solidifying as a distinct entity in the world. Yet the individual nation-states of Europe endure, as do their internal provinces and regions. So do the macro-regions of the continent – broad socio-cultural entities like 'Latin Europe' or 'the Nordic countries'. Broader international and transnational relations affecting the continent – some of them global in scope – have also been becoming denser. How can we grasp the relations between such multiple social networks in order to situate Europe in the world? To what extent is Europe beginning to constitute a distinct 'society' in the world?

Social scientists across the world have long wielded two main models of twentieth-century society. The first centres on the nation-state. It is the circumscribed field of study of most historians, the implicit society of most sociologists, the 'economy' of most applied economists, the unit-actor of political scientists and international relations specialists. The second view of society is transnational. This society is variously termed 'industrial (or post-industrial) society' or 'capitalist society' or the 'world system' or just 'the market' – constructs offered by Marxists, modernization theorists and neo-classical economists. Recently, most of these transnational theorists have been claiming that 'globalization' has been particularly eroding the society that was the nation-state.

But many European social scientists, especially those interested in global-ization, egged on by major changes in their continent, have added a third 'society'. Transcending the national, though often in league with the global, lies the place I shall call *Euro*, that unit defined by the boundaries of a succession of acronyms, the ECSC, the EEC, the EC and now the EU. This now occupies the bulk of 'Western Europe' (the small EFTA countries providing the residue). The third and broadest place, the whole continent, I shall refer to as 'Europe'. Yet at every turn the linked enthusiasts of the Euro and of the global are harassed by the dogged defenders of the nation-state, asserting that less has changed than might be supposed. Thus a contentious troika of the national, the Euro and the global currently dominate thinking about Europe's place in the world.

While such a troika has its utility, its combined resources are ultimately inadequate to comprehend the position of Europe in the world. We require a more adequate theory of human societies if we are to grapple adequately with such issues. This theory needs to be more general, yet also more concrete. My history of power in human society (Mann, 1986: esp. ch. 1, and 1993: esp. ch. 3) has advanced five main propositions which can help us in both respects:

1. There has never been a singular systemic network of social interaction which might constitute, as it were, 'a total society'. Neither the nation-state, nor the market nor the world system, nor Europe have ever remotely approximated to such an entity. Human societies have always consisted of multiple, overlapping, intersecting networks of interaction each with differing boundaries and rhythms of development. Many social scientists studying the present assent to such a proposition, since (for example) nation-states and capitalism today are clearly not coterminous, yet both structure our lives. But multiple, overlapping networks have actually been a universal feature of human life on earth. Just as there never was a nation-state society, just as (I will later suggest) there is not a global society, nor can there be a singular society called Euro, only at maximum a European network of interaction at the boundaries of which occurs a limited degree of cleavage. Thus *I investigate the degree of internal coherence and external closure of European social networks.*

2. Since there is no singular system, there has been no singular prime mover, no single overarching character to human society, no singular social structure or logic ultimately determining human existence. Ideally, we should avoid such terms as 'American society' or 'capitalist society', which suggest that 'society' has one essential property. Of course, it is difficult to do so when we are focusing practically on either the United States or the economy. We cannot trace the overall past, present or (probably) the future of the world in terms merely, or even principally, of the development of capitalism, of the world system, of the global, of the state system, of systems of cultural symbols etc. etc. All these matter and so constrain the influence of the others. As Talcott Parsons once famously remarked, such singular stories should belong to the kindergarten phase of social theory. Human interactions are extremely complex – and will of course be so within and across the boundaries of Euro.

However, we may usefully simplify this complexity in regard to both the content and the spatial configuration of social networks.

3. In terms of *content*, we can distinguish four major analytic types of social network, each forming around a primary source of power in human societies. Mobilization of ideological (the label 'cultural' would do almost as well), economic, military or political power resources enables human beings most effectively to achieve their goals. Thus around these four power sources form relatively specialized and especially durable networks of interaction, capable of combining intensive and extensive power mobilizations. Thus *I analyse the complex entwinings of ideological, economic, military and political power networks within and across the boundaries of Europe.*

4. As a rider to this, and since political institutions figure large in most accounts of Euro, I add two empirical political complications. First, what are conventionally called 'geopolitics' blend together military and political power. 'Hard geopolitics' (concerning wars and alliances) are predominantly military, 'soft geopolitics' (negotiations between states over the economy, the environment etc.) are more varied but politically organized. Second, since states engage in the authoritative regulation of social relations across defined territories, and these relations are multiple, states must be viewed as 'polymorphous' rather than unitary. This means that states 'crystallize' in multiple forms and institutions, as they successively respond to different sets of interactions between varied social constituencies. States may crystallize while discussing their banking laws as economic-capitalist; the following day they may crystallize while restricting abortion as ideological-religious. These may involve rather different parts of the state as well as the mobilization of very different constituencies. States need have no final unity – mainly because society does not. This is obviously true of the complex political institutions found in today's Euro. But it was also true of states in the nineteenth and early twentieth centuries – thus, for example, profoundly polymorphous states started World War One (see Mann, 1993: chs 3, 21). Thus *I use the notion of the polymorphous state to help explain Euro-politics today.*

5. Empirical analysis can be aided by a very concrete methodology: We can trace out power networks *spatially*. With whom in what places are Europeans linked in their macro-interactions? For most macro-sociological purposes we can identify five main spatial networks: the local (i.e. the subnational), the national, the international (i.e. relations between national units), the transnational (i.e. relations freely crossing through national boundaries) and the global (i.e. relations spanning the globe, which might be either transnational or international in nature).

Human history has seen an enormous secular increase in the breadth of these networks, moving humans away from a predominance of local networks of interaction toward the national, the international and the transnational – and most recently towards the global.

My specific concern here, to analyse contemporary Europe, requires the distinguishing of two additional supranational spatial networks. We need to distinguish Euro from 'Northern' networks. The 'North' has become a conventional, ultimately non-geographic, term encompassing the most advanced countries and regions of the world (which almost all lie in the Northern hemisphere). Both the Euro and the Northern can be distinguished from genuinely global networks, as well as from networks which serve to integrate other 'transnational slices' of the world besides the Euro-community and the North – as for example do the Catholic Church or the Spanish language. Thus *I examine the relative salience of a nested series of five spatial networks – the local, the national, the Euro, the Northern and the global – the last three of which may be constituted either transnationally or internationally, plus non-nested, crosscutting 'transnational slices'*. This may seem rather complicated but it is necessary, since all these networks may impinge significantly upon life in the continent of Europe.

How salient among all these are Euro networks, and what degrees of internal coherence and external closure do they possess? Obviously a single essay can only sketch out some of the main contours of an answer. I begin by summarizing (obviously briefly and crudely) the principal power networks of the continent before 1945.

Europe before and after the year 1945

There had long been a sense of common European *ideology*, centred on a claim to possess 'civilization', which helped Europeans commit both great and terrible acts in the world. This ideological identity had first centred on Christianity, then on claims to head the 'white race', to possess distinctive liberal 'freedoms', and to spearhead 'modernity' – 'the discovery of the future as a new place, attainable but never visited before' (Therborn, 1995: 19). As Therborn notes, all these conceptions have been perennially frayed and blurred around the edges, preventing tight external closure: 'Europeans' could include the inhabitants of Europe plus their descendants settled elsewhere; while the eastern borders of Europe always remained unclear. Thus 'European' often only indicated 'West European' rather than the entire continent – and we must acknowledge that both have always had blurred eastern boundaries. Or it might indicate a larger 'West', including the settler colonies scattered through the globe. Across this only semi-bounded terrain a common sense of identity and a spatial flow of ideological messages concerning religion, 'race', 'civilization', 'progress' and 'modernity' gave some minimal coherence to Western European networks.

But such ideological coherence as Europe or Western Europe ever attained came through the severest of 'civil wars', concerning religion, nation and class. These eventually undermined Europe as its claims to civilizational leadership also weakened, threatened by the rise of the United States, Japan and the Soviet Union. European identity became undercut by severe ideological schism. Christianity had long been divided into three: Catholic, Protestant and Orthodox (and only Catholicism was organized into a single Church). Europeans were also strongly divided by the ideologies of class. Yet the bloodiest twentieth-century conflicts were fought under ideologies of nationalism, which destroyed European claims to civilizational leadership and which almost destroyed Europe itself.

Other European ideological divisions reduced coherence without necessarily involving conflict. Under 10 per cent of Europeans were able to communicate any ideological messages with each other beyond the reach of their local vernacular language. In general we may say that European collective identity could strongly mobilize only when confronted by 'Others': rival religious communities, especially Islam, and 'less civilized' indigenous peoples elsewhere. Even these confrontations were declining through the twentieth century. Thus the year 1945 was not characterized by a very salient European ideological power network. Local, national, class, gender and other identities undercut its coherence very considerably, while broader international or transnational identities tended to reduce its external closure.

The *economy* of Europe had long been capitalist. Since property owners were autonomous of states and capitalism was market-oriented, in principle capitalism was a transnational interaction network, built on top of local networks. That is the view of neo-classical and Marxist theory alike. Yet in reality (as most have recognized) European capitalism had always come entwined with military and political power relations. Capitalism was partially segmented into distinctive national economies, while imperialism produced some military-political structuring of capitalism across the world. This complex mixture was thrown into crisis during the twentieth century by inter-imperial wars and by a Great Depression which enhanced protectionism (including imperial protectionism). Though capitalism and then industrialism began as distinctively European, and provided considerable internal cohesion to Europe, they had not encouraged European social closure.

Over the previous four centuries most *military* power had become gradually monopolized by states, and this proved the greatest subversion of

Europe. Conflicts between European nation-states had escalated into hi-tech mass mobilization warfare using terrible weapons of destruction. In 1945 Europe (and much of East Asia) lay devastated by internecine strife, occupied by the militaries of two only half-European Powers, the United States and the Soviet Union. Europe was in *no* sense a military 'society'.

Politically, Europe had been partially segmented into a series of bounded nation-states, each with a distinctive political economy, social stratification, national citizenship and ideology of nationalism. But in 1945 the most extreme form of nation-statism, fascism, had just been defeated in Europe. Its extreme corollary on the left, state socialism, lasted another forty years. 'Moderate nation-statism' (involving only mildly statist and mildly nationally-confined networks of interaction) triumphed in Western Europe in 1945 and in the whole of Europe from 1989. It was also diffusing as the most desired political model across much of the globe (Mann, 1997). Again, political activity did little to cement either the integration or the closure of European networks.

Wielding these plural power sources – a Christian/racial/modern sense of ideological civilizing mission, a capitalist, hi-tech militarism and nation-state rivalry – European imperialism had dominated much of the world. But great changes were set in motion by the settlement of 1945. World War Two solidified a smaller 'Europe'. The Continent was tired of war and Empire and its military powers had been humbled. Half-European troops occupied the continent, dividing it into two blocs, one capitalist, liberal democratic and Catholic/Protestant, the other state socialist and officially secular, though mostly retaining the Orthodox religion. The Western half lost its empires, separated itself economically and politically from its neighbours to the east and south and appropriated the term 'Europe'. Fascism destroyed, communism kept at bay, its politics formed a fairly narrow range around the moderate nation-statism of the Christian Democratic/Social Democratic centre. The war also climactically ended twentieth-century Europe's ethnic conflicts: mass migration and mass murder nearly completed the ethnic 'purification' of the continent. Outside of the state socialist countries only very old, institutionalized states (the UK, Spain and Switzerland, with Belgium the latecomer) remained very multi-ethnic. Western European countries now shared a very similar culture, if still expressed in different languages.

This growing similarity reinforced Western Europeans' sense of ideological identity. It especially strengthened their determination not to fight each other again. 'European' now conjures up a rather pacific, toothless community – the exact opposite of prior history. Since Europeans were rejecting much of the old geopolitical-military core of the state, the Euro acronymic unity project could take wing, aimed first at preventing the 'hard geopolitics' of war reviving – and at rebuilding a shattered economy. 'Hard' were replaced by economistic 'soft' geopolitics at the Euro level.

But the war was also consequential outside Europe. Under American military protection, capitalism greatly expanded. In the 'North' – fascism defeated, communism kept at bay – extreme ideologies of class and nation gave way to moderate, largely pacific compromise. Since Northern weapons were aimed against the state socialist enemy outside, the military was pushed to the margins of public life, becoming caste-like, quietly cultivating 'baroque arsenals'. Not Europe, nor even the 'West' (i.e. including the US), but the 'North' became the new core of a capitalist, somewhat de-militarized (apart from the US) and predominantly democratic 'advanced' world. It increasingly took a trilateral form, centring on North America, Western Europe and Japanese-led East Asia. The North provides over 80 per cent of world production, finance and trade. Much of life across the North has become essentially similar. It is regulated by 'soft geopolitics' between similar advanced blocs of countries. Thus we should not expect much external closure from Euro economic networks *vis-à-vis* the rest of the North.

But globalization also involves a more conflictual stratification hierarchy between the North and the South. All the Western European countries stand squarely in the Northern 'upper class', the richest quintile, of the world's nations – while the poorer East Europeans are firmly in the second quintile, the world's rather small 'middle class' (Korzeniewicz and Moran, 1997). The continent occupies a distinct place in global stratification networks – though only along with the rest of the North.

Contemporary ideological power networks

Euro identity today is neither very coherent nor very closed. True, Euro has border problems which may come to reinforce its Christian sense of identity – traditional uncertainty to the east (is the Orthodox Church of the same overall faith?) plus rising conflict to the south with fundamentalist Islam. This fault-line provides most of the evidence Huntington (1996) offers in support of his broader theory of emerging global 'civilizational conflicts' centred on religion. Yet Euro is a relatively secular Christian place, while its religious identity actually integrates Euro with large 'transnational slices' of the world – with the American and Australasian continents, most of sub-Saharan Africa and parts of Asia. The hierarchy and core of the Catholic and the major Protestant Churches are also becoming perceptibly less European. Though Churches may yet come to provide southern border reinforcements, they do not provide much closure against the rest of the world, North or South.

Indeed, much of Euro culture – democracy, white racism, etc. – is shared

with the United States and Australasia. Thus Eastern Europeans casting off
the Soviet yoke saw their desired political and economic future ambiguously
as European-cum-American. Economic (i.e. capitalist-dominated) culture is
also shared right across the North, increasingly including Japan and East
Asia. Other cultural identities centred on religion or language cross-cut
Europe: 'Anglo-Saxon', Catholic and Ibero-American networks connect
parts of Europe to wider transnational slices of the globe. The British, the
Irish, the French, the Spanish, the Portuguese all weaken potential Euro
boundaries by their involvement in such transnational slices.

Internal ideological coherence is also rather weak. Reviews of survey data
(Dogan, 1993; Laffan, 1996; Reif, 1993; Therborn, 1995: 246–50,
278–82) reveal, first, that Euro is not much of a community of sentiment.
'Europe' is generally portrayed as a rather abstract ideal by committed
federalists. They tend to see it as the direct inheritor of 'Enlightenment
values', hardly the basis for mass mobilization. True, its 'modernity' is quite
widely valued, especially across the more backward countries of southern
Euro (though their commitment is also influenced by more contingent,
material motives – they are net beneficiaries of the Euro-budget). Support for
Euro is also consistently higher among the most educated, the most urban
and the highest social classes (alongside more varying relationships with age
and gender). Nationalist *ressentiment* against Euro has been recently surfac-
ing among lower classes, who disproportionately support the new extreme
rightist parties. And Euro mobilizes intensive ideological commitment from
only a few. Surveys indicate that Euro attachments are dwarfed by attachments to local and national communities. One half of respondents across
Europe go so far as to say that they *never* feel European. More Africans claim
to share a continental identity than do Europeans, and about the same
number of Latin Americans.

True, the surveys reveal that European nationalisms have weakened
somewhat, especially losing their aggressive edge. But, unlike global or Euro
cultural networks, national sentiments are embedded in communities of
ritual and emotion shared by neighbours affirming a (mythical) common
experience, history and ancestry (Smith, 1990). As Therborn (1995: 233–9)
notes, of the three ritual occasions that are celebrated very widely across
Euro, only one, Christmas, is truly integrative, while the other two
(Armistice/Victory Days and May Days) celebrate divisiveness provided by
nations and classes. Tears well up at the sight of Christian, national and (to
a lesser extent) class symbols, not Euro symbols. Euro elections generate only
half the turnout of national ones. The new Euro banknotes cannot portray
human beings, only stylized architectural shapes, since human beings – like
the possible candidates Beethoven, Shakespeare or Leonardo – are seen as
having nationality above all other collective identities.

Vernacular languages remain national or local. Though English is becoming a shared language, this is predominantly under American influence, it characterizes global rather than just European communication, and it will long remain a formal, public and somewhat stilted language for almost all Europeans except the British and Irish. The language of the emotions, of love and humour, remains the national or local vernacular. 'You don't fall in love with a common market', observed Jacques Delors himself. The ideological coherence and closure of Euro remains very low *vis-à-vis* the national and the local. We will see below why this is likely to remain so.

Contemporary economic power networks

Economic integration has been the backbone of the acronymic Euro project. Despite numerous 'spillovers' into other spheres, especially law, the EU remains principally an economic power network. Its drive towards full economic integration has so far seemed unstoppable, leading to considerable internal economic coherence. Perhaps we should remain a little cautious, since Euro must now cope with economic stagnation worsened by shocks administered by the Soviet collapse. The absorption of East Germany has severely dented the German economy, while splits may emerge over expanding the EU eastward (more advanced EU national economies tend to be complementary to Eastern economies, less advanced ones tend to be competitive). The ambiguity of the eastern border remains, presumably to be reflected in closer association with the EU for Poland, the Czech Republic and Hungary than for a middling belt of countries, with the third belt, Russia and its Slav/Orthodox client-states, remaining largely outside. The countries of former Yugoslavia may be also differentially treated. The ambiguous position of Islamic Turkey will crucially affect the Euro border, with major repercussions on any future Christian–Islamic conflict along the borders. At present, however, in economic terms the eastern borders are ajar, not closed.

But Euro has now acquired considerable internal economic cohesion. It has largely replaced the nation-state in harmonizing economic regulations and providing economic protection. More direct Euro interventions in the economy (except for agriculture) have been feebler, if gradually growing. External economic closure depends mainly on broader trends, principally on whether global free trade continues to deepen. Though tariffs have been significantly reduced across the world – and Europe's are generally less than 5 per cent – the proliferation of subtler non-tariff barriers has so far cancelled out most of the free-trade gains. The Korean auto industry has been reportedly protected from imports by its government running tax audits on Koreans buying foreign cars! Can GATT overcome such national (or Euro) strategies – especially if neo-liberal ideology has now peaked?

We have quantitative data of varying quality on three types of economic networks: those centred on trade, multinational corporate organization and finance. The data on trade are the clearest, revealing that Euro trading-bonds are substantially tightening. Between 1958 and 1994 intra-EC trade rose from about 36 per cent to just under 60 per cent of all trade crossing its member states' borders. The EC has become a more exclusive, closed bloc than either North America (including Mexico) or East Asia – their intra-bloc trade in 1989 amounted to only 35 per cent and 42 per cent of total foreign trade (Busch and Milner, 1994: 261). Since the EU's largest 'foreign' partner has actually been EFTA, the organization of West European countries remaining outside the EU (mainly Switzerland and Nordic countries), total intra-West European trade has been around 70 per cent of all the area's cross-border trade during the 1990s (European Commission, 1996: Tables 45, 46; Tsoukalis, 1993: 282–3). Since Euro has been recently swallowing up much of EFTA, we can conclude that it has become a substantially bounded network of trade interaction, though it is unclear whether this results from the EU or from mere geographical propinquity (Therborn, 1995: 195–200 emphasizes the latter, Tsoukalis, 1993 the former).

Yet much of what should really be counted as foreign trade (but is not) consists of exchanges between branches of single multinational enterprises located in different countries. Including these may slightly reduce our image of EU internal cohesion. In 1988 the value of production of US-owned companies in the EC exceeded by eight times US trade exports to the EC (Hufbauer, 1990). To include multinational corporations in the overall trading equation would increase EU links to the US and, to a lesser extent, to Japan – though not much to anywhere else in the world (another indication of Northern exclusiveness). Yet we must balance against this the fact that genuinely Euro multinational corporations are growing. In 1983/84, of all manufacturing mergers and acquisitions occurring in Euro, 65 per cent were within a single country, 16 per cent occurred between Euro and elsewhere (mostly the USA, followed by Japan), and only 19 per cent were between Euro member countries. Yet by 1989/90 intra-Euro mergers outnumbered other types: only 39 per cent were now national, 20 per cent were with elsewhere, and 41 per cent were Euro (Tsoukalis, 1993: 103).

These Euro corporations also seem to involve greater internal integration than do more global ones. In Euro, full-scale acquisitions outnumber the less integrated 'joint ventures' between corporations and are increasing as the common market nears completion (Kay *et al.*, 1996). Many, perhaps even most, mergers and acquisitions between foreign countries are more tactical, being aimed mainly at avoiding those countries' tariffs. That is why the multinational corporation in most places in the world is an indicator less of a world that is transnational than of one that is still divided between national economies. Yet the Euro-corporations tend to be integrated, genuine 'Euro-champions': integrated productive enterprises spread across Europe, organized for global competition between blocs. Thus, though data on multinational corporations are less comprehensive than trade data, they probably only slightly reduce the degree of internal coherence and external closure suggested by the trade data.

Finance capital is the most difficult to quantify and evaluate. Electronically transmitted claims to economic ownership slosh relatively freely and trans-nationally across the world, their 'paper' value exceeding the value of all global trade by a factor of three hundred or more. Such astronomical sums are misleading, the result of the same stocks, bonds, futures, etc. being traded many times during a day. Whatever the real economic power such trans-national capital possesses, it is far less than its nominal value might suggest. Moreover, there is some regulation of finance capital. This still operates principally through the stock exchanges, the accountancy practices and the commercial laws of individual nation-states. Indeed, as Moran (1994) shows, as transnational financial velocity zoomed upwards, nation-state regulation actually increased, replacing the prior element of collective self-regulation by financial institutions themselves. The US government stepped in first. The regulatory model provided by its Securities and Exchange Commission then spread to Japan and Britain, and from Britain it spread to the individual nation-states of continental Europe. The loopholes left by this essentially national system are gradually being filled by intergovernmental agencies grouped around the Bank of International Settlements (head-quartered in Basle, but not part of Euro). Thus Euro has been quite marginal to this essentially national and international system of financial regulation. Euro is a much more salient network of trade and production than of finance capital.

These are all gross flows. Individual nations, regions and classes may differ in their positions. Some countries are more Euro than others. Smaller countries have more open economies than bigger ones and their openness has shifted toward Euro. Denmark used to be an outlier in the old EC, since much of its trade was 'outside', with EFTA countries; while the major ex-colonial countries, Britain, France and Spain, still retain relatively stronger economic links with the South than do their Euro partners. Italy and especially Germany have been recently developing greater trading and investment links across the Eastern borders. Indeed, some (e.g. Gretsch-mann, 1994) consider that a resurrection of German economic domination over the east will severely strain the economic coherence of Europe. But the UK stands out as the major subversive, with the least Euro-oriented econ-omy, the lowest proportionate trade with the rest of the EU (and with the EU+EFTA) and the most globally oriented multinational corporations – in

1996 it has once again become the number one foreign investor in the USA, recovering this position from Japan. Britain also receives most inward investment from Japan, and (above all) its stock market is easily the biggest in Europe and the most globally oriented. Britain is the North's and even the South's Trojan horse into Europe – as Germany may be the leading Trojan horse to the east. These contrasting pulls may undermine the utility of current spatial distinctions made between Euro 'core' and Euro 'periphery'.

Regional differences are also evident. Inequalities between regions have widened as a result of Euro integration. A central belt – the Low Countries, southern Germany, northern France and northern Italy (plus non-member Switzerland) – prospers at the expense of the north-west and the south. Euro regional policy could only reverse such a powerful tendency at the cost of enormous economic inefficiency. In this respect Euro looks a little bit like the old national economy, integrated at the cost of some internal tension by stratification relations between centre and periphery. The entry of the Nordic countries may somewhat confuse the geography of this, since these geographically peripheral countries are actually the most prosperous ones.

Yet these national and regional differences pale beside class differences. Though here we have fewer quantitative data, it seems that capitalists, top managers and professionals are the most Euro, transnational and global in their economic orientation, farmers the most Euro and national, with other classes and social movements remaining far more local and national.

Some of the evidence derives from studies of organized interest groups in Brussels and Strasbourg (Grant, 1993; Greenwood *et al.*, 1992; Grote, 1992; Visser and Ebbinghaus, 1992; and the articles on Denmark, Germany, Holland, Portugal and the UK in van Schendelen, 1993). Most commentators agree that agricultural interest groups are the most effective Euro-lobbies, having wormed their way inside the actual Euro policy formulation process. This reflects both the prize at stake (easily the largest part of the Euro budget) and traditional farmer domination of Ministries of Agriculture in the member states (which characterizes all Northern countries). The bigger capitalist enterprises come second in results and their lobbies are much larger than the farmers. Big corporations maintain their own Euro lobbies and also participate in the 'peak' and sector organizations of business. Together these three types of business lobby provide the vast bulk of the total Euro-lobby. Bigger corporations tend to be better represented than smaller ones, those in dynamic and hi-tech industries are better represented than those in declining industries traditionally dependent on the nation-state, and those in the larger countries are better represented than those in the smaller ones. All studies confirm that agriculture and business together dominate Euro lobbies.

In contrast, labour unions have puny Euro-organizations. Though on paper large, they are deeply divided by national traditions and interests, by sector and by ideology. They have made little impact on the predominantly business-oriented policies of Euro. Indeed, business is adamant that corporatism and welfarism will stop at the level of the nation-state – as the feeble 'Social Chapter' of the Maastricht Treaty reveals. Labour remains caged by the nation-state, outflanked by the Euro-reach of capital.

Nor have other popular social movements made much Euro-impact. Anti-nuclear movements are quite well organized but have failed utterly to impact on EC policy – defeated mainly by the large variations in nuclear policy between the member states. Consumer groups are poorly organized, with little Euro-effect. Poverty and welfare groups are welcomed by Euro agencies, but mainly as humanitarian window-dressing, to prove that Euro has a small soul as well as a wallet. Though Euro-policy on women's issues and environmentalism has been more radical, this results more from EU executives and national politicians than from Euro-pressure from below. Feminist movements in the United Kingdom, for example, direct almost all their pressure at London rather than Brussels. Regional government pressure groups have had much more impact in Brussels – largely because some major member-states are federal polities. Though the regional governments in federal Germany and Spain are active in Brussels, they have much less influence there than in their own national capitals. Only Britain offers the true reverse example, of a politically centralized country in which regional nationalisms can more easily organize at the Euro level (Bretherton and Sperling, 1996; Harvey, 1993; Marks and McAdam, 1996; Tarrow, 1995).

Euro would not support Marx's assertion that farmers have little capacity for collective organization. But it would support his notion that the state was but an executive committee for managing the common affairs of the bourgeoisie. Not only is Euro primarily a capitalist common market, but its 'multi-agency' and 'regulatory' government (see below) can *only* engage in *ad hoc* tinkering with capitalist markets. Euro cannot plan, cannot confront the capitalist market head-on. There is virtually no Euro political economy except market tinkering. Capitalists have finally hit upon the ideal government for pursuing their collective interests *vis-à-vis* labour: to prevent collective controls over market capitalism.

We must qualify this in two ways. First, the capitalist class is not uniquely dependent on Euro networks: it is both transnational and national as well. Between the Euro and the broader transnational is only a very limited degree of cleavage. Sklair (1997) believes that a truly global capitalist class is currently emerging. Multinationals increasingly encourage more mobility among their international operating units by their high-flyers; business schools encourage the flexible blending of American, Japanese and European management styles; and finance capital is substantially global in its movement. Nonetheless, mobility can be ranked: people are the least mobile, then goods, with finance (especially electronic entitlements to finance) being the most mobile. We badly need research on capitalists' and top managers' sense of their own identity, but most probably do still retain a strong sense of national identity – though national identity may be lower for capitalists and top managers inside Euro than for either Americans or (especially) Japanese.

Second, Euro also heavily involves professionals and would-be professionals. Professionals staff the lobbies and the Euro-agencies. They and students dominate intra-Euro population movement (apart from short-term tourism). Yet, once again, their movements are not confined to Euro. Though EU programmes have increased intra-Euro student mobility, gross student flows within and across Euro boundaries are dominated by four individual Northern countries. The USA, Germany, France and Britain absorb large numbers of students from the rest of the world, especially from the developing world, and they also exchange more students with each other than other countries do (Romero, 1990). This is probably also true of university-trained professionals, including academics. In their lives Brussels and Strasbourg are just two of the more important troughs in a truly global swill of contracts, grants and fees provided by industry and trade interest groups, IGOs, NGOs, foundations and professional bodies. The global village of each profession is restricted only by linguistic barriers and familial conservatism.

The lower middle class and the working class remain far more locally- and nationally-oriented, though their size means they dominate gross population flows. Tourism has become the largest flow, with all Euro countries now sending and receiving large numbers. Indeed, intra-European tourists may now comprise half of the entire world's cross-border tourists (they were 45 per cent, and rising, in 1985). Whether a short stay, often in enclave resorts dominated by fellow-nationals, reinforces much of a Euro-identity is uncertain. Long-term residential movement would be more significant but is actually rare: in 1991 over 90 per cent of Euro's 344 million officially counted population were nationals of their country of residence. Under 3 per cent were from other European countries (and this statistic bafflingly includes Turkey). Migration between Euro countries has actually been declining over the past twenty years. Before then the rates had been dominated by southerners moving north, especially Italians. Now under 20 per cent of immigrants come from within the EU. If we could count the illegal immigrants, those from outside may be not far short of 10 per cent of the Euro population (Eurostat, 1993; Philip, 1994; Romero, 1990).

The permeability of the eastern borders, illegal immigration, mass asylum-seeking and labour exploitation of immigrants all result in considerable socio-political conflict. This is beginning to produce tighter common immigration policies, though more from *ad hoc* inter-governmental agreement than from the EU. The implementation of Schengen inches forward, asylum seekers are curbed by intergovernmental agreements and member states impose restrictions in deference to emerging Euro rules (e.g. Spain and Portugal have restricted the rights of Latin Americans to opt for their citizenships). The result is less internal coherence than external closure. But since immigration policy has the potential to create a backlash among ordinary people, it might eventually increase internal coherence by strengthening a Euro identity – though hardly in an 'Enlightenment' direction.

Neither the Euro nor the global economy seem to have much positive impact on popular class identities. Routine employment in a multinational corporation seems to give little sense of international or transnational identity or interest. True, in countries like Sweden it may induce trade union members employed in profitable export sectors to abandon national corporatist bargaining structures in favour of free collective bargaining with one's employer. Tax resistance amid a stagnating Western economy is also tending slightly to reduce national corporatism. Yet pressure groups representing ordinary working- and middle-class people, like trade unions or age- or gender-organizations, remain overwhelmingly oriented to the nation-state, the regulator of their employment relations, the provider of pensions, unemployment and disability insurances and indeed of all family welfare entitlements. There is little evidence that middle- or working-class identities are shifting toward Euro or broader units. As many writers and politicians have noted, Euro remains primarily a network of upper classes and elites – of capitalists, top managers, top bureaucrats and professionals. Whether it will remain so in the long run is an imponderable. Many believe that rational self-interest will *force* subordinate social groups to focus their collective demands on Euro, since it increasingly and regressively determines their fate. But, seeing little evidence that interest, reason or equality do govern human societies, I remain sceptical.

Contemporary military power networks

These will not long detain us: Euro is obviously not a singular military power. Its military networks are US-led and Atlanticist-Northern rather than European in scope. The individual member states possess virtually the entire European military budget. Britain and France remain major military powers of the second rank, brandishing the entire arsenal of modern military weapons. Germany has the largest armed forces, while all the larger states retain armed forces of some size. Yet the tendency is towards smaller, more professional, caste-like militaries. Euro dresses more in civvies than do either the United States or Russia. Euro military integration is slowly proceeding at a technical level, as a singular military-industrial complex begins to produce more standardized weaponry. Led by the Franco-German brigade, harmonization of military training and tactics has also begun.

Yet there are virtually no Euro 'hard' geopolitics, only Euro-dithering behind American leadership. Since Bosnia did not threaten vital Euro interests, it was no real test of Euro hard-geopolitical will. But for the foreseeable future, both of the main potential geopolitical 'threats' to Euro – a revisionist Russia and an escalation of Islamic 'terrorist' pressure – would be met primarily by American military and diplomatic leadership. American withdrawal from Europe is likely in the long run. Then, if Europe's borders became tense, hard geopolitics conducted by Europeans would presumably reappear. At this distance from such an eventuality, it is impossible to judge whether they would centre on a single Euro-polity or on an *ad hoc* association of Great Powers (a British/French/German troika?).

In an era increasingly dominated by 'soft' geopolitics, Waever *et al.* (1993: esp. 71, 76–7, 195) suggest that our concept of security issues should also become rather softer, more 'societal' than 'statist'. It would include notions of 'cultural self-defence', organizable at either the national or the Euro level. As they observe, Europeans' 'insecurities' centre more on matters like immigration than on 'war and peace' issues. They further suggest that Europe may develop a political identity which would not require an ethnic-cultural underpinning like that of the nation-state. Instead they envision a Euro in which

> foreign and security policy become the focus of a 'republican' construction of a state subject . . . . To this belong citizens, a people who choose at the level of politics to identify with the values of this state subject, who are patriotic in terms of politics – but who do not necessarily feel they are in any organic sense one big family. It can be rather hollow as long as the shell is hard.

Yet could the present capitalist, undemocratic and decentred Euro-polity conceivably fill this role – unless 'patriotism' of a rather unpleasant racial-cum-religious type could cement it?

Soft Euro-geopolitics predominate, centred on economic and environmental diplomacy. At Brussels they entwine negotiations between the member states and Euro-agencies – though obviously the more powerful member states have a greater hand in the Euro-agencies. Overall, the Euro constraints on individual states have grown considerably, though unevenly and through a complex thicket of committees and regulations rather than through the formulation of authoritative geopolitical pronouncements. This is typical of Euro-politics, as we shall now see.

Contemporary political power networks

Euro does not not have a government like other governments. It has *two* main locations, national and Euro (i.e. Brussels/Strasbourg). Both member states and Euro agencies play major roles in soft geopolitical relations with the rest of the world. The member states predominate in negotiations occurring within UN agencies, while states and Euro agencies are closely entwined amid the Northern-dominated economic institutions – the IMF, the WTO, the World Bank, GATT, etc.

In many respects the individual member states remain alive and well. Like other states across most of the world, they seem to be changing and diversifying rather than declining, the result of three general and contrary trends (see Mann, 1997): (1) for most Northern states (though not most Southern ones) an increase in 'soft' geopolitics has replaced a decline in 'hard' ones; (2) globalizing tendencies are somewhat weakening state powers in the realm of political economy; but (3) most states are increasingly asked authoritatively to legislate in new areas like the environment, or in old ones traditionally considered 'private', inside the household or concerning intimate lifestyles. Thus the Euro member states remain the primary site of authoritative law, planning and redistribution, trimmed back by Northern/ global capitalism and by Euro economic regulation, yet also finding new legislative tasks. This national state makes more immediate sense to the mass of the people, whose life conditions it most directly affects: popular political identities are concentrated overwhelmingly at the national not the Euro level (Waever *et al.*, 1993: esp. 76–7, puzzlingly argue the opposite).

The second state, in Brussels, etc., has greatly exaggerated what are actually two qualities found in many states. Majone's (1994) term, 'the regulatory state', aptly describes the first quality. Euro is neither *dirigiste*, distributive or authoritative; it has a small budget and virtually no public assets. It scarcely plans or authoritatively allocates outside of agriculture and the regional funds. Its budget comprises only 1.3 per cent of total Euro GDP, compared to the average of 45 per cent of their national GDPs which the individual member states spend. Its overwhelming activity costs very little: it devises regulations for the Euro market, devolving most of the costs on to member states and private citizens and organizations. The member states have delegated to Euro institutions most powers of initiating regulation over their common market. They are generally quite happy with those regulations but if they became unhappy their only option would be the very costly strategy of exiting Euro. Brussels, etc. regulates what it is given – which is primarily economic regulation, plus spin-offs. Regulation has mainly indirect effects on the Euro population, who mostly experience the direct effects of the capitalist markets and property relations which have already been regulated. Thus it has far less political salience for the people of Euro – except for economic elites.

The second characteristic of the Brussels state is almost captured by Marks *et al.*'s (1996) term 'multi-level governance' – though since the 'levels' are not hierarchically arranged, perhaps 'multi-agency governance' would be more accurate. But this is not unique to Euro. In many states it is difficult to find a single authoritative centre – a parliament, an executive, a judiciary, perhaps a military may all have some fairly autonomous powers. But here lie a plethora of autonomous agencies. The relations between them – between the Commission, the Council, the European Court of Justice, the Parliament, and multiple *ad hoc* agencies – are ambiguous and emergent, contested more by murky multi-committee tactics ('commitology') than by head-on confrontation. Nor are the agencies nested inside each other. Thus pressure groups cannot concentrate on a single 'supreme' institution or relationship (like that between the US President and Congress). They will try to influence in *ad hoc* ways all relevant Euro agencies. Multi-agency also has two much-remarked consequences: the 'democratic deficit' and the unintended, interstitial emergence of Euro-agency autonomous power.

Let me note some of these emergent political powers within the multi-agency state. One is the persistent, somewhat mysterious, power that Euro exercises over national politicians. They often seem to act as ideological 'Europeans' rather than as preservers of national sovereignty (Marks *et al.*, 1996). This seems to reflect the hegemony of the notion of Euro-modernity among elites, which also forces anti-European politicians to appear reactionary, demanding a return to 'national traditions'. This emergent Euro-power seems to intensify when a country begins its six-month stint in the EU Presidency. Then its national politicians cultivate the 'national (and personal) prestige' they believe will flow from the Euro-achievements made during their Presidency. However, some politicians also find EU outflanking of national sovereignty tactically useful. Many have accepted neo-liberal wisdom while recognizing its unpopularity among their own electorate. Thus they pursue a monetary union embodying neo-liberal fiscal restraint so as to curb free-spending Social or Christian Democrat rivals without being personally blamed for the consequent welfare cuts or rise in unemployment.

The European Court of Justice is a different example. It has persistently acted as an autonomous power actor, gradually promulgating law which is far greater in scope than the treaties between the member states had initially envisaged. The ECJ probably wields more autonomous power than any other Euro-agency. It arrived at this position gradually, rather surreptitiously, in informal alliance with national courts, especially lower-level courts which became willing to send cases to the ECJ for 'preliminary rulings' (thus reducing the power of higher-level national courts). National politicians were then reluctant to act against rulings which had been actively sought, and then implemented, by their own courts. Alter (1996) argues that this is 'a classic story of bureaucratic politics'. Yet it seems to reveal something else too: the corporate organization of European lawyers, confident of their capacity to wield a body of legal norms which is independent of any single state. The lawyers' emerging corporate commitment to Euro-law surely played a large role in curtailing nation-state sovereignty.

The Agricultural Commission's powers seem more amenable to a bureaucratic explanation, since it has the one sizeable bureaucracy and budget in a Euro-apparatus which is geared towards regulatory rather than budgetary controls. Other Euro agencies employ few bureaucrats but many 'experts' linked to the thousands of pressure groups besieging Brussels. The intimacy of the connections between consultants/technocrats and pressure groups/ classes explain much of the considerable variability between agency powers. Some can mobilize Euro elite constituencies independently of national governments. Where the Commission formulates draft regulations in concert with powerful pressure groups (especially business ones), it is relatively unlikely the politicians will subsequently reject them.

Of course, despite such complexity of political institutions, internal Euro coherence might still be increasing if they were all separately converging towards a single political model. Meyer (1997) argues that across the globe state constitutions, functions and legitimations increasingly resemble one another. States, he argues, share in a global political culture. The Euro member states are clearly converging far more than Meyer suggests. They tend to be small-to-medium-sized neighbours in the same land mass, sharing the same history, barricaded by the Iron Curtain against the ambiguities of the East for forty years. They are economically advanced, liberal democratic, mildly 'statist' and welfarist (eleven of the fifteen governments' expenditures fall in the range 40–50 per cent of GDP). They are predominantly secular states in Western Christian countries. That their political actors should think, talk and act broadly similarly is perhaps to be expected. Perhaps only South America could rival such internal similarity of experience – and it contains far less cohesive economies and much greater internal inequalities.

Yet once again, many of these political similarities are not only shared by Europeans. Secular, though implicitly Christian, states are found elsewhere in the West, while economic development and liberal democracy have been creeping slowly outwards from the West to most of the North. Part of the democratic creep, occupying over a century up to the early 1980s, eventually integrated the whole of Western Europe into democracy. But creep has also stretched to neighbours, to 'kith and kin' and to ex-colonies. As long as the European Union requires its members to be democratic, eastern and south-eastern neighbours, including Turkey, will feel the weight of Euro socialization. France and Britain are also the hubs of distinctive Francophone and Anglophone associations of nations, each occupying a distinctive transnational slice of the globe. The British slice contains a disproportionate share of the stabler liberal democracies of the South (Rueschemeyer *et al.*, 1992). If Huntington's (1991) 'Third Wave' of democracy keeps surging – swelled by the current pro-democracy stance of the US and the Vatican – then democracy will become less distinctively Euro-Northern.

Naturally, we find more intra-Euro differences if we go into political details. Consider, for example, Europe's welfare states. These are often divided into three distinct types: Social Democratic, Christian Democratic and Liberal. These tend to inhabit different macro-regions of Europe – Scandinavia is the core of Social Democracy, south-central Catholic countries are the core of Christian Democracy. Yet the Liberal type extends beyond Euro, joining the British Isles with other 'Anglo-Saxon' countries – the USA, Canada and (more contentiously) Australia and New Zealand (Esping-Anderson, 1990; Huber and Stephens, 1997). East Asian welfare regimes may also increasingly share resemblances with Euro ones. Intra-Euro differences in welfare seem to be declining, as the political spectrum narrows and moves rightward, toward neo-liberalism (Müller, 1994). Three probable causes for this are not specifically Euro, but Northern or global in scope. Northern citizens are now reluctant to vote for the high taxes that more generous welfare regimes require; transnational capital flees from the more generous welfare regimes; and as the traditional family decays and women continue to enter the labour force, the differences between Christian and Social Democracy (until now centred on the position of women) will decline. Only two probable causes concern Euro alone: the Maastricht convergence criteria limit welfare options, while welfarists cannot challenge this in Brussels since its agencies have little competence in redistribution or planning.

In sum, Euro welfare regimes may increasingly resemble those of the entire North. However, we cannot be sure that such trends are strongly entrenched or that they will continue with great force in the future. Tight convergence criteria amid wildly different national unemployment rates (from 3 per cent to 23 per cent in 1996) – especially if inside a single currency union – might produce very varied political reactions across the member countries. Thus the future of welfare is unclear. It may preserve current intra-Euro and trans-Euro welfare regimes; or it may introduce a single Euro welfare regime; or new welfare regimes may come to inhabit the North or distinct transnational slices of the globe.

It is now very difficult to wield in Euro the traditional unitary state theories of political sociology, political science and International Relations. Euro's two states differ. Its nation-states are presently diversifying, while Euro agencies are multiple, unified more by a common elite culture than institutionally. The two states are not very clearly, constitutionally, related to each other. Though state-centric, realist, rational-choice and functionalist institutionalist models are still paraded, reality has become increasingly too messy for them. Yet such models *always* distorted reality. States have always been permeable, fragmentary and 'polymorphous', crystallizing in different institutional forms and with different policy outcomes according to the variegated pressures put by different social constituencies on their multiple agencies. These agencies have also usually had interstitial emergent properties. Euro merely exaggerates these traditional characteristics of states.

Within this complexity we can see that the Euro-agency state has two predominant crystallizations, reflecting its domination by the economically and politically privileged. Functionally, it crystallizes primarily as a capitalist state. Its function is thus rather simpler than the individual member states'. These, though also capitalist, leaven this crystallization with those of other classes, as well as with ideological and military ones (plus more mixed crystallizations involving region, gender, etc.). Of course, if the economic planning pretensions of the member-states are also being trimmed by the delegation of regulatory powers to Euro-agencies, then they may also become more capitalist. In a sense capitalist domination emerges out of the 'hole' left between Euro's two state sites. Institutionally, the Euro-state crystallizes in much more plural forms, as multi-agency networks of economic and political elites, wielding emergent power resources. But since having two states has only feeble parallels elsewhere in the world, it might be said that, for all its complexity, duality is essentially Euro – internal cohesion through unique chaos, perhaps!

Conclusion

My discussion has emphasized the complexity of interaction networks found in Europe today. We have not found an emerging singular society, whether in Euro or anywhere else. Yet some argue that a truly global network of interaction is emerging which might be capable of subsuming all the complex networks described above into one overarching 'society', of which the present Euro may be an early harbinger. These globalizing and Euro enthusiasts wield a two-part vision of a global future.

Globalization I emphasizes *external closure*. It envisions human networks of interaction as having finally arrived up against the limits of the planet Earth. These limits will increasingly confer an outermost external closure on human society. At least in some minimal sense this will comprise a singular 'society' shaped and constrained by global limits. *Globalization II* emphasizes *internal cohesion.* It envisions a global interaction network becoming internally coherent and systemic, in the sense of being dominated by a singular logic, hegemonic over the logic of all other networks. The logic of capitalism is the one most commonly placed in such a primary role – primary in a 'last instance' sense (Altvater and Mahnkopf, 1997).

I remain much more sceptical about Globalization II than about Globalization I. Global limits have indeed already been reached by military power (its weapons can destroy the earth), while global capitalism and the sum of its states endanger the Earth's global environmental limits. Yet the expansion is not internally cohesive. The saliences of global, Northern and Euro networks of interaction are all currently strengthening. Each of these is different and each contains both transnational and international elements. Nor are the local and the national in major decline across the world. Thus it seems that outer global closure is perfectly compatible with multiple inner networks each embodying limited degrees of closure and cohesion. One world is emerging, but composed of multiple, overlapping, intersecting – and often conflicting – networks of interaction.

Within this complex picture, Euro has been strengthening but does not seem yet to be a particularly coherent or closed network of interaction. It mobilizes few ideological commitments or military 'hard' geopolitics. Its economy has become more internally coherent, weakening nation-state economic cleavages within. But its external closure, especially *vis-à-vis* the North, has only slightly increased. Its polity is dual, with a gap between the two and pronounced institutional incoherence in one of them. Euro borders are largely irrelevant to networks of finance capital and somewhat porous to trade and production networks. Euro is much more a network of upper social classes and elites than of the masses. Yet even they are not specifically committed to it alone. The eastern borders remain blurred and German activities will prolong this; other borders are especially blurred by British activities. Euro is a rather specialized set of power networks, formed as a response to rather specialized social interests and constituencies.

Though all 'societies' are composed of multiple, overlapping, intersecting networks of interaction, Euro seems especially to lack overall internal cohesion and external closure. Doubtless, it will gain both in the foreseeable future. Perhaps it will eventually attain the moderate degree of cohesion and closure attained by nation-states during the relatively transnational phases of modern development – in the period after 1815, for example, or around 1900. My own guess is that Euro will be less than this, less salient as a network of interaction than networks constituted both by the North as a whole and by the more successful nation-states of the world. This is not meant to be dismissive of Euro. Euro is becoming one of the more significant macro-networks of human interaction in the globe. It is especially significant as a site of capitalist organization and exploitation – exploitation of its own workers and, in conjunction with the other two Northern blocs, exploitation of workers across the South. But I do dismiss those theories based on social scientists' longings for a singular, unitary society – whether constituted by the nation-state, by the world system or by Europe. Such societies would be easier to understand, but have never existed.

References

Alter, K. J. (1996) The European Court's political power, *West European Politics*, **19**.

Altvater, E. and Mahnkopf, B. (1997) The world market unbound, *Review of International Political Economy*, **4**.

Bretherton, C. and Sperling, L. (1996) Women's networks and the European Union: towards an inclusive approach?, *Journal of Common Market Studies*, **34**.

Busch, M. and Milner, H. (1994) The future of the international trading system: international firms, regionalism and domestic politics, in R. Stubbs and G. Underhill (eds), *Political Economy and the Changing Global Order*. New York: St Martin's Press.

Dogan, M. (1993) The decline of nationalisms within Western Europe, *Comparative Politics*, **26**.

Esping-Andersen, G. (1990) *Three Worlds of Welfare Capitalism*. Princeton, NJ: Princeton University Press.

European Commission, Directorate-General for Economic and Financial Affairs (1996) *Broad Economic Policy Guidelines*. Brussels: European Commission.

Eurostat (1993) *Rapid Reports (Population and Social Conditions)*, no. 6.

Grant, W. (1993) Pressure groups and the European Community: an overview, in S. Mazey and J. Richardson (eds), *Lobbying in the European Community*. Oxford: Oxford University Press.

Greenwood, J. *et al.* (1992) Conclusions: evolving patterns of organizing interests in the European Community, in *Organized Interests and the European Community*. London: Sage.

Gretschmann, K. (1994) Germany in the global economy of the 1990s: from player to pawn?, in R. Stubbs and G. Underhill (eds), *Political Economy and the Changing Global Order*. New York: St Martin's Press.

Grote, J. (1992) Small firms in the European Community: modes of production, governance and territorial interest representation in Italy and Germany, in Greenwood *et al.*

Harvey, B. (1993) Lobbying in Europe: the experience of voluntary organizations, in S. Mazey and J. Richardson (eds), *Lobbying in the European Community*. Oxford: Oxford University Press.

Huber, E. and Stephens, J. (1997) Internationalization and the Social Democratic model: crisis and future prospects, *Comparative Political Studies* (forthcoming).

Hufbauer, G. (1990) An overview, in Hufbauer (ed.), *Europe 1992: An American Perspective*. Washington, DC: Brookings.

Huntington, S. (1996) *The Clash of Civilizations and the Remaking of World Order*. New York: Simon & Schuster.

Kay, N. *et al.* (1996) Industrial collaboration and the European Internal Market,

Journal of Common Market Studies, **34**.

Korzeniewicz, R. and Moran, T. (1997) World-economic trends in the distribution of income, 1965–1992, *American Journal of Sociology,* **102**.

Laffan, B. (1996) The politics of identity and political order in Europe, *Journal of Common Market Studies,* **34**.

Majone, G. (1994) The rise of the regulatory state in Europe, *West European Politics,* **17**.

Mann, M. (1986) *The Sources of Social Power,* Vol. I: *A History of Power from the Beginning to 1760 AD.* Cambridge: Cambridge University Press.

Mann, M. (1993) *The Sources of Social Power.* Vol. II: *The Rise of Classes and Nation-States, 1760–1914.* Cambridge: Cambridge University Press.

Mann, M. (1997) Has globalization ended the rise and rise of the nation-state?, *Review of International Political Economy,* **4**.

Marks, G. *et al.* (1996) European integration from the 1980s: state-centric v. multi-level government, *Journal of Common Market Studies,* **34**.

Marks, G. and McAdam, D. (1996) Social movements and the changing structure of political opportunity in the European Union, *West European Politics,* **19**.

Meyer, J. (1997) The changing cultural content of the nation-state: a world society perspective, in G. Steinmetz *et al., State and Culture.* Ithaca, NY: Cornell University Press.

Moran, M. (1994) The state and the financial services revolution: a comparative analysis, *West European Politics,* **17**.

Müller, W. (1994) Political traditions and the role of the state, *West European Politics,* **17**.

Philip, A. (1994) European Union immigration policy: phantom, fantasy or fact?, *West European Politics,* **17**.

Reif, H. (1993) Cultural convergence and cultural diversity as factors in European identity, in S. Garcia (ed.), *European Identity and the Search for Legitimacy.* London: Pinter.

Romero, F. (1990) Cross-border population movements, in W. Wallace (ed.), *The Dynamics of European Integration.* London: Pinter.

Rueschemeyer, D. *et al.* (1992) *Capitalist Development and Democracy.* Cambridge: Polity Press.

Sklair, L. (1997) Social movements for global capitalism: the transnational capitalist class in action, *Review of International Political Economy,* **4**.

Smith, A. (1990) Towards a global culture?, *Theory, Culture and Society,* **7**.

Tarrow, S. (1995) The Europeanisation of conflict: reflections from a social movements perspective, *West European Politics,* **18**.

Therborn, G. (1995) *European Modernity and Beyond.* London: Sage.

Tsoukalis, L. (1993) *The New European Economy,* 2nd revised edn. Oxford: Oxford University Press.

van Schendelen, M. (1993) *National Public and Private EC Lobbying.* Aldershot: Dartmouth.

Visser, J. and Ebbinghaus, B. (1992) Making the most of diversity? European integration and transnational organization of labour, in Greenwood *et al.*

Waever, O. *et al.* (1993) *Identity, Migration and the New Security Agenda in Europe.* New York: St Martin's Press.

Index